Writing Desire

Wisconsin Studies in Autobiography

William L. Andrews
General Editor

Writing Desire

Sixty Years
of Gay Autobiography

Bertram J. Cohler

The University of Wisconsin Press

The University of Wisconsin Press
1930 Monroe Street
Madison, Wisconsin 53711

www.wisc.edu/wisconsinpress/

3 Henrietta Street
London WC2E 8LU, England

5   4   3   2   1

Printed in the United States of America

Library of Congress Cataloging-in-Publication Data
Cohler, Bertram J.
Writing desire: sixty years of gay autobiography / Bertram J. Cohler.
        p.   cm.—(Wisconsin studies in autobiography)
        Includes bibliographical references.
        ISBN 0-299-22200-4 (cloth: alk. paper)
        ISBN 0-299-22204-7 (pbk.: alk. paper)
1. Autobiography.   2. Gays—Biography—History and criticism.
    3. Gays' writings—History and criticism.   I. Title.
        CT25.C64   2007
        920—dc22   2006031470

TO MY COLLEAGUES
IN THE SOCIETY FOR PERSONOLOGY

For encouragement and support in the study of lives

and

TO MY COLLEGE AND
GRADUATE STUDENT COLLEAGUES
AT THE UNIVERSITY OF CHICAGO

Who have taught me about lives and social change

For narratives to flourish there must be a community to hear . . . for communities to hear, there must be stories which weave together their history, their identity, their politics. . . . There is an ongoing dynamic or dialectic of communities, politics, identities . . . gay persons create a gay culture cluttered with stories of gay life, gay history, and gay politics, so that very culture helps to define a reality that makes gay personhood ever tighter and evermore plausible. And this in turn strengthens the culture and the politics.

Ken Plummer, *Telling Sexual Stories*

Contents

Preface and Acknowledgments

This is a book about lives and life stories. It is also a book about the times in which lives are lived. It is particularly a book about the lives of ten men seeking sex with other men who were born across six decades, from the 1930s through the 1980s. Men born before World War II do not like to describe themselves as gay or queer in the manner preferred by gay men in more recent generations. Two of the men whose life stories I discuss wrote accounts of their life as they negotiated adulthood *before* the advent of the Gay Rights movement. Two writers born after 1970 are still young adults as they write about their life in a time following increasing social acceptance of gay lives and the possibility of gay marriage. Other men in this study have written their memoirs within the past decade and have benefited from the social change that has made it possible for them to publish their memoirs by the mainstream press; these men have been influenced as well by a younger generation of self-identified gay men more comfortable with their own sexuality and who have influenced their elders to move beyond their feelings of shame regarding their sexuality (Plummer 1996).

My understanding of these lives has been influenced both by my life-long experience as a gay man and as a social scientist and graduate psychoanalyst. My scholarly work has been informed by the studies of pioneering Harvard psychologists Gordon Allport, who emphasized the importance of studying personal documents such as memoirs in understanding lives, and Henry Murray. Murray and his colleagues coined the term "personology" for that discipline concerned with the study in depth of particular lives over time rather than reducing personality to variables. The contribution of this perspective has been enhanced in the important work by psychologists Amia Lieblich (Lieblich, Tuval-Mashiach, and Zilber [1998]), Ruthellen Josselson (1996a, 1996b), and Dan McAdams (1990, 2001). Understanding the dynamics of life stories in terms of social and historical change has been fostered by sociologist Glen Elder and his colleagues (Elder 1996; Elder,

Johnson, and Crosnoe 2003), together with the work of sociologists Ken Plummer (2001) and Dana Rosenfeld (2003), and writer and psychotherapist Doug Sadownick (1996). They have shown that lives of gay men cannot be understood apart from social and historical circumstances.

Certainly, for those of us with same-sex desire, there have been dramatic changes in the experience of our own sexuality as a result of the social changes occurring since the postwar period. As a graduate student in clinical psychology, working in a Harvard-affiliated mental health setting, at a time when psychiatry still classified such same-sex attractions as psychopathology, and later coming to terms with my own attraction to other men, I helped to organize an aversive conditioning study in which we attempted to change the sexual orientation of men finding other men attractive as sexual partners (Birk, Huddleston, Miller, and Cohler 1971). When behavioral intervention proved of little value in changing sexual orientation, we turned the study into a support group for these men (Birk, Miller, and Cohler 1971). Andrew Tobias (1998a, 1998b), a 1940s-generation lifewriter, remarks that a number of his fellow Harvard undergraduate friends had taken part in this study (although he incorrectly attributes this project to Irving and Tony Bieber, who were consultants to the study).

Born in the decade of the 1930s, historian Martin Duberman (1991c) describes his sense of shame when, as a Yale undergraduate, he furtively cruised the New Haven Green for a man with whom to have sex. His memoir painfully portrays his experience with psychoanalysts who not only viewed his desire for sex and relationships with other men as evidence of mental illness but also attempted to change his sexual orientation. I began my own psychoanalytic education on the cusp of this larger change regarding our understanding of sexual orientation. My analyst, while classically educated in psychoanalysis, shared few of the prejudices besetting Martin Duberman's analysts. He helped me to recognize and feel comfortable with my desire for intimate relations with other men.

Friends have asked me why I should undertake the arduous, lengthy education that psychoanalysis requires. I believe that psychoanalysis provides a unique method for understanding our lives and actions. From Freud to the present, psychoanalysis has been concerned with understanding the meanings that we make of desire, wish, and intention. Psychoanalysis offers a unique perspective on the human experience and focuses on those wishes and meanings that lead to enhanced self-understanding and to an increased sense of personal vitality. Readers will find my discussion of the life stories in this book informed by clinical psychoanalysis, which emphasizes understanding of self and desire through experience.

It is important to realize that enhanced self-awareness need not mean that such aspects of ourselves as same-sex desire should be viewed as pejorative simply because we seek to understand the meanings of this desire in our lives. For example, psychoanalyst Richard Isay (1986, 1987) writes about the emotional distance often reported by gay men regarding their relationships with their fathers. Isay suggests that this distance may reflect the father's discomfort with his son's early awakened erotic interest in him rather than in his mother as is more generally expected. The psychoanalyst Sidney Phillips (2001, 2003) adds to Isay's important observation and suggests that the consequence of the son's erotic interest in his father may be that he experiences this erotic tie to his father as overstimulating and thus protects himself by distancing himself from this attachment to his father. The gay son may then assume that it is his father who has pulled away from him, while it is equally possible that he has attempted to protect himself by pulling away from his father. This need to psychologically protect oneself from such overstimulation may explain why some gay men have difficulty in maintaining intimate relationships with their lovers. Fostering awareness of this issue, psychoanalysis may help gay men to realize more satisfying and intimate relationships with boyfriends or lovers.

I have been particularly influenced by Heinz Kohut, and the Chicago school of Psychology of the Self. Kohut and his colleagues have been careful to avoid reductionist study and to appreciate without pejorative assumptions all aspects of the human endeavor. Self-psychology focuses on how we experience others in order to realize enhanced sense of personal coherence. Work by Chicago psychoanalysts Dennis Shelby (1994, 2002) and Marian Tolpin (1997) has emphasized sexual and romantic ties as a means of fostering a personal vitality rather than viewing these ties simply as a reflection of a psychological deficit in relations with parents and others in the childhood years (Hagman 2002).

In the forty years since I began my own graduate education, homosexuality has been removed from the psychiatric nomenclature; the American Psychoanalytic Association no longer regards sexual orientation as relevant either to selection for psychoanalytic education or for certification and appointment as a training and supervising analyst. Meetings of the Association often feature panels by gay and straight analysts discussing their therapeutic work with gay and lesbian analysands. The University of Chicago was one of the first American universities to recognize domestic partnership and to support a mentorship program for undergraduates identifying with minority sexualities. In my courses on sexual identity and life course, and on the family, many of my students identify as queer or gay, and have little problem being "out" in the classroom and in their college houses. These students are respected and admired by their fellow students for standing up for their views. The world has changed since my time as an undergraduate at The University of Chicago when homosexuality was regarded either as a sickness or criminal offense!

This book describes, through the writings of men who lived in these times, the course of this change over the postwar period. In addition, the book provides in greater detail prescient observations made in an important book by Doug Sadownick (1996), who knew many of the life-writers whose stories I tell. Jesse Green (1999) has observed that "compiling a memoir is a way of deciding which of the lives one has had are true and which life to have in the future. It is also a way of pruning lives" (239). Two events are of particular significance in fostering this social change: the 1969 riots following a police raid on the Stonewall Inn, a Greenwich Village bar catering to men and women identifying with minority sexualities, and the sudden appearance in 1981 of an immune-deficiency illness, AIDS. The Stonewall Inn riots and the emergence of the gay rights movement in the ten or so years was itself preceded by significant social activism within the homophile movement of the earlier decades, which provided the foundation for the gay rights movement (D'Emilio 1983/1998).

It has been claimed that the new personal and sexual freedom for gay men, which accompanied the gay rights movement, unwittingly led to the emergence of AIDS. Writers such as Patrick Moore (2004) may have exaggerated the sexual license of that time. The gay rights movement did lead to more readily identifiable public spaces such as bars where possible sexual partners could be found. There is little evidence that such sexual spaces as bathhouses in themselves fostered the unsafe sex that resulted in a silent killer spreading through the gay community (Henrikkson 1995; Woods and Binson 2003). Life-writers born in the 1940s and 1950s were particularly vulnerable to the AIDS pandemic.

In the chapters that follow I narrate the stories of men born from the 1930s to the 1980s. Life stories offer a means for understanding social change and for showing the impact of this change upon both the experience and the writing about gay desire. Ever since sociologist Karl Mannheim (1928) wrote about the effect of being born at a particular time on personal outlook, there has been much interest in the impact of adjacent birth years (a generation-cohort) upon the sense that we make of lived experience. There has been much discussion regarding the number of adjacent birth years comprising a cohort. Recognizing the arbitrary nature of a

decade as marking a cohort, I have followed the observation of sociologist
Fred Davis (1979):

There is however the arresting fact that the commonly identifiable American generations of recent time all evidence a symbolic span of approximately ten years. . . .
The ten-year intervals over this limited span of historical time may, of course, be
purely coincidental, although they also suggest a certain inherent periodicity in the
generation-defining phenomena. It is probably of greater significance that despite
their approximately equal duration the intervals are bracketed in collective memory by major historical events rather than by simple chronological references. (113)

Using an approach borrowed from the social science qualitative method
known as grounded theory, I have followed the practice of selecting particularly salient life stories with each generation-cohort for discussion (Charmaz 2002; Plummer 2001). I have chosen noteworthy memoirs from two
life-writers within each decade from a larger group of twenty-seven such
narratives (including the 1970s and '80s in one chapter). The ten memoirs
I chose for this book are by men who, in writing about same-sex desire, are
particularly articulate regarding the interplay of social change. Selection
from among life-writers born in the 1940s and '50s was particularly difficult since there were a number of accounts of men living with and caring
for lovers dying of AIDS. Paul Monette, who died from complications attending the AIDS pandemic, and Mark Doty each wrote a volume about
their care for their AIDS-afflicted lovers and then wrote memoirs of their
own lives. Monette's (1988) detailed story of his lover's illness and death
provides important testimony regarding the many clinical trials and dashed
hopes among men who became ill in the early years of the pandemic. Mark
Doty's life story is particularly articulate and self-reflective about the complex problems of memory, desire, and the social context of narrating both
the story of his lover's illness and that of his own life.

Two additional problems are presented in working with these ten life
stories. In the first place, many of the memoirs I have selected for discussion are by men who are particularly accomplished as writers. These unusually well-written memoirs may make the best case for understanding
the interplay of history and understanding gay desire. I discuss the life
writing of one of the many men writing Weblogs about their own lives and
same-sex desire after the millennium. This particular "blog" is unusual in
that it is very clearly written, self-reflective, and extremely detailed. The
second problem is, of course, that presented by writing a life story backwards (Schiff and Cohler 2001). Clearly, social change taking place across a

lifetime has an effect upon the manner in which one's own life is presently understood, including those social changes of the past decade. Still, it is likely that life-writers who are part of different generations will experience social changes across the course of their life in ways distinctive to their own generation. Further, life stories such as these are shaped both by the emerging genre of gay life writing and the effect of particular, iconic, life stories written earlier.

There is need for a companion volume portraying the lives of women seeking other women as sexual and romantic partners. It would be difficult for me to undertake such a project, in part because social circumstances have combined to make it difficult for women to find their voice and to write their memoirs (although some memoirs [Blum 2001] have recently appeared), and in part because, as a gay man, I have particular empathy with the lives of men seeking men as sexual partners. Further, particularly across the postwar period and into the 1970s and beyond, Whisman (1996) has observed that the lives of lesbians and gay men have diverged, even though the scourge of AIDS may have reunited the community as both gay men and lesbians became caregivers of those afflicted with AIDS. Similarly, memoirs by transgendered men and women are only now beginning to appear (McCloskey 1999).

In order to preserve the engaging and informative observations regarding self and social change made by these ten gay life-writers, I have attempted to make sense of the significance that these men have made for their life-choices and sexuality and, at the same time, portray the richness of their personal experiences. Some of these life-writers have kindly reviewed what I have written about them. I am particularly grateful to them for telling me where I have erred in my account. I would like to thank Raphael Kadushin, my editor at the University of Wisconsin Press, for helping me to clarify my ideas and provide a readable account, and also Sheila Moermond at the Press who saw this book into print. I am particularly grateful to Bill Hensley who has been my "essential other," and who has patiently read and critiqued the many prior drafts of this manuscript.

Chicago, Illinois
July 2005

Writing Desire

1

Life Writing about Gay Desire

Telling oneself about oneself is like making up a story about who and what we are, what's happened, and why we're doing what we're doing . . . [o]ur self-making stories accumulate over time, even pattern themselves on conventional genres . . . [o]ur very memories fall victims to our self-making stories. Self-making is a narrative art . . . more constrained by memory than fiction is . . . guided by unspoken, implicit cultural models of what selfhood should be.

Jerome Bruner, *Making Stories: Law, Literature, Life*

We live the stories we tell; the stories we don't tell live us. What you don't allow yourself to know controls and determines; whatever's held to the light "can be changed"—not the facts, of course, but how we understand them, how we live with them. . . . What matters is what we learn to make of what happens to us.

Mark Doty, *Firebird*

Self, Experience, and Social Change

Stories of our lives both reflect and constitute what we call our "self." As psychologist Jerome Bruner (2002) observes, we strive to maintain a sense of our personal continuity over our lifetime. The very concept of our self is comprised of the story we tell about ourselves and explains our wishes, our feelings, and the meanings we make of our relationships with others. Across the course of life we remake our life story as a result of both expected and unexpected life changes. Unexpected life changes, such as personal or collective adversity, are likely to require that we remake our life story to maintain our sense of personal continuity. Most often, success in overcoming obstacles or surviving catastrophe provides impetus for telling or writing about one's life. This search for resolution is often presented as a journey resulting in enhanced sense of personal integrity.

This effort at remaking a life story is reflected in the personal accounts, for example, of those involved in the Holocaust. Recognizing the significance of telling one's life story as a means for realizing enhanced personal integrity when struggling with the impact of major adversity, Steven Spielberg used part of the proceeds of his film *Schindler's List* to fund a project to record the life stories of those who had experienced the Holocaust first-hand. Thousands of people accepted his offer. Our own life story may be told or may be written. It is as much the act of telling or writing as it is the story itself that is particularly important in maintaining our sense of continuity of self across the course of life. Psychologist Dan McAdams (1990, 2001) has suggested that life stories are concerned with turning points in the writer's life. For those experiencing the Holocaust, the struggle to stay alive represented an extreme challenge to survival. Remaking one's life story in the aftermath of this traumatic experience provided survivors with renewed sense of coherence and personal integrity. It should be noted that telling and writing one's life story represents self-making (Bruner 1990, 2001). Writing the life story is a different genre from the retelling one's life in an interview or oral history project. In the present study we are concerned with self-life writing.

Over the past century there has been particular interest in writing one's own life story. From Henry James's account of his confusing childhood, as his father moved the family back and forth between Europe and the United States, to the "Weblog" memoirs posted on the Internet in our own time, writing a memoir is psychologically fulfilling for writer and reader alike. The historian Peter Gay (1995) noted in his study of Victorian society that the social changes accompanying industrialization in the nineteenth century led to a profound sense of social and personal disruption, and required that people make sense of this time of change. Although the Enlightenment had promised that rational thought would resolve all social problems, rationality had not been able to resolve these problems. The result was that people began looking inward, focusing on self and the need to remake one's story of self and the social world.

Sigmund Freud's emphasis upon introspection and the effort to remake a disrupted life story through collaborative work between analyst and analysand was, perhaps, the ideal type of nineteenth-century solution to feelings of loss of integrity posed by the crisis of technological and social change. Freud's reports on the lives of his analysands raised the question of the role of the personal past for the story we tell in the present. Indeed, the life story is always a presently recollected account of the personal past. The very act of remembering, however, is influenced by our shared understanding regarding the meaning of the past, including the importance of experiences taking place earlier in life for later-life outcomes. Psychologists Jerome Bruner (1990) and Mark Freeman (1993) emphasize that there may be little relationship between the memory of the past and the past as it "really happened." Across the course of life, memory is reorganized in order to maintain a coherent story of oneself. Rewriting our life story over time we reorder the past; as Mark Freeman (2002) observed, we always impose the present on our memory of past events. At the same time, this does not mean that our present composed life story is a fiction. Unlike fictional accounts of a life, these autobiographical memories have some relationship to memories of real-life experiences (Conway 1998; Singer and Salovey 1993). We are less concerned with the accuracy of these memories than with the ways in which memories are used in writing a coherent narrative and one that is "followable" by oneself and by others reading this account (Ricoeur 1977).

While life writing may be traced back to antiquity, the term "autobiography" was introduced in the nineteenth century. The autobiography was presumed to be more enduring and philosophically profound than other forms of self-life writing such as the diary, journal, or memoir (Gusdorf 1956; Weintraub 1978). This concern with telling and, in particular, writing the story of one's own life has continued to the present time. The social changes of the past century, which have challenged our sense of personal and collective coherence, have also highlighted the significance of maintaining personal integrity. Rather than a formal autobiography reflecting on the meaning of one's own life in terms of some larger philosophic concern, such as Jean-Jacques Rousseau's *Confessions,* written in the 1760s, contemporary self-life writing has been represented by the diary and the memoir. The memoir as a genre of self-life writing is less formal than the classical autobiography, and it is concerned less with enduring political and social dilemmas than with portraying the course of one's life and reporting the impact of unexpected and expected social and personal changes.

We can understand why people write their life stories. However, we must also ask why people like to read these accounts of other lives. After all, life stories are written with a reader in mind, if only for oneself as reader. The literary scholar Nancy Miller (2002) has posed the question of why we like to read life stories. She notes that we particularly like to read personal accounts by others who are like ourselves. It is inevitable that the reader seeks a connection between his or her own life and that of the author. Readers most often find some similarity between the person whose personal account they are reading and their own life. For example, gay and lesbian readers look to the personal accounts of other gay life-writers in order to help us understand the meaning of sexual desire in their own lives, to learn about how others have dealt with issues of coming to terms with a gay identity, how they have disclosed their gay identity to family and friends, how they have dealt with stigma at school and in the community and, alas, how gay men have managed issues related to the AIDS pandemic.

The project of self-life writing poses some issues that we must consider in understanding the significance for us as readers of these accounts. Taking advantage of recent discussions in both the social sciences and the humanities, I have provided the background for understanding the self-life writing of those men, born in the time from the Great Depression to the 1980s, who have sought sexual intimacy with men. I have mostly avoided using the word "gay" to describe those born in the 1930s and 1940s since they often feel less comfortable with this term than with the term "homosexual." However, men born in the postwar period often find the term "homosexual" to be a label implying deviance and abnormality. The term used to refer to one's sexual identity raises the larger question of the place of social and historical change in the study of personal accounts. Studying the life writing of these men across the past six decades, we are faced with the problem that life experiences cannot be understood apart from the very language or discourse we use in talking about lives and experiences (Chauncey 1994; Linde 1993; Plummer 1995), which is shaped by social and historical context. As sociologist and psychoanalyst Nancy Chodorow (1994) has written, there is little to be gained from differentiating between social context "outside" or "inside" the person; self, society, and history are inextricably intertwined.

Furthermore, these life-writers often tell us about experiences far removed from the time at which they have written their memoir. We need to consider the manner in which memories of the personal and shared past are used in these memoirs, and to recognize the reason that certain experiences are written about; in so doing the life-writer realizes an enhanced sense of personal congruence. This recollection of the past is always written from the vantage point of present experiences, including the experience of reading the memoirs of other gay men. At the same time, men born earlier and later across this period of more than fifty years, and living in different areas of the country, have different experiences. For this reason it is important to consider how social and historical change, such as the emergence of the Gay Rights movement in the 1970s or the emergence of the AIDS pandemic in the early 1980s, affects the life story that we write.

There is a complex interplay between generation and recollection of these past experiences. At least to some extent, life-writers born across the adjacent birth years of a decade may remember their past in ways different from life-writers born in earlier or later decades. Life-writers born across those decades may all have experienced the same events, but they may understand and write about these events in quite different ways. My goal in this study is to show the impact of social and historical change upon the manner in which homosexual men have written about their lives. Men born across succeeding decades have made meanings of their same-sex desire in somewhat different ways. These meanings are influenced by their own life circumstances and also by the time and place in which they live. Even as they write their life story "backward," looking at a lifetime from the perspective of middle or later life, these writers are influenced by the very manner in which their generation has understood the meaning of sex between men and the impact of social and historical change upon the manner in which they understand this desire.

Finally, as readers we make our own meanings from the life stories we read. It has been said that there is no text apart from the reader. This has been an ongoing problem in the study of literature. We are able to find unique meanings in reading about these life-writers who are, in some respects, much like ourselves. Important for the present study, Nancy Miller (2002) has noted that *generation* is particularly significant in drawing together writer and readers. Again, the meanings of same-sex desire, which men born in different generations make by reading life stories, are influenced by both time and place of reading as well as that of writing. From this perspective both social context and particular circumstances of particular life circumstances enter into writing and making meaning as a reader of a life story.

Nowhere is Nancy Miller's observation more evident than in the tie that binds those men living in a particular time and place who have written about their own struggles to come to terms with their homoerotic desire, and readers who have encountered similar dilemmas in their own lives. Coming to terms with this desire is a turning point in the sense that psychologists McAdams and Bowman (2001) have noted in life writing. Reading, just as writing, helps us to remake our own life story and realize an enhanced sense of self-congruence from seeing how others have resolved problems. Reading about how men across succeeding generations have dealt with their same-sex desire may help us better understand our own sexuality and its expression in the time and place in which we live.

Writing a Life Story

The meaning of homosexual desire has been a contested subject that has changed in dramatic ways across the past half-century. From Oscar Wilde's portrayal of the sexual attraction of men for other men as "the love that dare not speak its name" to recent memoirs and mainstream magazine articles portraying the gay experience, there have been dramatic changes in the very manner in which we write about sex between men. This desire has become enshrined in the scientific and political term "sexual orientation" which, at the present time, is often portrayed as an innate or essential characteristic among some men. Men seeking psychotherapy to help them come to terms with this desire about which they feel confused, or even ashamed, often ask about the reason *why* they are attracted to other men. Scientific and popular accounts essentialize same-sex desire and stress such factors as genetics and prenatal experiences as the "cause" of this erotic tie, as if this desire were a disease whose origins must be explained. The danger in this essentialist approach to the study of same-sex desire is that scientific evidence supporting an innate or essentialist perspective is itself problematic (Cohler and Galatzer-Levy 2000). Further, as philosopher of science Edward Stein (1999) has noted, classifying men as either homosexual/gay or straight tends to portray this same-sex attraction as binary and "of a natural kind."

Psychoanalysis, particularly as portrayed by Heinz Kohut and his colleagues (Kohut 1984; Kohut and Wolf 1978; Shelby 1994, 2002; Tolpin 1997), may be of some assistance in appreciating the ways in which desire for a sexual relationship with other men is important in reconsidering this issue of cause. Freud had suggested that simply by living in culture we are forced to make compromises with our desire: neurosis is an inevitable result of social life. Sociologist and psychoanalyst Nancy Chodorow (1994) has noted that we know little about why men and women chose either same sex or other sex partners in playing anew that nuclear drama lived in personal experience of a family romance known popularly as the "Oedipus Complex." The preschool boy or girl inevitably becomes a rival with one parent, most often of the same sex, for the love of the other parent. Much of classical psychoanalysis focused on this choice of the sex of the person to love, and founded on presumably troubled relationships with parents or other significant persons in one's earlier life.

While consistent with more traditional psychoanalytic perspectives—concern with the meanings that we endow of lived experience—many of the problems associated with classical psychoanalysis, including critique of same sex relationships, are resolved when refocusing psychoanalysis as a way to appreciate the place of same-sex desire in fostering the experience of personal vitality or coherence, rather than merely as a reflection of interferences in the development of a relationship with another person. For example, 1950s-generation life-writer Mark Doty (1997) notes that as his lover lies dying, he looks out of his Provincetown window and comments with appreciation on a buff young man walking past their house. This experience adaptively helps his lover to feel an enhanced sense of being alive even as he struggles with his own morality.

Self-psychological perspectives share in common with more traditional psychoanalytic perspectives an understanding of one's own wishes and desires. Psychoanalysis maintains that we may not always be aware of these wishes. However, self-psychology focuses on those experiences of being with others that foster a sense of enhanced congruence and personal integrity, and particularly with the psychological use of essential others in cultivating a sense of continued well-being. Particularly significant for the study of life stories of gay men, self-psychology is concerned with feelings such as those of shame, which may not be acknowledged but which haunt adult life and interfere in realizing a sense of personal vitality. Psychology of the self is focused on understanding the experience of being with others in maintaining self-esteem rather than solely with those aspects of relationships with others earlier in life, which interfere in realizing satisfying relationships in adulthood. Disappointments are inevitable in both childhood and adulthood, and inevitably we need others as a source of sustenance and comfort at such times. Galatzer-Levy and Cohler (1993) view such psychologically sustaining functions as "essential others." Tolpin (1997) emphasizes that it is the ability to make use of the experience of others, such as lovers, as a source of continued personal integrity or coherence, which is the important factor in being able to maintain one's own psychological center. Concern with self and realization of a sense of personal vitality shifts the discussion of our relationships with lovers and friends from simply a replay of impediments to mutuality to the psychological use of others as essential for our own well-being.

Self psychology pioneers Heinz Kohut and Ernest Wolf (1978) have portrayed three characteristic modes of using others as a means of maintaining self vitality: (1) realizing a sense of well-being from basking in the glow of an admired and idealized other person, such as a teacher or psychotherapist; (2) realizing affirmation of one's own talents and skills in the support offered by an important person in one's life; and (3) realizing enhanced personal vitality through sharing experiences and personal views with an alter ego or soul mate. While such uses of others for maintaining personal coherence may be characteristic of those persons who are more psychologically fragile, we all make use of others in one or more of these three modalities in our daily life and at times of personal stress and difficulty. The experience of another's strength as a source of idealizations, a mirror for one's own talents or as an alter ego or "twin" (Kohut 1984) fosters psychological vitality from childhood to oldest age. For example, 1970s life-writer Kirk Read (2001) searches during adolescence for older men as lovers, men he can look up to and idealize, and who are able to appreciate and affirm or mirror his talents and interests as a nascent playwright. Other men search for a lover who can be an alter ego or psychological twin nurture an enhanced sense of self-coherence. Nowhere is this better stated than 1980s-generation life-writer BrYaN Phillips, writing in his Weblog about his relationship with his partner, Matt: "There are times when I feel that there is absolutely no way I can function without Matt. It's almost as if he completes my being."

Rather than assuming sexual orientation as innate or "hardwired," we might better understand the desire for sexual and social relationships with other men as a way of providing not only an enhanced experience of personal vitality but also a particular kind of shared life story learned within a particular time and place. This life story has been portrayed by sociologist Ken Plummer (1995) as a "sexual story." Plummer notes that we borrow from socially shared meanings to describe ourselves, our experiences, and the larger social world across the course of life. The story we learn to tell becomes our memory of the past; our memory is always a social memory that leads us to select particular aspects of our past as elements of the life story and which we continually remake with additional experiences and in accordance with the expectations of the social world of which we are a part. These shared understandings of self and social order are reflected in a "master narrative" of ourselves and the world around us, which we learn first from our parents and other family members, and later at school and in the community.

Psychologist Jerome Bruner (2001, 2002) has suggested that our identity is founded in the story that we tell about our life. The act of telling or writing a life story adds to our collective understanding of ourselves and re-creates the meanings that we make of such aspects of social life as our sexuality (Cohler and Hammack 2006). Nowhere is this perspective more clearly illustrated than in the life stories of gay men. Following the paradigm of folklorist Vladimir Propp (1928), Plummer (1995) has suggested that there is a dominant narrative that men learn of "coming out," typically telling the story of a journey of self discovery, including an epiphany or turning point, and then the resolution of this quest with the creation of a new identity. The media plays an important part in making the sexual story from the sepia-toned muscleman magazines and publications such as *One* (published by the Mattachine Society of the 1950s) to the emergence of gay pornography and contemporary glossy, sociopolitical magazines featuring mainstream advertisers. Media portrayal of the gay culture has been important in making this master narrative of a gay identity. Our sense of knowing what it means to be sexually attracted to other men and to tell a sexual life story (Plummer 1995) is governed by what we read, not just from viewing gay pornography (Cohler 2004b) or from what we learn from being in such venues as gay bars and bathhouses.

At least within generations of gay men born in the period following World War II, growing up in the turbulent 1960s and beyond, this master narrative of sexual desire for other men is a life story of coming out "gay." Earlier generations of gay men living outside urban areas often lacked opportunities for learning this master narrative. With the advent of the Internet, even young men growing up in small towns now have the opportunity to read about the experiences of other men with similar desires (oasismag .com). Readers of these Internet accounts are then able to use this master narrative as a means of organizing their own life experiences into a coherent story of oneself as gay. Reading these experiences, we remake our own life stories. At least to some extent the life stories discussed in this study have been written in the context of the life stories previously written by other men harboring desire for sex with men. Sometimes these life-writers of the past decade have themselves discussed the impact of these previously written life stories upon their understanding of their own life story.

It should be noted that until the past two decades, the social world of homosexual men was characterized by venues hidden from public surveillance. Often feeling ashamed for their same-sex desire, sexual encounters were furtive and anonymous. The life stories of men coming into a gay identity over the immediate postwar period reflect a secretive, subversive world. For example, Alan Helms (1995) has written of coming to college in New York in the 1950s from a small Midwestern community and raised in a Conservative Christian family. Invited to a party by a man he had recently met, on opening the door to a swank Park Avenue apartment where an elegant reception was taking place, Helms glimpsed a world like that of

Alice following the White Rabbit into the underground. Helms discovered that there was a whole new world, hidden away from mainstream society, in which men had met through furtive sexual experiences and were drawn into this secretive world. Similar accounts of this sub-rosa world in the hidden bars, tearooms, and baths of the postwar have been reported in the accounts of Brown (2001), Delph (1978), Humphreys (1970), Read (1973), and Styles (1979).

Being a part of this hidden world gave men an identity counter to that of the larger social world. Listening to stories of other men and learning what men did together sexually was an important aspect of the process of remaking the subversive life story. Frontain (2000) has suggested that the genre of gay self-life writing has been shaped by the historical experience of social opprobrium that forced men to have furtive, generally anonymous, sexual contacts. Gay men tell about these experiences in coded narratives, which, as Jolly (2001a) has suggested, are often told or written as a kind of confession. Writing about these experiences provides a way of remembering and making sense of a past and helps these men overcome feelings of shame.

Plummer (1995) has observed that being able to write a life story of how we remake ourselves offers a means for overcoming the secrecy imposed on gay men and hiding an important aspect of one's own life from friends and family. Publishing a memoir of the journey into accepting homosexuality is personally affirming and reflective of changing social circumstances in which men feel safe in writing their own life stories, whether formally published or available as a Weblog. In an earlier time, Andrew Tobias (1973) wrote his memoir under an assumed name (John Reid) to hide his gay identity from his family. With the social change of the past decade, Tobias felt sufficiently safe to reissue the memoir in the late 1990s using his real name, along with a second volume portraying his experiences since the first volume had been completed. Consistent with Mark Freeman's (1993) discussion of the self-life writing as an account of a particular life and an effort to resolve issues facing a shared community of writer and readers, these personal accounts are, at the same time, those of one's own life and those of that larger community.

Narratives of lived experience, including memoirs and autobiographies, are inevitably "political" in the sense that they use self-reflection to address some larger social issue salient at the time when life writing takes place (Williams 1977). Issues of identity, group solidarity, and enhanced sense of personal and collective empowerment become a salient feature of these narratives. Paul Monette (1988) wrote a detailed account of his lover Roger's discovery of being HIV positive, his own seroconversion, and of Roger's illness. It is also a historical account of life-threatening desire and the response by an indifferent government reflecting stigma and anti-gay prejudice to the emerging plague at a time when reliable information might have helped prevent others from becoming infected. Monette's account portrays the desperate search for a cure and the disappointment that Roger, and the community of men stricken with AIDS, felt as promising medical treatments proved worthless and sometimes increased the intensity of the symptoms of AIDS-related illness.

Historical and social change enters into the individual life story but in somewhat different ways for life-writers of different generations. The memoirs of men born in the late 1940s and the 1950s are replete with recollections of loss of lovers and friends to AIDS. Sometimes explicitly, as in accounts authored by Paul Monette (1988), Fenton Johnson (1996), or Mark Doty (1997), the memoir is itself an effort to work through the loss of lovers; in the case of Monette and Doty, their accounts are later followed by autobiographical memoirs. Consistent with psychoanalyst George Pollock's (1989) observation regarding mourning as a prelude to increased creativity, writing about the death of a lover may have made it possible to write one's own life story. Other memoirs, such as those of Andrew Tobias (1998a) or Tim Miller (1997), hint darkly at the issue of this loss shared by the community. Self-life writing among men born in the 1960s and coming of age in the 1980s, such as those of Scott Peck (1995) or Marc Adams (1996), both of whom grew up in Evangelical Christian Right families, are much more focused on issues of overcoming stigma and gaining family acceptance than on the issues of loss and mourning so common in the life writing of gay men born in preceding generations.

Understanding Time and Place

I have presented a view of the life story as an effort to make meaningful memories of the experiences of a lifetime. This is a somewhat daunting task for gay men whose very sexual being has long been stigmatized and who have felt ashamed of this desire. At the same time, even the most personal experiences must be understood in the context of a particular place and time. American culture is far more diverse than is often recognized. Southern writer James "John" Sears (1991, 1997) has demonstrated the importance of appreciating place in his collection of the personal accounts of gays and lesbians growing up in the South in the postwar period. Personal accounts based on interviews collected by Will Fellows (1996) point to the significance of understanding homosexuality while growing up in the rural Midwest and then relocating from farm to city in adulthood. These personal accounts are told in the context of the larger social changes and political controversies that they have faced in their own lives.

Time is as important as place in understanding the way we make our life story. Indeed, time is important in determining the ways in which we understand our very life. In this book I have described the ways in which the generation these men were born in has influenced both their understanding of their same-sex desire and the significance of this desire as an organizing force in writing a life story. For example, many gay men born in the 1970s and 1980s write about their gay sexual desire and identity in much less stigmatized terms than those life-writers born in earlier generations. A primary concern among these younger gay life-writers is having the same opportunities and rewards as their straight counterparts. Life-writers such as Kirk Read (2001) have grown up at a time when it was possible to disclose their gay identity while in high school or college. They report that they have found community support and acceptance for their gay sexual orientation.

Social theorist Karl Mannheim (1928) was among the first to write about the importance of generation in the study of social life. He maintained that there is a continual interplay between history and autobiography; each generation has experienced unique social and historical circumstances that determine its outlook. While Mannheim had pointed out the importance of generation in determining the manner in which we write about our own life, the dynamics of this interplay between generation and one's view of self and society have been most clearly described by sociologist Glen Elder (1996), who refers to a group of persons born in adjacent birth years (generally within a decade) as a generation-cohort. People within this cohort may share common experiences and travel in a sort of convoy together across the course of life. While they share certain experiences in common, they maintain a distinctive understanding of experiences taking place at a particular time in the course of their life. While there may be wide variation within a generation, which reflects both geography and family background, there are also some similarities in the meanings that these members of a generation make regarding personal and social changes.

Social psychologists Howard Schuman and Jacqueline Scott (1989) and Martin Conway (1997) have shown that events taking place during young adulthood have a particularly important impact on the manner in which members of a generation later remember the past. These experiences of young adulthood, roughly between the ages of nineteen and twenty-five, represent a "reminiscence bump," which becomes a kind of filter for a distinctive worldview unique to this generation, and which members of this generation carry across the course of their life and into old age. Members of this generation then understand subsequent social and historical change in terms of memory of this early adult experience. Youth is a time of particular sensitivity to social and political movements; youth are more willing than older counterparts to be involved in social innovation. Such institutional settings as college or the military bring young people together in a place where new ideas can be learned from consociates. Successive generations are each founded on the salient ideas and experiences common for that genera-tion during young adulthood, which are then maintained throughout their life. These generationally based solutions for personal and social dilemmas may come into conflict as each generation seeks to press its own solutions for shared dilemmas upon both older and younger generations.

This generation-cohort perspective has been developed most com-pletely by sociologist Glen Elder. Elder (1974) had used the Depression as an event experienced by a large number of people but one that had a quite different impact upon those who were young children or teenagers at this time of this national calamity. Elder showed that this event had a distinc-tive impact on the way in which each generation viewed itself and others, and the manner in which each generation negotiated its own life course. Just as the Depression was a historical event leading to wide-scale social change in American society, two historical events have been of particular significance for the gay community: the gay rights revolution that followed in the wake of a protest riot in June 1969, when the police attempted to raid New York's Stonewall Inn, a gathering place for people of minority sexualities (Carter 2004; Duberman 1994); and the emergence of the AIDS pandemic in 1981 (Boxer and Cohler 1989; Cohler, Hostetler, and Boxer 1998; Cohler and Hostetler 2002).

This perspective for studying the impact of generation on sexual iden-tity and expression of same-sex desire has been used by the Hall Carpenter Archives Group (1989), by Nardi, Sanders, and Marmor (1994) and by Ro-senfeld (2003) in their reviews of the personal testimony of gay men across the twentieth century. Will Fellows (1996) has also used this perspective in his account of men growing up on Midwestern farms and moving to the city as they sought connection with a community of gay men, as well as by journalist and gay activist Douglas Sadownick (1996), who has reviewed interviews and written accounts of gay men across successive decades from the postwar period to the 1990s. Two interested observers of the lesbian life course (A. Stein 1997; Parks 1999) have discussed the meaning of self and sexuality across several generations of lesbians.

Social disruptions, such as the Stonewall riots and the creation of a visible protest movement, intersect with the course of life in ways that challenge one's understanding of self. The Stonewall riots and the dramatic social changes inspired by this resistance to the police were, in turn, foreshadowed by events taking place earlier in the decade. At that time, many courageous gay men and women, using the model of the civil rights movement, picketed the White House demanding equal rights. Indeed, the Mattachine Society and the Daughters of Bilitis, semisecretive organizations formed in the postwar period, had tried to bring the plight of homosexuals to the attention of policy makers. However, the political activity inspired by the generation of gay men born in the 1940s and 1950s was able to bring about this revolution in gay rights by advantage of the dramatically changed social conditions of the late 1960s and the 1970s (Clendinen and Nagourney 1999; D'Emilio 1983; Loughery 1998).

The AIDS pandemic followed the advent of the gay rights movement by a decade. There has been much controversy regarding the outbreak of this scourge, first within the gay community and, more recently, throughout the world. It may be that the virus responsible for this assault on the immune system, leading to opportunistic and inevitably fatal illnesses, had been present in the population for several decades. Journalist and gay activist Randy Shilts (1987) may not be correct in his portrayal of a flagrantly promiscuous gay flight attendant as "case zero" and the source of the HIV virus in the gay community. However, he portrays the spread of the virus among health workers in Africa and homosexual men in the United States, in the previous decade, as well as the government's indifference to this health hazard, even as it was spreading among gay men across the nation. What we do know is that a bulletin from the Centers for Disease Control and Prevention (CDC) reported in June 1981 that a rare form of pneumonia had infected five men, all active homosexuals in Los Angeles; three of the five men had shown compromised immune systems.

Andrew Tobias (1998a) recalls a sunny morning at breakfast over the long Fourth of July weekend in 1981, sitting with his housemates on the veranda of their Fire Island home overlooking the tranquil Long Island Sound and reading the *New York Times*. One of them reported a brief item, buried on page 20 of the *Times,* about a rare illness striking homosexual men. He remembers that a chill went through him as he immediately grasped the significance of the account of the CDC bulletin in the *Times*. AIDS would eventually claim four of his housemates and about half of his Sunday brunch list. It was only a matter of a few weeks until the magnitude of this health crisis was publicized in the alternative press by physician and activist Larry Mass and others. Soon the newspapers were full of obituaries of men dying from the consequences of AIDS (the stigma attached to this gay disease was often coded as death from pneumonia or an unstated illness). This second cohort-defined event can be dated from the publication of the CDC bulletin and the reports in the *Times* and Mass's article, which alerted the community of this emerging health crisis.

Among those men and women seeking same-sex social and sexual intimacy, the emergence of a gay identity as a visible social movement called for a new story of self. *The Best Little Boy in the World,* first published in 1973 by recent Harvard graduate Andrew Tobias under the pseudonym John Reid, and Arnie Kantrowitz's (1977/1996) memoir *Under the Rainbow* are particularly dramatic exemplars of the impact of this social change. These narratives, in turn, have become icons for later self-life writing by gay men seeking sexual partners. Across the past decade, as gay identity and lifestyle has increasingly become a part of mainstream contemporary society, a number of publishers have accepted memoirs of gay men for publication.

Some of these accounts, such as those authored by Tobias and Kantrowitz, were written contemporaneously with the events portrayed. Other men have written memoirs looking back on their experiences over half a lifetime. These accounts are "written backwards" and inevitably raise questions regarding the accuracy of events so dependent upon memory and recollection. These more recent personal accounts have also been influenced by accounts previously published by other gay men of their own and other generations. We ought to find, however, that gay men of particular generations may look back at the past and discuss sexuality and self in ways more similar to other life-writers of their own generation yet different from the way in which men of other generations make use of the past in writing their life story.

Using the concept of generation-cohort as a means for understanding the impact of time upon the experience of self and others in the meaning we make of sexual attraction for other men, I have chosen to discuss the life writings of six generation-cohorts who have experienced same-sex desire within the sociohistorical changes of the past half-century. The oldest generation of men born in the 1930s came of age following the end of World War II. These men may have served in the Korean conflict and were already middle-aged at the time of the Stonewall riots of 1969 and the emergence of the gay rights movement (Carter 2004; D'Emilio 1983/1998; Duberman 1972/1993; Clendinen and Nagourney 1999; Hall Carpenter Archives 1989,

Harwood 1997; Kantrowitz 1977/1996; Nardi, Sanders, and Marmor 1994; Young 1995). Many of these men had no name for their same-sex attraction. If they were urban residents, they might have known of particular places, such as bars or Turkish baths, that were "safe" for finding others seeking intimate sexual relationships (Brown 2001; Chauncey 1994; Read 1973/1980). Political activity was difficult for this generation since homosexuality was often defined as illegal and subject to criminal prosecution.

Among men of the 1930s generation, homosexuality was classified as a psychiatric disorder, and homosexual men were often remanded by family and community to psychiatrists seeking to convert these men to heterosexuality. Frequent police raids on bars where these men went to find sexual partners often resulted in criminal prosecution and publication of their names in the newspaper. Because of the social taboo on intimacy between men, this furtive experience of sexuality led to a disconnect between sexuality and intimacy, the remnants of which have echoed across succeeding generations of gay men struggling to reconcile sexuality and enduring intimacy (Sullivan 1998).

A second generation of men born in the 1940s, the leading edge of the "baby boomers," came of age at about the time of the Vietnam conflict. Along with some of the men born in the 1950s, men in the '40s generation were particularly likely to be affected by the dramatic social changes of the late '60s and '70s (Marotta 1982; Monette 1992; Tobias/Reid 1973, 1998a, 1998b). As young adults in the late 1960s, the '40s generation was on the leading edge of social change at the time of the Stonewall riots (Carter 2004; Duberman 1994). In the wake of that event and the emergence of the gay rights movement, the social change realized by the members of this cohort led to greater freedom in acknowledging their gay sexual identity to family and friends. Alas, they shared with the 1950s generation the impact of the AIDS epidemic as a result of their increased sexual freedom (Gagnon 1990; Moore 2004) and may have contributed to the spread of a silent killer that began to take its toll a decade later. Reaching middle age, members of this cohort have experienced large numbers of losses due to the death of partners and friends from AIDS-related illnesses (Doty 1997; Monette 1988, 1992, 1994; Odets 1995). Sadownick (1996, 107) reports that these men at midlife often feel guilty that their youthful heady rush into newly accessible encounters led to the AIDS pandemic, a generational-defining event that structured the personal accounts among men reaching young adulthood during the 1980s.

Commenting on men writing their autobiography portraying their sexual desire for other men, Mary Evans (1999) observed:

The changes in sexual mores and sexual behavior that became part of the common culture of the West (and the changes were emphatically Western rather than global) made it possible for gay men to discuss openly the nature of their sexuality and its implications in terms of their relations to others . . . there has always been a substantial literature about the nature of gay relationships and gay subcultures, but until recently it has had to exist in a coded or submerged form . . . little explicit discussion of homosexuality was possible . . . [but] the transformations of the 1960s and 1970s made a new openness and revelation possible. . . . HIV (and AIDS) brought a new, tragic dimension to autobiography in that many of the men who now came to write it were either infected or closely involved with the afflicted. (92)

Evans demonstrates the significance of generation as a means for understanding social change. As Plummer (1995) has noted, mention of one's own sexual orientation in those early days was sure to invite social exclusion and even risk criminal sanctions or forced medical treatment. The result was that men attracted to other men could not tell others about this attraction; indeed, many men could not even admit this desire to themselves. Secrecy kept this desire hidden, hence the metaphor of the "closet" (Loughery 1998). Particularly in the life writing of men born in the 1930s and 1940s, but to some significant extent for men in all six cohorts in this study, life stories told of being forced to maintain a subversive identity.

A third generation of men, those born during the 1950s, came of age following the emergence of a gay rights movement; they celebrated the enhanced personal freedom made possible by that revolution and the increased opportunity of "coming out" or disclosing gay identity to family and friends, and possibly within the workplace as well, but they also bore the brunt of the AIDS pandemic (Odets 1995). Men in this generation believed that it was possible to adopt a gay lifeway (Herdt 1997; Hostetler and Herdt 1998). Often concerned with issues of finding a life-partner or "husband," participants in this cohort may be the first to have assumed an adult life-course little different from that of so-called straight counterparts. Members of this generation were also among the first to believe that it was possible for gay men to be parents (Green 1999) and to enjoy the social change that permitted them to adopt children.

A fourth generation of men, those born during the 1960s and presently in settled adulthood (Cohler and Boxer 1984) or early middle age, came of age at a time when sexual intimacy enjoyed with other men had become "virtually normal" (Fricke 1981; Herdt and Boxer 1996; Miller 1997; Peck 1995; Savin-Williams 1998; Sullivan 1995). Within this generation, enjoying the benefits of the gay rights movement, concern with finding a life-partner and achieving career success have replaced the shame and stigma felt by previous generations.

A fifth generation of gay men, those born in the 1970s, and a sixth generation of gay or questioning young men, born in the 1980s, have come to adulthood at about the time of the discovery of antiretroviral medication. As result, young men in these two most recent generations have seldom experienced the tragedy of witnessing lovers and friends succumb to AIDS. These two generations have also experienced somewhat less stigma regarding an alternative sexual identity than prior cohorts of young adults (Dew 1994; Lawrence 1999; oasismag.com 1999; Savage 1999; Shyer and Shyer 1996). Many members of this generation of gay youth, particularly those growing up in more affluent, socially sophisticated urban and suburban communities, have found acceptance from family, school, and community for their alternative sexual identity and have enjoyed the support of such organizations as Parents and Friends of Lesbians and Gays (PFLAG) and the Gay, Lesbian and Straight Education Network (GLSEN) (Herdt and Koff 1999).

For many of these young people, the issue is less one of being "out" to self and others than of being able to realize satisfying and lasting relationships. These two generations of young adults have also known since childhood that expression of sexual desire must always be qualified by insuring "Safer Sex." For these men, the murder of Matthew Shepard in October 1998 was particularly terrifying (Kaufman 2001; Loffreda 2000). They identify with college student Shepard and believe that they too could be potential targets of hate crimes. The Shepard murder may be the event of young adulthood that defines their generation. At the same time, the impact of Shepard's murder, while uniting the gay community in response to this hate crime, has had quite different meanings for men belonging to older generation-cohorts who respond in terms of their particular life experiences as a "convoy" moving together through the course of life (Plath 1980).

The Significance of Personal Narrative

Olney (1972, 1998) and Weintraub (1978) maintain that the formal autobiography is the ideal form of self-life writing since it is self-reflexive and concerned with the interplay between one's own experiences and the time and place in which the autobiography is written. However, the contemporary idiom of life writing among men portraying their life and the personal significance of being homosexual is most often a blend of memoir and autobiography. This genre of life writing reflects the same self-consciousness characteristic of autobiography in former times. Memoirs such as those by the life-writers in the present study generally make explicit reference to the interplay of lived experience and the larger social and historical context in making meaning of their desire for an intimate relationship. Indeed, the awareness of stigma and possible sanction simply on account of an alternative sexual lifeway has itself fostered heightened awareness of social and historical context (Read 1973). At the same time, life-writers vary in the way they look backward to their own or a shared experience in constructing a coherent life story. This is particularly true of the two younger generations of life-writers who have not reached that point in life where such concern with accounting for the past is likely to be salient (Lieberman and Falk 1971; Neugarten 1979).

Identity or self is founded on a sense of personal coherence, which is realized through a life story remade over a lifetime in response to both personal circumstances and social and historical change (McAdams 2003). A life story includes events in both our own lives and our experiences living at a particular time and in a particular place, and written or told within a shared understanding of what constitutes a good story. Writer and reader alike each bring a unique perspective to a life story. Our own life experiences, particular generation membership, and the time and place of the reading all enter into the manner in which we make sense of a life story. In some sense, the life story does not exist outside of our present reading of the story at a point in our own life and as a member of a generation experiencing some larger social and historical changes in common, and in which events of youth assume significance in shaping the outlook of that generation.

The significance of social circumstance in the construction of personal narrative has been well portrayed by Plummer (1995) in his discussion of sexual stories and by Flannigan-Saint-Aubin (1992), who notes that both writers and readers need to be considered in discussing any text. Indeed, both self-life writing and reading assist in constructing the lifeways of any particular generation or cohort. Writing becomes reading, and reading becomes the template for understanding self and others. As Plummer (1995) observes: "We consume stories in order to produce our own; we produce stories in order to consume them. Stories can be appropriated in a multiplicity of ways" (43). For example, understood as text, the ubiquitous male pornographic video has become the script for what gay men understand as the expected sexual experience (Burger 1995; Cohler 2004b, 2004c). In the same way, the so-called coming out story has achieved the status of an icon among men narrating the course of their dawning awareness of same-sex sociosexual desire, although somewhat differently interpreted across generations (Savin-Williams 1998).

Following Mannheim's (1928) discussion of generations and the dynamics of social change, I suggest that generations succeed each other, that younger generations are a source of social change, and that these changes become part of the shared experiences of each successive generation-cohort or consociates (Plath 1980), while recognizing that there is important intracohort variation such as that founded on geography, ethnicity, or social status (Settersten 1999). Generation shapes the social outlook and narrative of lived experience among members of a generation-cohort, and these generation-based differences in social outlook and timing of role transitions, such as age of leaving school or retirement, are reflected in the personal accounts of successive cohorts. Nowhere is this more evident than in the experience of the generation of men now in midlife, many of whom have suffered the loss of partners and friends through AIDS. Experiencing losses more typical of men within the heterosexual community and who are in their seventies and eighties, these men at midlife express a foreshortened sense of time as a result of their many early adult losses (Borden 1989).

Writing and reading life stories regarding epiphanies or "turning points" experienced in resolving issues of sexual identity fosters an enhanced sense of personal integrity for the writer *and* an enhanced sense of community for the reader. Readers of particular generations identify with the exemplary stories of their consociates; these life stories reflect and elaborate the particular memories of a generation. At the same time, following Mannheim (1928) and Settersten (1999), and recognizing the impact of variation due to region of the country, ethnic background, and family position, understanding of self and the experience of sexual desire is understood in ways that are in most ways similar to others of their generation. Plummer (1995) notes that there is always "a flow of negotiations and shifting outcomes" (27), which enables stories to be told—in particular ways at particular times and in particular places; at least to some extent, these personal accounts make up the way in which gay men understand their life experiences.

Men in the two oldest generations in the present study, growing up before Stonewall and the emergence of the gay rights movement, presumed that awareness of their same-sex desire was innate, present from earliest childhood and the source of enduring shame and social stigma. Men coming of age in the wake of the gay rights movement, particularly those born after 1960 and living in more affluent and liberal communities, were better able to express same-sex desire with somewhat less personal conflict and social opposition then was experienced by men born in the 1930s through the 1940s.

The views of these younger generations have increasingly altered the views of the older generations regarding their sexual desire for other men in a kind of "backward socialization." Increasing numbers of middle-aged and older men have begun to report first awareness of same-sex desire only in the second half of life (Cohler and Galatzer-Levy 2000). These men may decide upon divorce in order to realize this lifelong attraction or make this decision following the death of their spouse. As members of a generation in which heterosexual marriage was believed the only acceptable sexual lifeway, other middle-aged and older men report awareness of this homosexual attraction from childhood or adolescence, but have continued to suppress it or to seek furtive outlets in bathhouses and with "escorts."

The present study discusses the self-life writing of ten men aware of their own sexual desire born across six generations from the 1930s to the 1980s. This discussion is supplemented, where available, by life-story accounts that my colleagues and I have gathered in our study of aging, same-sex desire, and the course of life, and also by my own psychotherapeutic work (Cohler 2004c; Cohler and Hostetler 2002, 2006). Robinson (1999) has commented on self-life writing among writers of twentieth century literature for whom same-sex desire was implicitly significant in their writings.

The life stories are authored by men self-identifying as homosexual or gay—seeking other men for social and sexual intimacy—and whose accounts have appeared from the postwar period to the present time. While some of these life-writers are accomplished and well-recognized writers, other accounts have been authored by first-time writers. I have followed the suggestions of Harvard social psychologist Elliot Mishler (1999) and sociologists Cathy Charmaz (2002) and Ken Plummer (2001) in selecting life stories among men writing about self and sexual desire within a particular generation, which are "information rich" in the sense that these life stories provide particular insight into an important issue or critical life experiences salient for that generation. As Plummer (2001, 133) observes:

Qualitative researchers only really seek samples that are "information rich"—they are much less concerned with representativeness. So life stories may provide "intensity sampling" where key informants provide great insight into a particular area or "critical case sampling" where stories are selected on the basis of providing detailed information on key, critical experiences.

In addition to being information rich, the accounts selected for discussion here have been included on the basis of the following criteria: (1) the personal account must be completely self-authored (2) it must provide an account of a life from childhood to the present living in an American community, and (3) it must include both discussion of efforts to come to terms with same-sex attraction and also means used to maintain personal coherence when confronted with awareness of this desire.

Clearly, no claim can be made that the self-authored accounts I have chosen for discussion are representative in any statistical sense for any generation of self life-writers. Following the perspective of Harvard social psychologist Elliot Mishler (1999), we rely on trustworthiness as defined within the tradition of the narrative study of lives, rather than standard assumptions regarding validity characteristic of quantitative inquiry. As Mishler has observed:

The view of validation I have advanced suggests that the questions to be asked about my study and of any study within any research tradition are: What are the warrants for my claims? Could other investigators make a reasonable judgment of their adequacy? Would they be able to determine how my findings and interpretations were "produced" and, on that basis, decide whether they were trustworthy enough to be relied upon for their own work. . . . The primary reason is the visibility of the work: of the data in the form of texts used in the analysis . . . available to other researchers, of the methods that transformed the texts into findings; and of the direct linkages shown between data, findings, and interpretation. (429)

Consistent with Mishler's (1990) discussion of inquiry-guided validation, most of the memoirs that I discuss are available in print; URLs for the blogs of life-writers born in the 1980s are listed in the references but are no longer available.

2

Born in the Thirties
Coming of Age in the Fifties

A . . . major example of stories of sexual suffering concerns gay and lesbian "coming out" stories. Although same-sex experience probably exists universally across time and space, the notion of "the homosexual" is a very modern thing . . . it is not really until the advent of a host of political activities in mid-century symbolically linked to Stonewall and the gay liberation front-that the full blown public "gay" and "lesbian" comes into being.

Ken Plummer, Telling Sexual Stories

I was eager to be liberated *from* an unorthodox sexual life. I saw therapy, not fringe politics, as the instrument of that liberation and would have rejected . . . any gesture to include homosexuals as a part of a virtuous, oppressed underclass.

Martin Duberman, Cures

New York Is a Wonderful Town

For the cohort of men born in the 1930s, reaching young adulthood in the 1950s meant coming to adulthood at a time of both unprecedented prosperity in the postwar era and also pronounced focus on conventionality in personal and social life. For men and women aware of their homoerotic desire, this time also meant heightened feelings of estrangement from their own desire (Duberman 1986, 344). As Duberman later observes in his diary while looking back at this period of his youth, "to have grown up gay in the Fifties was to view oneself as emotionally shallow, stunted" (Duberman 1986, 362).

It is ironic that this postwar prosperity also presaged significant social change in the succeeding decades: society in 1970 looked markedly different from 1960. The war years had led to unprecedented population shifts, including the urban resettlement after the war of single men and women who had served in the armed forces, had enjoyed shore leave in these cities, and who were reluctant to return home to small towns where life-chances were less promising. For gay men, the allure of the large city was particularly important. Historians John D'Emilio (1983/1998) and Alan Bérubé (1990) have documented the impact of World War II on gay lifestyles, the mass movement of the American population that led to the enhanced possibility of meeting other men of similar sexual persuasion within large seaport cities as New York and San Francisco, and the consequent development of such settings as bars and bathhouses catering to this emerging social group.

Urban Life as Refuge

Nowhere was social change better represented than in New York, an urban magnet for single young men looking to make their way in the world. Much of this postwar excitement was anticipated with the 1944 opening of composer Leonard Bernstein's musical *On the Town*. Three sailors on a twenty-four hour leave explore the enchantment of this magical place and time. The 1953 Bernstein musical, *Wonderful Town,* borrowing a phrase from its predecessor musical and crafted by ostensibly gay Jewish men, portrays a much more domestic New York of the 1930s in which two sisters leave Ohio for New York and a bohemian Greenwich Village. *On the Town,* developed by two men whose own sexuality was rumored to tend toward homosexual, anticipated the arrival of three men whose lives are recounted in this chapter. Consistent with Tierney's (2000) reading of Meriwether Lewis's suicide as a response to unrequited love for William Clark following his return from his cross-continent expedition with Clark, the gay patron watching *On the Town* is struck by the reluctance of the hero to succumb to the wiles of his guide who seeks through the musical to entice him to her apartment. Is it possible that there is a subtext to this musical, that of the man who seeks a man rather than a woman as his companion and who would enjoy going with a man to his apartment?

At the same time, as the social commentator John Loughery (1998) has observed, the postwar period stressed not only the end of the restlessness of the war years in the new housing estates but also the importance of the heterosexual union, which may have sharpened the difference between homosexual and heterosexual. Social and psychiatric commentary alike stressed the importance of the "normal" family, with a husband working and a wife at home caring for their young children. Failure to live up this model meant stigma as a social outcast. The big city offered an alternative to the idyll of suburban America in these years.

The two life-writers of the generation born in the 1930s came from strikingly different backgrounds, yet each ended up in New York in the heady 1950s, a time when there was a vibrant underground homosexual community largely out of the public purview. Young men struggling with the conflict between their own sexual desire and community expectations of conformity were drawn to New York where there was social support and opportunity for an alternative lifestyle. Alan Helms (Helms 1995) arrived in New York from middle America and came of age as the oldest son of a Presbyterian family struggling through the Great Depression. Helms was able to win a college scholarship to Columbia and first ventured to New York in the late 1950s. Writer and activist Martin Duberman (Duberman 1991c, 1996) grew up in an affluent suburban New York Jewish family in which his immigrant grandparents had realized economic success in their adopted land. A native New Yorker, Duberman never strayed too far from the city, venturing as far as Harvard to the north and Princeton to the south. Each of these life-writers ended up as professors of literature (Helms in Boston, Duberman in New York). Born in the 1930s (Duberman in 1930, Helms in 1937), these men came to adulthood along with the growth of the American metropolis in those postwar years, which provided anonymity, diversity in lifestyle, and enhanced possibility of finding others with similar inclinations.

In the wake of the social change created by World War II and its aftermath, including migration to the city, a nascent homophile movement emerged during the 1950s. Kaiser (1997) noted three critical events of this decade that made a difference in the lives of men and women realizing same-sex erotic desire: (1) the organization in 1951 of the Mattachine Society, the first explicitly homosexual social and political organization; (2) the publication of the Kinsey reports on the sexual practices of American men along with the publication of the first widely available book discussing homosexuality as an urban lifestyle (Cory 1951); and (3) the psychological studies of the Los Angeles psychologist Evelyn Hooker (Hooker 1956, 1957). These three things helped gay men across the country realize that they were not alone in their homoerotic desire. The formation of the Mattachine Society in Los Angeles made it possible for psychologist Evelyn

Hooker to design a study of homosexual men not seeking psychotherapy, which would show that sexual orientation had little relationship to psychological adjustment.

The first landmark event was the founding in 1951 of the Mattachine Society in Los Angeles by the longtime Communist Party activist Harry Hay. Autonomous local cells fostered radical political action using the model of the American Communist Party (Loughery 1998). Hay chose the name "Mattachine" after "mysterious medieval figures in masks whom Hay speculated might have been homosexual" (D'Emilio 1983, 67).

The second landmark event, publication of the Kinsey reports and the trade book *The Homosexual in America: A Subjective Approach* by Donald Webster Cory [Edward Sagarin], was important in making known a social minority long invisible in American society. Even though based on rather skewed data, often using men in jail as informants, the Kinsey report suggested that upwards of one-third of all men had experienced some desire for sexual intimacies with other men during their life with about 10 percent explicitly identifying with same-sex erotic desire. In the first volume of his memoirs, Martin Duberman (1991c) notes the importance of the Kinsey report for his generation in showing that same-sex desire was a "normal" aspect of human experience.

Cory's book was the first mass-marketed book to document the nature of the homosexual community in America. Widely available in bookstores and libraries, written by a homosexual married man under a pseudonym, the book went through seven printings between 1951 and 1957. D'Emilio (1983) and Duberman (1999a) have discussed the impact of this book on a generation of gay men and women participating in the construction of a new identity politics. Sagarin's description of his desire, which he had been aware of from his youth, his feelings of shame engendered by an unforgiving society, and his call to action became a beacon for gay young people. It provided assurance that there was "nothing wrong" with us, even though our fantasies differed from those reported by our heterosexual high school peers.

Access to members of the Mattachine Society made possible the third important event of the 1950s, the pioneering social psychological reports of the Los Angeles psychologist Evelyn Hooker (1907–96) (Boxer and Carrier 1998). Hooker realized that prior psychological study of the association between homosexuality and psychological adjustment had been based largely on groups of men seeking psychological intervention (common at a time when homosexuality was presumed to be "unnatural" and a form of psychopathology). Through her research assistants at UCLA, several of

whom were homosexual and in contact with the newly organized Mattachine Society, Hooker was able to recruit a group of homosexual men who
had not expressed the need for psychological help and a matched compari-
son group of men self-identifying as not having homosexual desire.

Psychologists, who did not know the self-defined sexual orientation of
these men, attempted to differentiate the psychological test protocols of
these homosexual and nonhomosexual men but were unable to sort protocols on the basis of sexual orientation. Indeed, some of the apparently best-
adjusted men were within what later emerged as the homosexual group.
Again, reports of this study in the media had a major impact on both the
public and the mental health professions, and led to a federally funded
conference on homosexuality and mental health sponsored by the National Institutes of Health (Hooker 1968). Findings from this conference
showed that sexual orientation and personal distress had little relationship
apart from the stigma attached to men and women with same-sex desire.
Martin Duberman (1991c) credits reports of Hooker's research with fostering his own self-esteem and realization that his desire was not "unnatural."

Martin Duberman: Making the Gay Identity

There have been few more articulate, activist, or self-reflective leaders of
the gay rights movement than Martin Duberman. Born in 1930, Martin
Duberman provides important details regarding the impact of social and
historical changes over the four decades covered by his memoirs of writing
about same-sex desire. Duberman was born into a wealthy, Jewish, suburban New York family. When Duberman became depressed as an adolescent, his family found the best-qualified psychotherapist for their son.
Later, continuing to seek psychotherapy for himself, his talent and education attracted the interest of the most senior but also the most antigay
psychoanalysts of the time. Duberman's story has the same tragic elements
as others of his own generation: homosexuality was presumed to be evidence of personal disturbance, which should be resolved through psychiatric treatment designed to foster the appropriate heterosexual adjustment.
Misguided efforts by mental health professionals stalked the life of this gay
pioneer.

Duberman's life story is reported in two volumes. The first, *Cures: A
Gay Man's Odyssey* (1991c), was an extension and revision of a personal
memoir included as a coda in his 1991 collection of historical documents
and essays *About Time: Exploring the Gay Past*. The second volume, *Midlife*

Queer: Autobiography of a Decade, 1971–1981 (1996), extended by a decade Duberman's reflexive account. Duberman also published several collections of essays, primarily on gay American history, including a classic account of the Stonewall Inn riot of June 1969 and based on the life histories of some of its major participants, and a number of plays for the American theater. *Cures* is based on a detailed diary that focused largely on his life through young adulthood, while *Midlife Queer,* also autobiographical, centers more on Duberman's contributions to theater and historical writing than on his own personal development. Considered together, the corpus of Duberman's life writing embodies the themes of engaging in a contest, primarily in opposition to the misguided psychiatric profession that sought to change his gay desire and, reflecting the theme of arriving at a new identity, finally establishing a personal home as a gay man comfortable with his newly found "true self" (Plummer 1995; Winnicott 1960). Indeed, as much as any person in the gay rights movement of the past three decades, Duberman has fostered construction of a new identity and a new community for men with same-sex desire.

Seeking the "Cure"

In the first (1986) edition of his essays *About Time,* Duberman reports being aware of his homoerotic desire from about the age of twelve when, at summer camp, he enjoyed rubbing his body against those of his cabin mates. He writes that later he had an unconsummated and anxiety-ridden fellatio experience with a high school classmate. While a Yale undergraduate, Duberman sought furtive contacts on the New Haven Commons. It is important to read this coda together with *Cures,* for the coda provides the background of the book and shows the importance of Doberman's diary as the basis of *Cures* (1991c). Duberman dwells much less on his childhood and his relations with other family members than is characteristic of other gay life-writers in this study. Other than noting that his father was a distant man and that his mother was attentive to his needs, there is not much discussion of his early family life. There is little more information than the cryptic remark (108) regarding repressive silence in society in the 1960s, "an order long familiar to gay people, who had learned how to read a father's silent disapproval of a son's voice pitched too high. Duberman is concerned less with an "explanation" for his gay desire than with the conflict between his desire and the opprobrium of a heterosexist society reflected in the attitudes of the several psychiatrists who tried to change his sexual orientation.

In his discussion of gay autobiographies of the twentieth century, the historian Paul Robinson (1999) comments on Duberman's cursory reference to his childhood and his relations with his parents. Robinson suggests that this is a literary device designed to silence those who might be tempted to view Duberman's life-history in terms of a failed and even personally destructive experience, a position that Duberman explicitly rejects. With the exception of brief mention of boyhood sexual exploration, Duberman tells us little about his life until the time of his graduate studies and his first sexual liaisons.

These two autobiographical volumes are part of a much larger corpus that includes *Black Mountain: An Exploration in Community* (1972), Duberman's personally meaningful account of New Left philosopher and social activist Paul Goodman and his pioneering North Carolina educational community, which lasted from the Depression through the mid-1950s. It was in this book, begun while Duberman was teaching at Princeton and struggling with the important issue of the psychological significance of teacher, student, and the classroom, where Duberman first publicly acknowledged his homosexuality (261, musing on his own teaching in a course on American radicalism). At that time, Duberman had been struggling with the possibility of disclosing his homosexuality to his seminar and the possible adverse impact of such a disclosure upon the students' own personal development. One the one hand, he was critical of Goodman's preoccupation with the confession of his sexuality and laments that Goodman had confused confession with autobiography. Goodman, an ostensibly arrogant, patronizing ideologist, was rude to Duberman in at least one public forum. But Goodman's disarming, honest approach regarding his sexuality resonated with Duberman's concern regarding his own split life, successfully plying his craft as a historian and playwright during the day, while at night exploring New York's gay bars and bathhouses.

The publication of his book on the Black Mountain community represented an epiphany following a journey of suffering (Plummer 1995). Duberman recognized that *Cures* was precisely the kind of explicit, confessional, personal book that he had earlier criticized in connection with Paul Goodman's writing. Duberman was troubled by Goodman's provocative use of his bisexuality as a confession, and reflecting on his critique of Goodman's work a quarter of a century later, he mused that identity was not merely the sum of socially disapproved acts but that "we *must* tell our secrets, must come out of our 'shameful' closets if a more humane, genuinely diverse culture is ever to emerge" (*Cures,* 80).

Duberman was inspired to make this revelation regarding his sexual identity in the book and in a *New York Times* article published at about the same time on the radical teaching ideas at Black Mountain. He believed that he was making an innovation in historical writing, showing how the life and personality of the historian inevitably influences the manner in which historical evidence is presented. Recalling this decision to disclose his gay identity in a preface to the 1993 reissue of *Black Mountain,* Duberman notes his distance from the incidents recounted in the book that provided, at the time, an outlet for his anger on learning of the arrest of a gay man in the community. Duberman expressed regret that reviewers neglected more important aspects of the book, an experiment in historical writing, focusing instead on those few lines in which he had revealed his own homosexuality.

At about the time that he was working on the page proofs for *Black Mountain,* Duberman had also written a play. Liberal friends, apparently not aware that he was gay, had invited him to stay with them while the work was premiered. When he arrived with his then boyfriend, his hosts told him he was not welcome in their home and would have to stay at a hotel since they were concerned about possible seduction of one of their sons. He reports that this experience led him to write his autobiography, relating what it was like to grow up gay in America, a project he completed two decades later. The incident with his friends represented a turning point when he finally was able to come to terms with his gay sexual identity.

Duberman also recognized correctly that reviewers would indeed pounce on this disclosure of his gay sexual identity in their critiques of *Black Mountain.* He warned his mother of this possibility, which marked his disclosure of his sexual identity to her (Duberman 1991c, 116–17, 223–24, 244–50). Duberman also assumed that reviewers would sharply criticize this disclosure and his own involvement with the history of the radical social and educational community that he was describing. Some critics excoriated him for defining himself in unconditional ways by disclosing his homosexuality, while others noted that Duberman was able to enjoy the luxury of being openly gay as an academic and intellectual, a freedom that was denied to those in more sensitive social positions. In the early 1970s, any disclosure of one's own sexual identity as homosexual would lead to being stigmatized. In the remarkable social change of the intervening decades, it is all too easy to forget Duberman's courage in his decision to disclose his sexual identity.

Following the publication of *Black Mountain* and an essay for the *New York Times Book Review* exploring psychoanalytic and social perspectives on homosexuality, Duberman again disclosed his sexual identity and became "irrevocably out" (Duberman 1991c, 257). Shortly thereafter he joined the Gay Activists Alliance, one of the earliest gay rights groups. This step into social activism within the emerging gay community, which he had resisted in the time immediately after the Stonewall Inn riots, marked a significant change and provided evidence that he was finally coming to terms with his homoerotic desire as something other than a disease to be cured. Yet Duberman still struggled with his sexual identity. Following the prejudiced remarks of one therapist who said that he would never be able to develop a satisfying relationship with another "gay" man, Duberman analyzed his relationship with hustlers, most of whom identified as hetero-sexual. He acknowledged that his desire for these men represented his hatred of his own sexual desire; it was, in effect, an effort to identify with the hustlers' heterosexuality and thus overcome being gay.

While Duberman's personal account is replete with suffering (McAdams and Bowman 2001) as a part of realizing a turning point in life and in his discussion of suffering in sexual stories (Plummer 1995), much of his distress was a consequence of the misguided efforts of psychological healers attempting to convert his sexual desire. Duberman's memoirs re-flect dramatic social change taking place throughout his adult years. This change is to some extent a direct consequence of Duberman's resistance to the prevailing view within the larger society that homosexuality was a form of psychopathology. He reports (Duberman 1991c, 22) that he used the term "gay" with a determination not common for his generation (Cohler and Hostetler 2003). At the same time, Duberman continued to have great difficulty accepting his own same-sex desire. His remarks (Duberman 1991c, 108–9) on social movements, psychotherapy, and his own homosex-uality suggest self-loathing, which led Duberman to persistent efforts to change his sexual orientation through psychotherapy.

Kaiser (1997) observed that this self-hatred and continuing sense of discontent was one of the most important attributes of the 1950s genera-tion of men with homoerotic desire. This was a time when psychiatry and psychoanalysis maintained that men seeking same-sex relations must have serious psychopathology (Socarides 1988). Duberman continued to pursue the elusive psychological cure through ever less conventional modalities of "people changing." As Duberman observes in the first edition (1986) of *About Time:*

I remember long talks with my gay friends at Harvard about whether we could achieve any sort of satisfying life, "stunted" as we were. We accepted as given that as homosexuals we could never reach "full adult maturity"—whatever the fuck that means. The it means what everybody said it did: marrying, settling down, having a family. We knew we'd never qualify, and despised ourselves for it. But it's too simple to reduce "growing up gay in the fifties" to a one-dimension horror story. (344)

Even while trying to change his sexual orientation, his public persona was that of a social activist countering the claims of those who maintained that sexual orientation could, or should be, changed. In 1972 at a conference for college counselors (Duberman 1991c, 269), Duberman (1999a) disputed the claims of purported psychiatric "experts" who advanced the theory that the "cause" of homosexuality was the parents' relationships with their prospectively homosexual son (Bieber et al. 1962). Psychiatric experts often made claims regarding the number of homosexual "patients" seen in treatment, which Duberman sagely described as their naive approach to the study of the development and family life of gay men and women. Duberman (1999a) describes a dramatic moment at the 1972 conference. Irving Bieber, one of these experts on the origins of homosexuality who maintained that the "cause" of homosexuality was an overbinding mother and an emotionally distant father, arrogantly reiterated his claim that he didn't know any homosexuals who had good relations with their fathers. At that point in the presentation a man in the audience stood up, disclosed that he was gay, and reported a continuing good and close relationship with his father.

It took another decade for psychiatry to undo the damage that had been done to the lives of gay men and women, and three decades for psychoanalysis to rid itself of this pathological bias (Cohler and Galatzer-Levy 2000; Terry 1999).

The theme for the first volume of his memoirs, and to some extent for the second volume as well, is established when Duberman recounts the experience at age fifteen of being sent to a psychiatrist; his parents were concerned that their son was "too quiet," perhaps even depressed. (He did not reveal his conflict with his sexuality to his first psychotherapist.) His second "therapeutic" experience took place at age eighteen, while on a cross-country journey, when he consulted a gypsy fortune-teller. The seer pronounced that he had a trouble that could be cured by joining the gypsies; Duberman chose Yale instead. Later Duberman sought the help of three other psychiatrists, each in his own way more destructive for Duberman's fragile self-esteem than his predecessor. We can understand all too well Duberman's unerring search for hypercritical psychiatrists rather than for psychiatrists more understanding of homosexuality whom Duberman would have known about through his immersion in New York's gay community. Quoting from his diary in the early 1970s after the third of these self-punishing therapeutic experiences (Duberman 1991c, 212):

I've internalized for so long the social definition of homosexuality as pathology and curse that I'm unable to embrace a different view, though I'd honestly like to. . . . The best I can honestly manage is to insist that I'm "caused," my imprinting so deep as to preclude any change in sexual orientation—yes, a change I'd still grab at, if perhaps a little less certainly than before. I've progressed to the point where I can (occasionally) relieve the guilt and shift the castigation from me to society.

This disparity between his self-loathing and his social activism is the theme of his life story. Duberman went on to a distinguished career in American studies and in the theater. His psychoanalysts at the time would likely have attributed his social activism to a "reaction formation" against his own unacceptable sexual desire. However, it is significant in understanding this split between self revulsion and social activism to recognize that he was a very talented writer, and this was not sufficiently appreciated by a succession of psychiatrists, less schooled in empathy than in assuring a heterosexual adjustment.

Unexplained is how Duberman was able to become involved in his work even as he was trying to make peace with his desire and to conform to the demands of the larger community. As among so many of his consociates coming of age in the postwar era, Duberman tried to appear heterosexually oriented. He even bravely attempted an experience in a whorehouse where, to his shame, he was unable to perform. Duberman's memory of his own sexuality is of homoerotic longing, reaching far back into his childhood. This insistence upon "always having been gay" is the dominant or master narrative of many men telling the gay sexual story (Moon 1998; Plummer 1995). This master narrative then serves to explain all subsequent concerns and conflicts.

Duberman's first tentative homoerotic experiences had been unsatisfactory contacts with older men on the New Haven Green. In graduate school, studying American history at Harvard, he began to explore the secretive Boston bars where homosexual men gathered. In the 1950s, one picked up information on gay bars from conversations overheard, or from off-hand homophobic comments among fellow students. Duberman cannot remember how he heard about the Napoleon, a bar catering to the collegiate crowd, and the Punch Bowl, a working-class gay bar. Cruising at night in two locales well known in Cambridge, Duberman's sexual experiences were furtive and shameful. Believing homosexual desire to be a problem, and guilt-ridden following satisfying and pleasurable experiences with fellow graduate students and working-class men from the community, Duberman once again sought psychotherapy, yet another of his many efforts at a "cure" for his homoerotic desire. Duberman notes that the 1950s was a time when psychotherapy was presumed to be the solution for all emotional problems. Not unexpectedly, "Dr. Weintraupt" was the stereotyped psychoanalyst of the time, devoted to curing patients of their problems—in Duberman's case, homosexuality, which reflected intrapsychic conflict leading him to avoid "normal" heterosexual desire.

His therapist urged him to terminate his tormented relationship with Larry, a fellow graduate student, also Jewish, but comfortable with his gay sexual identity. Duberman was unable to comply with this demand. Writing in his ever-present diary, Duberman recounts the struggle between his therapist's demand that he give up his relationship with Larry and also cruising for sex. Rather than helping Duberman to have good and satisfying gay relationships, the relationship with Larry became the stereotype of all gay relationships and his therapist regarded this as evidence either of a psychological conflict or a deficit in personality development. Social pressures of the time, including Harvard's overt antigay prejudice (Shand-Tucci 2003), would have made it difficult for any gay man to realize a satisfying relationship—even in the absence of a therapist's condemnation of gay desire.

Completing his doctoral studies and returning to Yale as a faculty member, Duberman once again sought a psychiatrist's assistance, inspired in part by the reality of academic life during the 1950s when, as he reports (Duberman 1991c, 43), there was particular sensitivity to the possibility that homosexual faculty would attempt to seduce students; colleagues had been summarily discharged from their positions once their homoerotic sexuality became known. Duberman feared that this might happen to him. The Yale psychiatrist, with whom he worked throughout the five years Duberman was back in New Haven, only affirmed his psychiatrist's view of gay desire as evidence of personal psychopathology. While "Dr. Igen's" affable demeanor and apparent neutrality regarding sexual orientation promised a more satisfactory resolution than in his previous therapeutic experience, the message was much the same: homosexual forays represented an "acting-out" of his neurotic conflicts. Duberman himself indicates (chaps. 3 and 4) that patronizing bars and bathhouses was associated with his despair. Empathic failure on the part of several well-meaning psychoanalysts only increased his feelings of personal disruption and helplessness, which were assuaged by these sexual forays.

Rebuffed and unappreciated, his psychiatric treatment adding to his own self-contempt, Duberman's search for fulfilling sex was intensified in the wake of these experiences with psychoanalysts. At the same time, Duberman's self-loathing prevented him from realizing sexual satisfaction with other men. He notes (49) his inability to appreciate his own body image in spite of the fact that he was indeed attractive. The problem is less that Duberman sought pleasurable experiences in a public sexual setting (Cohler 2004c) than that he sought out such pleasure but felt too inhibited to enjoy them.

Consonant with the attitudes of the 1950s, the criticism of his psychiatrists, academic culture, and society at large, Duberman faced continuing social opprobrium regarding his homosexuality. The McCarthy hearings at mid-decade echoed the sentiments of the larger society. Duberman, as so many other young men of his age, led a life divided between his career as a university faculty member, teaching and writing, and his gay pursuits. Leading such a split existence, denying an aspect of oneself, ultimately takes its toll on morale; Duberman reports feeling a lack of connection between these two facets of himself.

It is hardly surprising that "Dr. Igen" was little more successful than his predecessors in changing his patient's sexual orientation. The doctor dutifully attempted to connect his patient's story of disappointing gay relationships with his disappointing relationship with his father. Three decades later, gay psychoanalyst Richard Isay (1986, 1989) suggested that such emotional distance might stem from a father's discomfort with his son's erotic attraction to him rather than to his mother during the critical years of the preschool epoch, while Sidney Phillips (2001, 2003), another Yale psychoanalyst, suggested that this erotic attachment to his father may be a source of traumatic overstimulation for the little boy who then protects himself against such overstimulation by himself maintaining emotional distance from his father. It is painful to read of the psychiatrist's insistence that Duberman find a woman companion and try to become sexual with her as a way of curing his homosexuality.

Offered a tenured position at Princeton in 1962, Duberman moved into a new decade and a new job at a university. Duberman's ongoing pain was exacerbated both by his experiences with his Yale psychiatrist and the current press flurry reporting on the work of psychoanalysts Irving Bieber and Charles Socarides, who proclaimed that homosexuality was a psychological malady that could be "cured" or reversed. Duberman tormented himself: fifteen months had elapsed since he had last enjoyed sex. This personal restlessness was compounded by Princeton's isolation from the social changes of the 1960s. Fortunately, Duberman found pleasure in his scholarly and literary achievements.

Duberman survived nearly a decade at Princeton before finally moving to New York where he received considerable recognition for his accomplishments in the theater. His move provided Duberman respite from a dreary life in Princeton's history department. Even as he was set-tling into the emerging gay world in the city, with its bars and bathhouses, there was renewed police harassment of men in gay bars. Read (1973) has described the uneasy tension between the bar owners and the police be-fore and during the 1960s. Duberman traces his later social activism to this harassment. His activism led to enhanced self-awareness not even re-alized through his experiences with psychiatrists. As Duberman (1991c) comments:

I got to find out more about myself from involvement in political work than I did through formal, obsessive analysis of who I was. I also got to like myself better. The analytic view of me, of all homosexuals, as "truncated" human beings felt stale and mistaken when measured against the competence I displayed in and the respect I earned from my work in the movement. (78)

With the emerging Civil Rights movement, Duberman turned to the study of the radical tradition in America. He became the ideal type of the 1960s social activist protesting discrimination and affirming the need for social justice (D'Emilio 1983/1998). Consistent with Kaiser's (1997) iden-tification of important social changes taking place in the decade of the 1950s, Duberman credits the Mattachine Society, even with all its schism, with providing some counterforce to that represented by psychiatry. On the East Coast, the early gay activist and Harvard-educated astronomer Franklin Kamney organized a branch of the Mattachine Society in the mid-1960s. He had been fired from his position as a government astrono-mer in 1956 because he was in a gay bar at the time of one of the police raids of the time (D'Emilio 1983/1998; Read 1973). Kamney's activism in fighting discrimination, together with publication of magazines such as *ONE,* provided early support for social activism among gay men.

Turning thirty-five, an age that is often viewed by gay men as the onset of middle-age (Harry and DeVall 1978), and depleted by his experi-ence with several male prostitutes, Duberman once more turned to psy-chotherapy for a cure of his homosexuality. This third psychotherapy expe-rience was particularly painful. His therapist was, again, inappropriate, and the therapy intensified Duberman's own self-loathing. It is puzzling that Duberman could not have found a gay-supportive psychiatrist in the underground network of gay and gay-affirmative therapists. His choice of therapists may be explained by his low self-esteem and the need to find a therapist who would punish him as he was punishing himself. A group and individual psychiatrist, "Karl," as he is called in Duberman's book, tried to effect conversion to heterosexuality in ways that were reprehensible. Duberman understood better than his psychiatrist what conversion therapy for homosexuality had yet to learn: while it is possible to refrain from homosexual activity, reparative therapy cannot extinguish fantasies about having sex with other men (Cohler and Galatzer-Levy 2000).

Finally, at age forty, Duberman entertained the idea of finding an appropriate life-partner. The emerging drug scene beginning in the 1960s made it all too easy to escape into the bizarre world of hallucinations, which offered little more solace than psychotherapy. This search for personal fulfillment and a means for assuaging his continuing restlessness led him to turn to one-night stands with hustlers, which often led to longer-term rescue relationships as he tried to help these intelligent but disadvantaged and troubled youth to realize their own ambitions. Then came Stonewall. The author of one of the most detailed and important of the books written on this event (Duberman 1994), Martin Duberman frequented the Stonewall Inn. The events of that day in June 1969 when the Stonewall patrons resisted the police raid were all the more personally significant—he might well have been one of the patrons rounded up by the police that night and charged with resisting arrest. In the wake of the ever larger demonstrations against police interference in the life of New York's gay bars in the days following this raid (Carter 2004), Duberman avoided taking active part in this radical gay social protest only a few short blocks from his apartment; instead he immersed himself in his historical and creative writing.

Duberman attributes his hesitancy to join the emerging gay rights movement to his individuality. He also attributes his reluctance to becoming involved in gay politics to his continued self-criticism for being gay. Homosexuality was then, as now, too often identified solely with a preoccupation with sexuality. Believing himself to be psychologically crippled, he had identified with the aggressive antigay position of his psychiatrists and the society. This may explain Duberman's penchant for selecting therapists who were so avowedly hostile to homosexuality. Later, after becoming a central figure in the gay rights movement, Duberman helped spur the movement to restructure attitudes toward social and sexual minorities through his leadership in the Gay Academic Union, the National Gay Task Force, and other activist organizations. His efforts, together with those of journalist Ron Gold, a fellow gay activist, were important in advancing the 1973 decision by the American Psychiatric Association to "declassify" homosexuality as a psychopathological condition (Bayer 1987; Kutchins and Kirk 1997).

Hopes Stymied: A View from Middle Age

The second of Duberman's two-volume memoir reports on his life in the 1970s. More concerned than the first volume with the meaning—for him—of his sexual identity, the very term "queer" represented a problem in understanding the interplay of history and life history. A preferred term among younger men and women identifying as a sexual minority within the '70s and '80s generations, "queer" avoids portraying a duality in sexual identity as "gay" or "straight" and implies that such an identity is essential or of a natural kind (E. Stein 1999). Published in 1996, this second volume of his memoirs represents Duberman's retrospective consideration of his life during the 1970s when much of his activism was expressed through his writing, which, together with that of other '70s-era gay historians, was disparaged by the orthodoxy in the profession as not sufficiently academic.

One of the threads of continuity between the first and second volume of memoirs is Duberman's continuing search for a cure for his homoerotic desire. Although he had been able to accept a public gay identity, he continued his search for some resolution of the tension that he felt about his desire. In keeping with the time, having tried psychoanalysis, quasi therapeutic groups, encounter groups, and yoga, he tried LSD with the hope that it might free him from his guilt, and then he moved on to body therapy. Ultimately, he gave up these quick-fix therapies in favor of working out at the gym. (Duberman alludes—in an afterword to his essay reporting on the trial of Leonard Matlovich [1999c]—that he was eventually able to find a therapist who was helpful in his effort to make peace with his same-sex attraction.) Having had a "bad trip" in a movement-based quasi-religious group, and an unsuccessful excursion into the bioenergetic therapy of Alexander Lowen (a quasi-religious spiritual therapy popular during the 1970s), Duberman poses the problem of much of his search for a cure: "I was as by nature an 'impossibilist': a man who continues to seek what cannot be had; whose tenacious will refuses to capitulate to the preordained; who insists that he *can* still be 'happy' when all the evidence suggests he can't" (*Midlife Queer,* 147).

While the bioenergetic therapist appeared more understanding than previous therapists regarding Duberman's homoerotic desire, the therapist's bias against cruising or brief relationships reflected continuing social opprobrium against any sex outside of a permanent monogamous relationship. Duberman himself was caught in the dilemma separating intimacy and exploration/adventure. Psychoanalyst Dennis Shelby (1994, 2002) has noted that this dilemma confuses the meaning of cruising by viewing it as a reflection of problems in forming intimate ties with others, presumably founded on experiences within the family in early childhood, rather than realizing that the psychological meaning of cruising is to feel alive and vital, and to protect oneself against feelings of impending fragmentation.

The second volume of memoirs concerns Duberman's struggle with his feelings about himself as a man in middle age ends with Duberman's heart attack and difficult recovery, and with a physician unable to appreciate the psychological issues posed for gay men who become ill at midlife. The slow but steady recovery is juxtaposed with a postscript alluding to the appearance within the homosexual community of an immune-deficiency illness, which would later be termed AIDS. Taking stock in 1980, Duberman pessimistically characterizes his life at the end of the decade as one of personal loss. These losses include his relationship with Gary, his Catholic lover who left him for the priesthood; his own illness; his mother's death; and the country's turn to the right following the presidential election of 1980. At the end of *Midlife Queer,* Duberman fails to find a lover. That he did eventually find a partner is clear from the dedication to Eli Zal some two decades later in the 1996 publication of his book and also in the most recent collection of essays, *Left Out,* published in 1999.

Commenting on Duberman's quest for a relationship from a feminist perspective, Conway (1998) notes the tragedy of Duberman's life, which is characterized by romantic stereotypes. He chooses to pursue beautiful young men who are clearly not able to respond to his romantic overtures. Still, Conway muses, Duberman writes with humor and a capacity for self-reflection absent in most romantic narratives.

In his scholarly life Duberman felt compromised: his compilation of gay and lesbian history was stymied by lack of documentation. At the same time, he felt unable to write for the theater with his earlier enthusiasm. His personal life provided him with few sources of satisfaction. He lamented his lack of responsiveness for those men who wanted to love him, while continuing with his penchant for those men too preoccupied to form relationships or for street hustlers with whom contact only supported his own self-loathing. At the conclusion of this second volume of memoirs, reflecting on his heart attack, Duberman ponders whether, in retrospect, his heart attack was the result of continuing tension and worries about his own future and that of the gay community. AIDS emerged much as he had presaged, but the 1980s and '90s were marked by significant gains in gay rights (Clendinen and Nagourney 1999); Duberman became one of the most prominent figures in gay arts and letters, whose contributions fostered enhanced civil rights for gay people.

Finally, echoing the word of the homoerotic writer E. M. Forester in the epigram at the beginning of his novel *Howard's End,* Duberman was unable to connect the prose and the passion; the rationality that marked his scholarly work failed to illuminate his feelings about himself and others. This had been a theme in his innovative teaching at Princeton and the City Colleges of New York, a reason for his involvement in the Black Mountain project, which represented his "coming home," and the resolution of his earlier suffering through his disclosure of his sexual identity. He observes (Duberman 1996, 223) that "much had happened but little had changed. . . . I continued to feel trapped and deprived." Resuming his diary after several years lapse, rather than finding solace, he sees only miseries.

Paul Robinson's Reflections on Martin Duberman

Former student and later associate of Martin Duberman, the historian and psychoanalytic scholar Paul Robinson has written about Duberman as one of a number of gay autobiographers across the twentieth century. Robinson (1999) recounts his relationship with Duberman from the early 1960s when he was Duberman's undergraduate student at Yale, through the turbulent '70s and beyond. In a book in which Robinson, Lyman Professor of Humanities at Stanford, is reluctant to talk about himself, or his being gay, he notes the many ways in which his life has overlapped with that of Duberman's. However, Robinson notes that he had less difficulty than Duberman in recognizing his homoerotic desire, deciding to end his marriage, and moving with a lover to San Francisco in the 1970s; Duberman, on the other hand, continued to torture himself for his failure to find a "cure" for his homoerotic desire.

For the present study, it is important to realize that Robinson was born a decade later than Duberman and represents a different cohort of gay men who viewed their sexuality in terms quite different from men born in the 1930s. Educated in psychoanalysis, Robinson wonders about the reasons for Duberman's bitter rejection of that discipline. A succession of analysts were unable to help Duberman reconcile reason and passion in his life.

Robinson assails Duberman's account and failure to comprehend his unambiguous homosexuality. What he does not understand is the extent of Duberman's low self-esteem. It is the same self-hatred that leads Duberman to seek the opposite of himself in sexual encounters with strong "Anglo-Saxon" working-class men. Robinson criticizes Duberman in *Cures* for not discussing his undergraduate experiences at Yale in the same detail found in the work of Paul Monette (1992), a member of the generation born in the 1940s. Robinson appears not to appreciate the purpose of

Duberman's first volume of memoirs (Robinson doesn't discuss the second volume). In choosing the title *Cures,* Duberman addresses the problem of the prejudice present in postwar American dynamic psychiatry regarding the lives of gay men and women.

Robinson also criticizes Duberman's rationale for the breakup of a succession of relationships with working-class men as a consequence of social rather than personal forces. He fails to fully appreciate the interplay of the personal and the social; feeling depleted, Duberman sought in his working-class lovers the strength and manliness that he believed might assist him buttress what he felt to be his own lack of masculinity. Ultimately, unable to capture the strength that he so desperately sought, these relationships ceased to be fulfilling for him.

Robinson is impatient with Duberman's problematic experiences with psychoanalysis. Robinson suggests, without sufficient justification, that Duberman had not actually read the work of analysts such as Bieber and Socarides, who were so critical of homosexuality as a lifeway, even though Duberman blamed them for his own difficulties with his three analysts. However, Duberman reports that on at least one occasion he debated Bieber in public and clearly was well informed of Bieber's position that homosexuality was a psychological symptom founded in family processes, which distorted the course of a boy's personal development. Further, in other essays Duberman shows a solid grasp of the work of these analysts who were prejudiced against gay lifeways.

It is possible that even with his sophistication in psychoanalysis, Duberman unconsciously sought out analysts who would play into his own self-hatred. After all, fellow life-writer and academic Arnie Kantrowitz (1973) was able to find a gay psychoanalyst. Duberman was also a highly desirable candidate for analysis because of his social position and intellectual abilities. While a Harvard graduate student, Duberman had turned to the local psychoanalytic society for a referral. As an academic at a prestigious university, he would have been referred to a senior analyst who likely would have espoused the conservative psychoanalytic tradition of the 1950s, a time when homosexuality was understood as evidence of personal psychopathology. While the Yale psychiatrist was more open-minded than the Boston psychiatrist, the result was the same: their efforts to convert Duberman to heterosexuality simply played into Duberman's self-hatred.

Robinson charges Duberman (1999, 348) with "writing cultural history as much as autobiography," and of writing a saga representative of his generation of gay men. That, however, is exactly the point Duberman stresses and is central to the argument made in the present work: self-life writing must always be understood in the context of particular social and historical circumstances. Duberman's reflexive life writing shows the significance of the concept of an intellectual generation-cohort in understanding any personal account of lived experience. While Duberman has not written of his childhood experiences within his family and community, which might have contributed to understanding his adult confrontation with a fragile self-regard, his continuing search for an idealizing mentor-therapist and his attraction to strong working-class lovers points to the long-standing need for assistance in realizing personal coherence. He struggled to make sense of such disparate aspects of his identity as his professional dedication to American history, his success in the theater, and his quest for sexual and personal intimacy.

Alan Helms: A Gay Icon in New York

Born in 1937 and growing up in rural Indiana, Alan Helms found his way to New York in the 1950s and published his memoir, *Young Man from the Provinces: A Gay Life before Stonewall,* in 1995. The adult lives of Helms and Duberman, both born in the 1930s, are in some ways parallel, while their origins could hardly be more striking. Each came to New York in the 1950s and became university professors. While Duberman's family was benign and affluent, Helms grew up in a family suffering the poverty of the Great Depression and in which violence and abuse was a regular occurrence.

Duberman, a regular patron of the Stonewall Inn, was certainly aware of the 1969 riots there, but he chose to avoid participation in the activism that was central to the emergence of the gay rights movement in the subsequent decade. Helms, in order to assuage the lingering pain of his abusive childhood, was too preoccupied with the search for admiration and the pursuit of pleasure to have given much thought to this event. Coming of age in the 1950s, Helms eagerly participated in New York gay culture, including its bars, bathhouses, and summers on Fire Island, all of which attained new heights of hedonism in the early '70s (Moore 2004). Helms's detailed account of his life as a "golden boy" provides valuable details about gay society in postwar New York.

Helms was the ideal type of this "golden boyman"—beautiful, brilliant, and self-absorbed, seeking only his pleasure. His account, just as that of Duberman, portrays a generation of gay men on the East Coast coming to adulthood in the postwar years. Helms provides sufficient detail regarding his deprived childhood and his troubled family to understand his need as an adult for the admiration of others, including the search for a mentor whom he could idealize. Helms used his sexual relationships to bolster his deficient sense of self-regard. Just as fellow life-writer Martin Duberman, Helms sought psychiatric treatment in an effort to understand his desire. However, while Duberman's young adult experiences with psychiatry were mostly misdirected, Helms had mixed results but was able to find significant support with a therapist he could idealize and who in turn appreciated Helms's many talents. Both Helms and Duberman composed memoirs, following lengthy psychodynamic treatment that inevitably focused on childhood origins of their adult psychological distress and which, in retrospect, influenced their descriptions of their lives and their desires; writing a life-story "backward" in the aftermath of this perspective gained in psychotherapy regarding self and desire is particularly evident in Helms's memoir.

While Duberman led a double life, with his furtive, guilt-ridden, nighttime trips to New York alternating with his life as a university faculty member compounding his self-loathing, Helms enjoyed a glamorous life as a gay blond idol, which he reported in an account replete with sexual and social encounters. In a tone of nostalgia and somewhat critical of his former escapades even while mourning his lost youth, Helms contrasted his staid life as a university faculty member with his flamboyant adventures in the company of some of the most prominent members of the New York theater world. Duberman ends the second volume of his memoirs at the end of the 1970s, a time of unbridled sexual excess, with a chilling postscript noting the outbreak of AIDS. Helms narrates the experience of living in the midst of the pandemic as friends and former lovers succumbed to the plague.

Clearly, one impetus for Duberman's memoir was to write a morality tale exposing the unforgivable and destructive role of postwar psychiatry that added to the psychological burden of experiencing homosexual attraction but feeling ashamed of this desire. Helms's stated purpose, on the other hand, in writing his account is to acquaint the reader with an intimate account of gay New York from the postwar years to the beginning of the gay rights movement. Following Plummer's (1995) taxonomy of plots in sexual stories, Helms's account is a classic tale of a journey, that of self-acceptance and contentment as a gay man. We come to share with Helms his dawning self-understanding of the motives underlying his flamboyant but ultimately empty life.

Parental violence and alcoholism throughout Helms's childhood and adolescence contributed to his vulnerability and sense of personal depletion, which he later sought to assuage through a variety of sensation-seeking experiences. Helms disavowed his feelings of emptiness and turned instead to the frenetic life of postwar gay New York. Helms's memoir begs for a psychological interpretation in order to understand his frantic pursuits.

Helms's account is organized into three parts, plus a prologue and an epilogue. The first section narrates his experiences during childhood and youth, through his third year at Columbia when he discovered the magical world of gay, affluent, New York. The second section narrates his life through the glamorous years of the 1960s, while completing his doctoral studies in English at Rutgers, when he traveled within the still-hidden world of gay New York and Europe in the company of rich and famous men. The third section portrays his life following completion of graduate study, his first academic job in Boston, and his effort to resolve the doubts about his life. The account ends with an epilogue, bringing the reader up to date with his present life situation as a professor of literature.

Helms's life story begins with an historical account of his family. Writing a memoir, published in 1995, but recalling a time when the psychiatric literature had portrayed homosexuality as the outcome of adverse childhood circumstances, Helms attributes his homoerotic desire to the effects of a particularly scarred childhood. Implicit in this account is the presumption founded in much of the psychiatric literature, with which Helms and Duberman are clearly familiar, that adverse early childhood experiences may presage adult personal distress. Less explicitly recognized is the source of the resilience of these life-writers, including Helms's success in overcoming the effects of a traumatic childhood.

While Duberman's mercantile Jewish family was largely untouched by the Depression, Helms's fundamentalist, Midwestern, Protestant family faced the full brunt of this economic and social crisis. His mother never knew her own father; her mother had married a hard-drinking, ill-tempered gambler who frequently quarreled with his wife. On at least one occasion, he pulled a knife on her during a drunken fit. Helms's miserly maternal grandmother, Bernita, lived in abject poverty—no running water or plumbing. Rather than hire a babysitter, Bernita, unable to care for or have any affection for her daughter, locked her in a closet. (Oddly, Bernita left Helms's mother a quarter of a million dollars when she died.) Helms's mother had grown up without affection and was poorly educated, her youthful beauty her only asset.

If his mother had grown up under the conditions of poverty, Helms's father had a somewhat more conventional childhood and lived in better economic circumstances. Midwestern German Protestants, Helm's paternal great-grandfather was a German baron who, according to family legend, had been kidnapped by gypsies as a child, ran off to sea before settling in Indianapolis, and became a rich and powerful contractor. Married to a wife-battering railroad worker who was unemployed in the Great Depression, Helms's paternal grandmother maintained some social pretensions. Helms enjoyed these pretensions and early identified with her purportedly glamorous childhood, which he later sought to recapture in his own flamboyant youth, while she, in turn, became his friend and protector.

Helms's father showed marked academic ability, but his hopes for higher education ended with the Depression. Grandfather Henry was laid off, and the family lost nearly all its income. His father's older sister worked in a department store while his father sought out odd jobs. A "Bible-thumping" Protestant fundamentalist, Grandmother Bead took care that her children should have both a religious and a cultural education. She taught Helms to read while he was still a toddler, taught him world history, and told him about the wonders of the natural world. Alas, Grandmother Bead also instilled a frightening fundamentalist Christian conception of morality and encouraged him to obey the voices inside his head that God had planted there to insure that he would always do what was right. As Helms reports: "[The voices] were like companions who lived inside my head. They talked to me often, and when all else failed, they told me what to do. The voices were always dependably present" (Helms 1995, 25). Those punitive voices stayed with Helms all through his youth.

Helms's parents married just out of their teens, at the height of the Depression, and his earliest memories are of poverty. While money was scarce, parental affection and affirmation of Helm's considerable charm and abilities were even more difficult to obtain. His parents were often violent with each other. The household was disrupted on his father's return from work at the post office or following a drunken night out when he roused his wife and physically threatened her. Their arguing became so loud that the neighbors would call the police, whose intervention led to denials regarding the violence. Sometimes Helms would try to get between his parents in order to stop the violence, while at other times he hid in a closet in a futile effort to protect himself from his father's rage. Helms himself knew something of this violence: on at least one occasion his father dragged him out of the closet and mercilessly beat him. Helms tried magical incantations in an effort to stop the violence that was taking a terrible toll upon him. Anticipating his father's drunken bouts, Helms developed nervous tics and twitches.

At times the family denied this discord: denial was evident in the photo of a smiling family including Helms, his brother, Kent, five years younger than he, and his sister, Debbie, sixteen years younger than he. There was also an erotic element in his parents' near nightly quarrels, which were sometimes followed by sexual encounters in the presence of the children; these experiences led Helms to dissociate. His account of an often violent, seductive childhood—including his mother's inappropriate demands that her young son care for her, wash her while bathing, and conspire with her to prevent his father's drinking—all provide the background for understanding Helms' life as a golden boy. It is also important to understand how Helms was able to overcome the impact of a traumatic childhood. An intelligent, diligent, hard-working student, Helms impressed his teachers who extolled his virtues and provided him with the praise he had missed at home. Helms does not explain how he was able to concentrate in school in the aftermath of tumultuous, frightening, often sleepless nights.

Instructed by the voice of conscience his grandmother had instilled in him, Helms believed he was at fault for the violence that wracked his family. He became superstitious, believing that stepping on a crack in the sidewalk *would* indeed make his parents die. He tried diligently to behave, working harder in school, seeking to placate the forces of evil that he felt threatened his family. Even as he was terrified and full of rage at his parents, he kept hoping that his own suffering would come to God's attention and that mercy would finally be shown. As he observes (Helms 1995, 23): "the voices told me what to do. And, at night, when I asked in my prayers if I'd suffered enough, the voices said 'almost, almost.'" The death of a pet chameleon he had won in a contest at a state fair symbolized his great sadness. Even those rare good experiences with his family were overshadowed by the fear that the violence would soon begin again. It was the classic story of a little boy growing up in an alcoholic family. He found safety only in his mother and grandmother, and in his butterfly collection.

Helms also tells the story of gender nonconformity, which presaged his later gay identity. A sensitive boy, he had little interest in competitive sports and was often violently attacked by classmates. Helms reports that in response to his parent's constant demands that he be a real boy and play "rough-and-tumble" games, he began to apply the term "sissy " to himself. He discovered his grandmother's homemaking magazines, which featured seminaked men posing for mattress ads, images that he memorized for masturbation. For the present-day gay reader of Helms's account of his youth (Tierney 2000), Helm's story is a modal one which fits well with Corbett's (1997) portrayal of the master narrative of the boyhood of gay men, presumed to be sissies, unable to whistle through their teeth, dribble the basketball (a sacred activity in Indiana), and preferring play with girls rather than boys. Helms loved working in his garden or admiring the beauties of nature. He even dressed up in his mother's clothes, the very essence of a girlish boy.

Helms's epiphany arrived early in adolescence. Escaping from the house one Friday evening, he saw the movie *The Heiress* with Montgomery Clift and Olivia de Havilland. In this movie the heroine, a wealthy but naive woman, is courted by a heartless man, who abandons her upon learning that she will be disinherited if she marries him. Some years later, after her father has died and left his fortune to her, the heartless suitor returns, seeking to renew old ties. (Horrigan [1999] has written about the impact of going to the movies on his development as a gay man.) Helms's experience at the movie that fateful night bears out Horrigan's observations. In the movie, the heroine gains self-confidence and is able to turn her former suitor away. For Helms, this movie featured "the hateful father, innocence betrayed, cruel abandonment and the long slow wait until one day— vengeance triumphant" (Helms 1995, 42). This movie also featured cruelty between a couple much like that of his parents, together with the woman's newfound ability to remain cool and collected, and to patiently wait in order to gain revenge over the cruel man. The heroine's firm control over her feelings became an inspiration for the sensitive young Helms. He recollects that the movie became a turning point in his own life; as an adolescent he was able to keep a tight rein on his feelings, never revealing affection, love, or sadness, or permitting himself to be hurt by an unfaithful suitor. As he reflects:

I mulled the movie over for days and then I made a vow. I would never again let my parents into the secret places of my mind and heart, never let the sadness or pain of that home enter me, never again experience such turbulent feelings. I would keep them out at all costs, would never, so far as I was able, permit the humiliations and the violence to affect me. I would feel nothing rather than risk those riptides of sadness and despair. That was how I could stop the pain, and that would be my final vengeance on that home and that life . . . in reality I was vowing never again to show pain, or accept, or forgive, or give satisfaction, or feel deeply or love. I would henceforth count on no one and nothing but myself. (Helms 1995, 43)

The lesson that Helms learned from this movie was a costly one. From this point on, he felt increasingly estranged from his feelings. Even though he became popular in school and in the community, he felt more and more a false sense of self (Winnicott 1960). His newfound determination made it possible for him to bury himself in books while chaos and violence swirled around him. He took a more assertive stance when his father became violent. At one point, when his father was particularly aggressive, Helms bloodied him with a baseball bat; his father flew into a rage and threatened his life. Thereafter, his father showed Helms a newfound respect.

Helms's fascination with the far-away places and his experiences at the movies, seeing people who overcame tough odds, inspired him to think that "there *had* to be some way out of my life. If only I were popular . . . if only, if only . . ." (Helms 1995, 39). When his grandparents took him on a trip to the locks at Sault St. Marie, Helms heard French spoken and became intrigued with language. He taught himself the rudiments of the language from a book borrowed from the library. This was yet another step in his effort to escape his repressive Midwestern childhood. Always the good boy, he was unable to carry through on his plans to run away from the escalating violence at home and his parents' continuing derision of his personality and interests. He continued to dream of rescue; Helms reports that his first adolescent masturbation fantasies were based on rescue by an empathic, gentle, caressing Batman.

Helms accepted a scholarship to Columbia University and began his new life in New York, but not before he had rectified the belief by family and peers that he was an inept sissy. Much to the consternation and dismay of his high school teachers, Helms used his newfound determination, which he had learned that evening at the movies, to reverse his image. He carefully engaged in minor infractions expected of schoolboys, which would earn the esteem of his peers. He delighted his classmates with a pornographic picture found in his father's dresser. Within a year he became popular; while shunning competitive sports, years of running away from the bullies who taunted him in elementary school had prepared him for success at track. Even his parents noticed his popularity.

Once, during his high school years, Helms was invited to a party celebrating a fellow student, his hero, the captain of the football team. The previous summer the two of them had participated in a "circle jerk." He was able to entice his drunken hero into an upstairs closet where they enjoyed mutual fellatio. Even that experience, and a later, somewhat frightening overnight experience with an older man, still did not awaken him to the reality that these homoerotic experiences were more than a passing phase.

Realizing that a college scholarship provided a means for his escape, Helms made the last two years of high school an increasing academic success while cultivating his popularity with his peers. He had developed into a strikingly handsome, tanned teenager, with a good physique improved by persistent weight lifting. In his charcoal suit with pink shirt, now skilled at the jitterbug, Helms became highly desirable as a date and friend. He was aware that none of the other boys worked as hard as he at weight training, and certainly none of them pored over male muscle magazines as carefully as he did. Ultimately he became president of the Student Council, voted Indiana teen of the year, and excelled in his College Board exams; thus he was able to garner scholarship offers from Wabash College, a conservative men's college close to home, and prestigious Columbia University in New York.

In order to assist him in making a decision, Columbia invited Helms for a campus visit. The Indiana teenager was immediately struck by the excitement of New York. One trip was enough for Helms to decide to accept Columbia's generous offer. Inviting a friend he had met at a student leader's conference to visit during the summer before college, Helms realized he couldn't bring his friend to stay in his own home. He arranged for the two of them to stay with his grandparents in Indianapolis. Helms recalls looking back as he drove away from home to pick up his friend, seeing his parents standing close together; he knew that they must have realized that he was ashamed of them if he was unwilling to have his friend stay with them. A few weeks later, exchanging hugs with his younger brother and sister, Helms set out for New York and a life that was still punctuated by the voices that were the cursed gift of his grandmother.

Journey into the Gay Life

New York in the mid-1950s reflected the sparkle and verve of the Bernstein musicals. Helms was giddy with relief at his escape from his family. At the same time, he still felt a nagging doubt as to whether he could succeed at college. Understandably, as with most students beginning college, Helms was at first uncertain that he would be able to live up to the intellectual standards of this elite college. Plagued by concern and uncertainty regarding his intellectual abilities for the first half of the term, and lacking in the social graces in the sophisticated Columbia community, the voices of self-doubt were relentless. He was concerned that others could see through his bravado, but determined control learned from the movie he had seen in early adolescence enabled him to overcome these doubts. Aware that he was extraordinarily handsome, he was able to ingratiate himself with others, and set about building a reputation. His determination and concentration, together with support offered by attentive, admiring, faculty, buttressed his self-esteem and led to respectable midterm grades . . . and to freedom from required class attendance.

Helms's transformation from naive Hoosier to urbane New Yorker was accomplished with the support of a professor who encouraged him not to give up and the help of his Swedish roommate, a "god" who was a member of the swim team. Aware of sexual longing for Dick (called "Bill" in Helms's [2003] critique of the gay porn industry), Helms discovered love following a Saturday night tussle and shower. While sitting together wrapped in their towels, Dick reached over to touch him. With Dick's support, and unwavering confidence in him, Helms gained self-confidence. He recovered the quick wit, composure, and self-control that had marked his high school career; he launched into a brilliant undergraduate career. Even an unpleasant Christmas visit home did little to dent his new self-confidence. Indiana now seemed even more petty than when he had left it a few months earlier; he longed for his sophisticated life in New York.

Returning to Columbia, totally entranced by his relationship with Dick, he was overjoyed with the discovery of two masculine men able to love each other. Helms now realized that his desire was not just a passing phase but rather an enduring aspect of himself. Instead of returning to Indiana over the summer between his first and second year at college, Dick invited Helms to live with him and learn to be a lifeguard. Lifeguarding together at the community beach by day and loving each other by night, the summer was a blissful one, even though finding ways to be intimate was difficult while living with Dick's parents.

Over the next year as Dick began medical school, the two were no longer roommates and found it increasingly inconvenient to be together. Even when they roomed together, love had been sometimes interrupted by disagreement. One particular disagreement brought Helms to the attention of the administration, a reflection of the difficult social circumstances of the time for gay men. Suspecting that the relationship between the two roommates was something more, an entry had been made in Helms's academic record; this black mark came back to haunt him when, as a senior applying for a Rhodes Scholarship, and a finalist in the competition, he was rejected without explanation. Dick's mother was also suspicious and did not want Helms living with them again during the summer between his second and third year.

Forced to return home for the summer, where he worked as a construction laborer and a lifeguard at a pool, Helms became aware of his family's further deterioration. His brother and sister were showing the impact of growing up in an alcoholic family. Helms discovered that his grandmother had tormented his mother ever since she had enjoyed a brief relationship, during adolescence, with another man. The same emotionally destructive force that led his grandmother to instill those voices in him had also been applied to his mother, who remained wracked with guilt throughout her entire life for this transient youthful encounter. Vowing never to return home to Indiana and the misery of his wretched family, Helms was sustained by memories of Dick. He worked at keeping fit for Dick, bought a new suit that he was sure Dick would like, and wrote an endless stream of letters.

With summer's end, Helms anticipated returning to college for his third year, and particularly looked forward to his reunion with Dick. Dick had promised to meet him at Grand Central, and he was indeed there to greet Helms, but with the awful news that he had decided their relationship was only a phase in his life and that he was determined to be "straight." Plunged into despair by Dick's news, Helms felt more alone than ever and was terrified by the thought that he was correct in his assumption that he alone desired other men as more than a passing phase. A suppressed fear had been lurking in the background that his wonderful, passionate, relationship with the godlike swimmer would not last. This fear was heightened by that lesson he had learned in early adolescence — he closed off his capacity to love himself or another person. In the wake of Dick's rejection, Helms became reclusive, drinking heavily, pining for Dick, and hating himself for the fantasies that emerged as he encountered desirable men in the shower or at the pool. His grandmother's voices of self-defeat and guilt once again clamored for attention.

In the midst of his despair, he received a phone call from Ronnie, who introduced himself as Dick's friend. He had grown up in Indianapolis and said that Dick had suggested he call his fellow Hoosier student. Ronnie suggested they meet, perhaps even work out together that day at the gym he frequented. Helms hesitated; something seemed strange that he couldn't explain. After a pause, Helms suggested an alternative, perhaps a cultural event like the ballet. Ronnie readily agreed and suggested that they first attend a cocktail party hosted that evening by a friend. Helms scrambled in his usual resourceful way and managed to snare two tickets to the ballet. Ronnie was gorgeous, dressed in the stylish manner of New York in the fifties, and a sharp contrast with Helms's own Ivy League tweeds. As they dashed off to the cocktail party in the company of Ronnie's roommate, a psychoanalyst, Helms felt that a window had opened in his life, one leading to a life quite different from that which he had anticipated. Opening the door to an elegant apartment on New York's fashionable East Side,

Helms encountered a group of about fifty stylishly dressed men who were enjoying cocktails. As Helms observes, recalling his entry into this world:

Without any preparation or the slightest hint of what was about to happen, I had just walked into a world of men like me, and I simultaneously experienced two overwhelming, diametrically opposed responses: "My moral universe has just been turned upside down," and "Thank God, I'm no longer alone." The dread of a new fear, the euphoria of an immense relief. (Helms 1995, 81)

At that moment, the second turning point in his life, Helms realized that he was not alone as a man desiring same-sex intimacy. He walked into a new world, albeit one still secretive and characterized by furtive, fleeting sexual encounters.

The second section of Helms's memoir begins with that cocktail party that provided Helms entry into a social wonderland; before leaving for the ballet a movie producer offered him a job and lodging at St. Tropez. Over the ensuing weeks, as Ronnie introduced him to gay New York, he discovered that he was wanted everywhere. He was invited to the theater, sought after by European princes, and offered modeling opportunities. What could be better than an Adonis with brains to match?

Helms provides a detailed picture of gay New York in the 1950s and '60s. He believes that this section is the most important contribution of his memoir. It is clear that the distinctive social and historical circumstances of this time shaped the expression of same-sex desire as an activity that needed to be furtive and illicit. A number of well-known men in the arts and in politics shared his desire for social and sexual intimacy but were required by their careers to keep this desire hidden. This is also the most troubling section of the book, however. Helms claims that his beauty and brains gave him access to the salons of many of the most significant figures in the arts and entertainments of the postwar period.

Helms was too dazzled by his popularity to be concerned about the meaning of being gay. Finally liberated from small-town Indiana, Helms was drunk with his own success in this heady world. He reports that a typical evening would begin with drinks and dinner, accompanied by fine wine, then a trip to the bar, perhaps dancing until dawn. Sex was everywhere: at the gym, in the supermarket, or just walking down the street. What was of greatest importance for Helms, though, was his sexual prowess and the opportunity for meeting the elite of New York theater and opera. As he observes: "If you were a presentable young gay man with manners and a good suit, there wasn't anywhere you couldn't go in the worlds of art and entertainment and those worlds easily opened up other vistas" (Helms 1995, 97). Helms sagely observes that he got much further being gay than he would have if he had been straight. There was no way to know what prominent niche in the New York world would be occupied by the man met at a bar or cocktail party and with whom he would go home for an evening.

Helms developed the art of being all things to all men, regarding life as a kind of theater in which, by turns, he was able to be the star student, college athlete, soulful aesthete, tortured intellectual, and nice kid from the Midwest who might grace the covers of the *Saturday Evening Post*—just the sort of wonderful guy who could and did make it for a while as a male model with his ego stroked and his body admired. He claims that he had become the most celebrated young man in all of gay New York (Helms 1995, 104). Even as he enjoyed his sexual conquests, Helms was troubled by the realization that he was sought after because of his appearance and sexual appeal rather than for something more tangible.

Life became little more than a round of sexual encounters. Helms became acutely aware of his stunning looks. Even as he perfected his status as "golden boy," he felt more and more estranged from himself. The harder he tried to please, the more fraudulent he felt. His academic talent led to prestigious academic awards, even though he was preoccupied with his glamorous life. He dissembled, keeping his academic success apart from his hidden gay life. With few exceptions, gay men he met expressed the need for secrecy and spoke of the terror of being discovered. Men would marry in order to maintain the pretense of being straight. He notes that he never met anyone who was "out" to his family.

The failure to win the Rhodes scholarship, the loss of his best friend at Columbia who had shunned him after learning that he was gay, and ultimately his family's rejection when finally they knew that he was gay all led Helms to cut himself off from the straight world. This need to keep his gay life and his academic life separate further added to his sense of self-estrangement. It was important to learn how to be secretive, how to find those "discreet signs of shared identity" (Helms 1995, 140), so that it would be possible, for example, to pick up a man met in the aisles of the neighborhood supermarket. Helms shared the experience, also reported by Duberman, of being subjected to police raids. As he notes, "There was no place in public where it felt safe to be gay. Even inside the gay world, there was little guarantee of safety since bars and parties were raided all the time" (Helms 1995, 92). Those who were caught had their names published in the newspaper. Entrapment, blackmail, and mugging were all a routine part of this life for gay men. Threatened with exposure, it was each man for himself.

Commenting on this paramount need for secrecy, Helms observes that when men told about seeing a "shrink," it was because of the need to go straight, which Helms connected with the terror of being "found out" and of being disowned by one's wealthy and socially prominent parents. Helms's view of homosexuality, shared by psychiatry, further supports Duberman's experiences: "Of all the enemies we had, psychiatrists were among the most dangerous . . . homosexuality was an abnormality to be corrected at all costs; the most barbarous treatments were justified in the name of destroying such pernicious tendencies" (Helms 1995, 92–93). Helms details electroshock and aversive conditioning therapy as barbarous examples. Helms also notes the cost of these treatments:

There were gay men walking the streets of Manhattan in those days who had been rendered incapable of sex or who had their memories obliterated by electricity. For some, it would take years to put their minds back together again; for others, the effort was hopeless. (Helms 1995, 92)

Following a failed love affair, Helms himself had such an experience. His psychiatrist meddled in his affairs and was overly involved in his personal success. Later, a Jungian therapist, a retired older woman who had been analyzed by Jung himself, was more sympathetic and cautioned Helms to slow down lest he burn out while still a young man.

Following his graduation from Columbia with highest honors and a prestigious fellowship for graduate study, Helms's life became a giddy round of parties. He regales the reader with the famous men and women who had become part of his life. His tale reads like a column from the *National Inquirer*. The reader is alternatively entranced, seduced, and repulsed by these escapades: visits with his upstairs neighbor and newfound confidante, Noël Coward; Tony Perkins, fresh from an affair with Tab Hunter, fell for him, as did Leonard Bernstein and a succession of the most well-known gay porn stars of the time; he was ultimately rejected as a lover both by Rock Hudson and Robert Redford. Apparently straight movie producers tried to seduce him and promised him bit parts, more out of their desire to have his body than for his acting skills. In turn, he basked in the admiration of these famous men. There was much about him to admire; brilliant and articulate but without intellectual pretense, strikingly handsome and radiating sexuality, able to converse in three languages, his many lovers found him an insatiable partner.

This talent as a golden boy is epitomized by the story he tells of making the acquaintance of an elderly man while traveling in France. Discovering that his fellow traveler spoke English, Helms inquired in the brazen manner of American tourists regarding his companion's occupation. Upon learning that he was at Cambridge and a writer, his companion acknowledged that, yes, he had written a famous book, *A Passage to India*. Astonished by his discovery he marvels at his luck in stumbling across his literary hero, homoerotic writer E. M. Forester, who, of course, invited him to tea in Cambridge.

Helms sums up his life as at the time as "sex, and more sex, and still more sex" (Helms 1995, 130), always a transcendent experience in which he was able to lose himself completely in the pleasure of the moment. Helms sees this as a time devoted to finding the self-acceptance that he had missed in his childhood. Still, it is hardly surprising, as Helms tells us, that this exhausting search for pleasure had terrible costs. Dreading those times when he would be "stood up," Helms relates the devastation he felt following these incidents to the frequent rejection and abandonment by his parents during his childhood (Helms 1995, 99–100). This psychodynamic explanation reflects his awareness of the origins of his difficulties, which he has observed in retrospect, writing his memoirs following his psychotherapy. At the time, sometimes suicidal, unable to be alone, frantically cruising for sex, alternating insomnia on those rare occasions when he slept alone, addicted to pill, liquor, and sex, he realized he had to get away from the rampant materialism of his life in New York. He fled to Europe.

Predictably, while he spent much of the next three years in aimless travel between Italy and New York, and occasionally around the world in the company of an incredibly rich, cultured, and generous Italian businessman whom he met in the course of his travels, Helms was unable to find the peace for which he was searching. More sex, more materialism, more sleeping pills, occasional suicide attempts leading to an overnight stay in the Bellevue psychiatric ward, more wasted nights with the rich, famous, and gay—all these things increased his sense of dissociation and loss of center. He looked at his life as an apparently disinterested observer, kept alive by the admiration of others, while he sought to make up for the lack of affirmation of his talents that he had experienced with his parents during his childhood years.

Stopping in Indianapolis while on one of his cross-continent excursions, Helms was overcome with despair when he encountered his mother, now living a disorganized life in a virtual junkyard, separated from his father, and wasting her mother's bequest with luxury items. He concluded that as much as he despised his present life, it was far better than the misery of his family, and he once again returned to New York.

On the verge of turning thirty, Helms met Brian, another golden boy who had just enrolled at Princeton for graduate study in history. The two self-absorbed gay men began a stormy relationship that lasted nearly four years. During this time Helms enrolled in a doctoral program in literature at Rutgers. He was encouraged to attend Rutgers on the advice of a Rutgers faculty member he met at a gay social event. Although at first experiencing the same uncertainty as upon beginning college, Helms soon realized his talent in writing about literature, helped along by "uppers" prescribed by a doctor to counteract his depression. Helms turned to marijuana—Brian's drug of choice. This was, after all, the 1960s, and nearly everybody in his circle of friends was into drugs. Over time, Brian and he became frenetic users of grass, and then moved on to a variety of designer drugs. During the early years of graduate study, with Brian as a constant companion, the two of them (no longer young), explored New York in the winter and Fire Island in the summer, amid the varieties of lovemaking while so stoned that they had little awareness of their surroundings. Then, if Brian was away, there was no end of other admirers and sexual contacts, including an aspiring porn star and an admiring grocery store clerk who recognized his name and had read one of his published poems.

The breakup with Brian was inevitable. The voices once again gained the upper hand, and Helms felt renewed self-doubt. Nearing thirty-five, a well-known watershed in the life of gay men (Harry and DeVall 1978; Weinberg 1970), he was plagued by doubts regarding the meaning of his life. Trips to the bathhouse relieved the psychic pain that he felt. Helms was entranced by the baths, where social position mattered little and body and sexual attractiveness was everything. This was the time of the ascendance of gay baths as a cultural space in urbane New York. The Continental was perhaps the best known of the bathhouses; Bette Midler, beloved in the gay community, often performed in the bathhouse cabaret, where on one side of the bar there were men clad only in towels and on the other side were straight couples in evening wear. However, even Helms's sexual success at the baths couldn't long sustain him. Becoming middle-aged at the height of the sexual revolution was difficult enough, but losing Brian to younger lovers only compounded Helms's sense of loss of his youth and heightened his anticipation of lonely aging.

Finding Affirmation

It is not clear how Helms got the name of Robert Coles, a Harvard psychiatrist who was on the brink of achieving international acclaim for his reports on the lives of children in contemporary American society, but Helms felt that Robert Coles could understand his pain. Psychoanalysis in its infancy had been conducted as a kind of conversation rather than as a medical procedure, although a conversation of a rather unusual sort and completely without pretense. Sitting in Coles's comfortable study in his suburban Boston home, and able to talk with this understanding and wise mentor who appreciated his talents and goals and understood his struggles, Helms believed that he had finally found the affirmation that he had so long sought. Virtually penniless, Coles agreed to see him for no fee. Coles even provided office space and access to the Harvard library in an effort to encourage Helm's dissertation work. Coles clearly recognized Helm's talent. For Helms, there was at least the hope that if this famous doctor could admire these talents, maybe he could begin to admire himself as well. He moved to Boston where in 1970, at the age of thirty-three, he entered into long-term intensive psychotherapy.

In the midst of writing his dissertation, able to make use of Coles's admiration and support in repairing his deficit in self-regard, Helms was able to put aside the excitement and admiration he had sought in New York. It must be pointed out, however, that while Coles was a wise and compassionate psychiatrist, he *was* also famous. Helms, with a talent for finding men who had attained recognition and basking in the success of his famous mentor, used Coles's appreciation of his talent to realize some feeling of self-worth, which he previously tried to find in his frenetic life as a golden boy. Coles's willingness to offer himself as an admirable mentor, able to affirm Helms's talent, provided the strength to examine his fragile sense of self, to repair the trauma of his childhood, and to find a new center for his life (Tolpin 1997, 2002). Working with Coles, Helms was able to craft a new story of his life, which permitted greater sense of well-being than had been possible prior to that time (Schafer 1980, 1981).

Accepting a job teaching at a local university while he completed his dissertation, Helms reports that he was not only terrified in the classroom but also disappointed that his university colleagues were so petty. In an effort to maintain his new sense of personal vitality that he had gained from his work with Coles, Helms determined to rid himself of all the symbols of his previous glamorous life: he disposed of his clothes and burned his letters from his famous admirers. Looking back at this time, he observes that he could never have considered that his life would be worth writing about. However, even while attempting to purge the past, Helms continued through the decade of the '70s to hold on to his earlier experiences as a golden boy. Weekends at Fire Island were marked by a constant round of drugs and sex with the most beautiful men in New York. He describes himself trying in his mid-thirties to integrate his life:

The effort to balance or combine three entirely different lives: the new life of teaching and scholarship, the old life of gay celebrity, and an ideal, almost saintly life I'd conceived on Cruft Street [Indiana] and revived in therapy with Bob Coles. New York Alan (getting older but still looking great) found class preparation and student papers boring; Boston Alan (now enjoying teaching but still worried he wasn't bright enough) was dismayed all the time New York Alan frittered away in the bars and baths. Saint Alan wanted nothing to do with the other two guys and constantly urged me to give up all worldly concerns and retire into a monastery for the good of my soul. The "me" being urged was a fourth Alan living yet another life that wound around and through the others. (Helms 1995, 196)

Struggling with the realization that he was no longer young and desirable, Helms reports feeling at that time that "my beautiful body was aging before my eyes. I was filled with revulsion" (Helms 1995, 215). Confronting his aging, Helms was also confronting the reality that a new generation of gay men had come of age, less burdened than previous generations by feelings of shame and revulsion regarding their sexuality. His own self-hatred for his gayness was projected onto a culture that he criticized as shallow and consumer-oriented. There were still the gay baths and gyms where a sexual contact could be assured. However, Helms felt a profound sense of sadness as his fabled beauty began to fade. Sometimes alcoholic, sometimes anorexic, often insomniac, always full of rage, it appeared that the efforts that he had made with Coles to develop a new life story had floundered. He was caught in what he termed "spiritual exhaustion" (Helms 1995, 214). He tried to hold on to the past rather than grieve its passing and put it to rest. The more he tried to recapture his remembered fabled youth in New York, the more depressed he felt in his present life. Underlying this distress was Helms's desperate longing for a lover, particularly for a younger man who could help him recapture his glamorous past.

Outwardly, everything seemed to be going right. He had received his doctoral degree and a university teaching position, which later led to tenure. He was still absorbed by the feeling that he was going through the superficialities of life; as he lay in bed at night he had visions of being with the golden boy of his dreams. Once again those grandmotherly voices proclaimed that his life was doomed. His self-hatred once again gained the upper hand. In ways reminiscent of Duberman's musings, Helms's life, his desire, and his aging all support Kaiser's (1997) observation that feelings of self-hatred were characteristic of the generation of men growing up in the postwar epoch and coming of age in the 1950s, and who were particularly likely to have experienced overt antigay prejudice.

The search for the ideal relationship appeared possible with a glorious young man who reminded him of himself when he had been twenty-five. This relationship turned sour when they ran into each other in the gay baths, which left Helms in despair so palpable that he once again considered suicide. His problems were compounded by family difficulties, including his father's consuming alcoholism. Ironically, attending a self-help group for the family members of alcoholics following one particularly depressing phone call from his father, Helms was jolted to a stark realization:

Suddenly I saw how much fear I'd carried with me throughout my life—the years of childhood fearing that I wasn't loved . . . the years in school fearing I would never be popular or bright enough. And the years in New York fearing I was a sham and would never live up to my reputation as a golden boyman, and the increasingly desperate years in Boston fearing I was losing my remaining chances at happiness and would end my life a lonely, bitter old man. (Helms 1995, 229)

At that moment, standing on a Boston street, Helms experienced a true epiphany. Breaking into tears, he was finally able to grieve a life wasted by fear and self-loathing: "And with those tears came immense relief, for the moment I became aware of my burden, that moment I began to be free" (Helms 1995, 229).

And then there was AIDS. Just as in Duberman's memoir, Helms's account of his experiences of the 1980s seem an afterthought with a journey already completed. More than eighty of Helms's friends had succumbed to the plague. Helms attributes blind luck to the fact that while he had been in the midst of the frenetic sexual activities of gay men in the 1970s, he had remained healthy.

Just as in Duberman's memoir, Helms's story concludes with an epilogue summing up his life to date. Preceding the epilogue, the reader encounters six diary entries from May 1988 describing a particularly difficult visit home, some months after he had formally disclosed to his parents that he was gay. He was unable to quell his grandmother's voices. Returning to Boston, he remembered that when his father was drunk, he used to go after the family with gun in hand. His sister also remembered these terrifying incidents. Shortly after this visit, his mother was diagnosed with an advanced cancer. Helms was awed by the dignity and grace with which his mother faced her own death. Her last words were ones of comfort; she assured the family that while she would not be there, they would still have their memories of her to ease their grief.

Grieving his mother's death, Helms gained some comfort from such memories as that of his mother quietly piecing a quilt. Writing his memoir was for Helms an activity similar to that of quilting and provides a similar sense of quiet reflection; a memoir involves putting odd pieces together so that they tell a story. What better than a story of adversity overcome! If Helms's story is one of a journey to self-fulfillment and resolution of the self-hatred so characteristic of self-identified gay life-writers of that generation, he assures us in the epilogue that his journey has been a successful one. The end of this story is a relatively promising one. He reports being less tortured than in the past, and even at times able to feel joy and contentment. With his mother's death, Helms was further able to mourn and make peace with his past, and to bring to the fore his present ability to love and to work. There is no information whether the voices his grandmother taught him have finally been silenced.

The End of the Beginning

These two life-writers, Alan Helms and Martin Duberman, of the generation born in the 1930s, shared young adulthood during the 1950s and active participation in the culture of gay New York in the 1960s, when they led somewhat secretive lives in a culture still largely hidden from mainstream society. In the 1970s they enjoyed newfound personal and sexual freedom accompanying the gay rights movement. Writing life stories with a theme of ending a journey and finding a home (Plummer 1995), both of these life-writers were ultimately able to resolve feelings of self-hatred, assisted by psychotherapy, which supported their gay identity and lifestyle. Duberman and Helms each also had experiences with misguided psychiatrists who believed that homosexuality was an illness, which must be eradicated, and who sought to convert them to heterosexuality rather than to help them to understand and realize satisfaction from their homoerotic desire.

Each became university educators: Duberman is one of the most important figures in contemporary American gay studies, with a bibliography that includes essential work on the course of gay and lesbian lives in the postwar era. Essayist and author Alan Helms wrote a moving portrait of the struggle to enhance a self-righting tendency whose foundation he attributes to his mother. While Martin Duberman had a reasonably uneventful childhood and certainly little experience with overt misfortune, Alan

Helms grew up in an alcoholic family; his life story reflects enduring scars of his early adversity. The religious fundamentalism of his family was quickly converted by Helms into self-hatred. Duberman, however, shows an enduring sense of shame learned simply through prevailing social atitudes regarding homosexuality.

While each of these life-writers benefited from the social change in the wake of the 1969 Stonewall Inn riots, only Duberman ambivalently acknowledges this event. While Duberman knew what was taking place and could have taken part in the protest against police intrusion, he did not do so, and does not tell us about his personal response to the Stonewall rebellion that was, even then, generally recognized as a cohort-defining event. His now-classic narrative of the Stonewall riots (Duberman 1994) might be understood as an effort to atone for failure at the time to have supported this protest against police raids on the Stonewall Inn.

Martin Duberman and Alan Helms are representatives of the last generation to become adults and to reach middle age before the gay rights movement. Silence and shame, which surrounded recognition of homo-erotic desire, pervaded the community of life-writers born in the 1930s, was palpably experienced during their youth, and contributed to the development of the self-hatred particularly characteristic of their generation (Kaiser 1997; Rosenfeld 2003). This self-hatred is perhaps most dramatically reflected in the voices that Alan Helms's fundamentalist grandmother had instilled during his childhood and which reflected the hatred of a repressive society. While the generation of men born in the 1940s also came to adulthood before Stonewall, the advances in the gay civil rights movement of the 1960s had already created social circumstances different from that of the preceding generation.

Gay life-writers born in the 1940s, reaching young adulthood in the 1960s, read about an active homophile movement, visible in newspaper pictures of protests in front of the White House by lesbians and gay men demanding civil rights, and in other evidence from both the mainstream and an emerging gay media that members of this generation need not feel alone with their homoerotic desire. At least to some extent, the lives of those gay men were changed as a result of the social change by those born in subsequent generations. Men born in the 1930s learned from younger generations, through "backward socialization," a different way for understanding their selves and their homoerotic desire. And men born in the 1940s have lived without much of the burden of shame and self-accusation characteristic of the 1930s generation.

3

Born in the Forties

Finding a Voice

We have found ourselves . . . we stand forth as homosexual members of that generation of Americans who came of age after World War II. We had our elementary and secondary school years in the fifties and early sixties, when there seemed no limit to what America could accomplish. We went to college and usually graduate school believing that we could make the American dream ours, and everybody else's. Not least because we grew up in such affluent, peaceful times, we were unusually well-educated, idealistic, ambitious and self-confident.

Toby Marotta, *Sons of Harvard: Gay Men from the Class of 1967*

Acknowledging that you're gay, if you are, and coming to accept it is only part of the challenge. Learning to have reasonably uninhibited, mutually satisfying sex is another part. Making and keeping great friends is even more important . . . the real trick . . . is finding someone to share your life with and making that work.

Andrew Tobias, *The Best Little Boy in the World Grows Up*

Creating an Identity at the Beginning of the Gay Rights Movement

The decade of the 1960s marks a turning point in American history. There was a sense of renewed energy and social commitment marked by the Kennedy inauguration and the idealization of Camelot in Washington. Kennedy's command, "ask what you can do for your country," fostered a broad social awakening. This increased social awareness was nowhere better reflected than in the creation of the Peace Corps and in the recruitment of young adults into the emerging civil rights movement. Alas, Martin

Luther King Jr.'s "dream" was shattered by the murders of President John Kennedy, Attorney General Robert Kennedy, and King himself, and by the violence of the Mississippi summer of 1964 that led to the death of three civil rights activists (Gitlin 1987). In the wake of these tragedies and the controversy regarding the Vietnam conflict, the nation turned toward brooding introspection. Indeed, we are still "getting over the sixties" (Tipton 1982). The intellectual outlook of this generation is well summarized in Toby Marotta's (1982) afterword to his report on his gay Harvard classmates. Marotta dwells on the soul-searching of this generation, its psychological mind-set caught between the conventional and liberal attitudes of the postwar years, and seeking a new and more honest morality in personal and civic life.

Coming Out in the Sixties and the Emergence of Gay Rights

The civil rights movement fostered political opposition to suppression of political and social minorities. This opposition was evident in the raid on New York's Stonewall Inn in June 1969, which marks the beginning of a visible gay rights movement in the United States (Carter 2004; Duberman 1994; Kaiser 1997; Loughery 1998). At the same time, the Stonewall rebellion was itself a result of social and political ferment within an ever more cohesive gay and lesbian community, which had emerged in the later half of the 1960s (D'Emilio 1983/1998; Loughery 1998; Shand-Tucci 2003). Marotta (1982) maintains that gay men of this generation deliberately promoted social change through their disclosure of their sexual orientation. As he observes (1982, 285):

What most makes us a new breed of gay men is less our liberation than our desire to let others know about it. It is our conviction that by being open and outspoken about our homosexuality, we can contribute to a reduction in suffering . . . and the advance of both humanism and productivity.

This generation of men becoming adults in the 1960s created a new conscious gay identity, a courageous social and political activism, and public discourse inspired by this activism. For those participating in alternative sexual lifeways (Herdt 1997; Hostetler and Herdt 1998), this activist discourse brought about a dramatic change in self definition from the term "homosexuality," regarded by the rising generation as a stigmatized medical-moral discourse, to the term "gay." While older men and women still preferred this more traditional definition of their sexual orientation and identity, younger men and women embraced the new label as a reflection of changing shared understandings of sexual identity and social life. During this decade the "homophile" movement, seeking acceptance of gay women and men as legitimate members of society, turned away from the secretive world of the Mattachine Society to an activist stance. Among the activists, Frank Kameny, a homosexual government astronomer with a Harvard PhD, was fired as a presumed security risk because of his alternative sexual identity. Overtly and visibly gay, Kameny protested in front of the White House, wearing suit and tie and carrying a placard affirming his gay identity. Every Fourth of July through the remaining years of the decade, Kameny organized annual protests at Philadelphia's Liberty Bell (Kaiser 1997).

Men and women born in the 1940s reached young adulthood in this tumultuous decade of the 1960s. Those born at the beginning of the decade were caught in society's continuing rigid opposition to alternative sexual identities (Kantrowitz 1977/1996); those born later in the decade experienced greater overt social support. Across this decade, gay men and women were finally able to overcome the prevailing view that their homosexuality was an intrinsic character flaw of their own making. Particularly for men struggling to understand their gayness, often believing that they were the only ones who felt this way, media coverage of an emerging national awareness of something called "being gay" led these men to realize that they were indeed not alone. D'Emilio (1983/1998) describes how a combination of counterculture and antigovernment poets and artists in San Francisco, many with fluid sexual identities and supported by members of the city's liberal establishment, joined to defeat police intimidation and raids on gay bars. Eventually this movement succeeded in electing an openly gay man to the city council.

The media helped to make a concept of gay identity. D'Emilio (1983/ 1998) and Kaiser (1997) surveyed many articles appearing in the *New York Times* and *Time, Life,* and *Look* in the late sixties, all of which portrayed the growing, visible, "homosexual" community. Even if at first critical of this emerging gay visibility, these media reports provided images of particular gay venues in New York, Chicago, and San Francisco, and helped to create a network for gay consciousness and identity. National television featured discussion of the pros and cons of this emerging gay lifeway with visible, self-identified gay commentators arguing with conservative antigay opponents. These media reports testified to the growing vitality of the gay community and unintentionally provided guides to gay venues.

In the 1950s gay men had furtively read Donald Webster Cory's [Edward Sagarin] 1951 book *The Homosexual in America*. Following the Supreme Court ruling on obscenity, a more visible gay literature emerged in the 1960s, ranging from John Rechy's (1963) dark novel *City of the Night* about the gay urban underground to *The Boys in the Band,* Mart Crowley's (1968) bitter play about gay life in New York and to the scientific studies of Masters and Johnson.

This was also the decade in which the study of gay men became a subject of particular interest in the social sciences and in psychiatry. Irving Bieber and his colleagues (Bieber et al. 1962) published a report of "homosexual" men in psychoanalysis. This report claimed to show that these men were psychologically troubled and that their homosexuality was the result of upbringing by mothers who smothered them and fathers who were emotionally distant. Although the so-called scientific status of this report was called into question, the portrayal of the early family life of gay men became a part of the "master narrative" of turning out gay, which was told in any number of personal accounts (Dew 1994). The Bieber report appeared to contradict earlier work by the psychologist Evelyn Hooker (1957), who found little relationship between sexual orientation and mental health.

Hooker was critical of generalizations regarding the mental health of homosexual men based on their own reports of personal distress and subsequent psychotherapy (Minton 2002). Throughout the 1960s, this issue of homosexuality and mental health was fiercely debated with senior psychiatrists inveighing against the position that sexual orientation was related to a psychiatric malady. Responding to this controversy, the National Institute of Mental Health appointed a scientific panel led by Evelyn Hooker (1968/69) to evaluate the scientific evidence regarding homosexuality and mental health. The panel was unanimous in its conclusion that apart from personal distress evoked by stigma experienced by gay women and men, sexual orientation itself was not associated with impaired mental health.

This chapter documents the dramatic social changes marking the 1960s in the self-life writings and portrayals of the same-sex desire of social activist and college professor Arnie Kantrowitz, born in 1940, and economist, entrepreneur, and author Andrew Tobias, born in 1947. Kantrowitz and Tobias have written life stories that have become icons for later gay self life-writers. Kantrowitz's account is sobering, even painful, as he struggles to accept his same-sex attraction. Tobias's account of coming to accept a gay identity is clever and irreverent, yet portrays a similar struggle. Tobias has brought his life story up to date with an additional account published nearly twenty-five years later, in which his personal growth both parallels and highlights the social and political changes of the gay community. The personal accounts of Kantrowitz and Tobias have the advantage of being written close to the time of the events that they narrate.

Reviewing the life writing of the men of this generation, Robinson (1999) is critical of the genre of life writing during the postwar period in which he sees little more than testimonies of "coming-out." Expressing a penchant for the elegant self-life writing of British and French writers in the interwar period, Robinson observes that British and French authors "don't agonize over their sexual secret with anything like the same intensity. Some of them . . . pretend to be indifferent to public opinion" (311). Robinson views postwar American life writing regarding same-sex desire largely as a reflection of a uniquely American penchant for "psychic puritanism" (311), focusing on confession and efforts to reconcile public and private while seeking psychic integration and unity. Again, he finds the work of such recent writers as Tobias to be little more than tiresome conversion narratives (even the work of his own one-time idealized Yale professor Martin Duberman is included in this indictment).

Robinson overlooks the interplay of social and historical change and life-circumstances in writing life stories. His critique does not adequately distinguish between historical periods, which have quite different traditions. Robinson (393) complains that "the great problem with coming-out autobiographies, as of all conversion stories, is separating their psychic truth and political effectiveness from their formulaic, even oppressive, predictability." He maintains that the AIDS pandemic is the only thing that punctuates these more recent stories of attaining sexual enlightenment and overcoming social oppression.

Robinson acknowledges that the issue of oppression is more significant among men writing about coming to adulthood in the postwar period than those coming of age earlier in the century. As Chauncey (1994), D'Emilio (1983, 1989), Kaiser (1997), Loughery (1998), Rosenfeld (2003), and Sadownick (1996) have shown, the increased visibility of homosexuality in American society in the postwar period eventually reduced antigay prejudice.

To some extent, Robinson's critique of postwar self-life writing fails to consider the particular historical and social changes taking place at that time and which led to quite different understanding of same-sex desire than earlier in the twentieth century (Chauncey 1994). Plummer (1995) observed that from the 1970s on, there was increased emphasis on the politics of being gay, together with increased visibility of gay institutions that vitiated the clandestine world of previous times. The homosexual life-writers most admired by Robinson (1999) learned how to live in the understated, furtive world prior to the advent of gay politics.

Plummer's (1995) discussion suggests that the postwar period has led to a quite different tradition of self-life writing from that favored by Robinson. This tradition relies upon metaphors of suffering and a journey to self-acceptance, struggles with opponents, search for transcendence, and making a new identity, characteristic of the life writing of self-defined gay men born across the postwar period. These men have lived at a time of open discussion of homoerotic desire, as contrasted with the experiences of earlier generations of life-writers. This tradition assumes complete honesty and little tolerance for maintaining disparate public and private selves. It is in contrast with earlier subtle American and, particularly, European writing, which carefully preserves this distinction between public and private life.

Arnie Kantrowitz and a Decade of Social Change

Seldom has one personal account so well documented the impact of social change upon writing about homoerotic desire as that of college instructor and social activist Arnie Kantrowitz in his account *Under the Rainbow,* first published in 1977, reprinted with a new introduction and afterword in 1996, during a time when many gay men published their memoirs. This is an account of a Jewish boy growing up in suburban New Jersey, coming to terms with his gay sexual desire, and becoming an articulate spokesman of the emerging gay rights movement of New York of the late '60s and '70s. Perhaps to a greater extent than any other life-writer in this study, Kantrowitz was at the center of the social protest leading to the gay rights movement. He writes about feelings of guilty self-deprecation similar to those reported by other life-writers born in the '30s and '40s. It is all the more remarkable that he was able to move from this position of pain and self-doubt to that of an articulate leader of the gay rights struggle. Kantrowitz has donated the entire corpus of his work, including letters, drafts, and published essays, to the New York Public Library where the collection occupies more than fourteen feet of shelf storage.

The title for Kantrowitz's narrative recalls "Somewhere over the Rainbow" from *The Wizard of Oz.* Released in 1939, the film opens with a monochrome portrayal of Dorothy, played by Judy Garland. A tornado transports her to the land of Oz, and the movie takes off in Technicolor. Alan Helms (1995) and Patrick Horrigan (1999) both acknowledge that movies were central to their understanding of self and desire. Arnie

Kantrowitz's gay "reading" of the journey portrayed in *The Wizard of Oz* (Tierney 2000) promised him a new home over the rainbow, where an empathic Wizard would understand his pain and grant him permission to realize his gay desire. Boys experiencing dawning awareness of some strange sensations acknowledged, in time, this sensation as sexual desire for other boys and men. They sought escape from a world in which they felt out of place to one in which their desire could be understood, just as the movie Wizard understood the desires of his four strange petitioners. Viewing the film of Dorothy's journey to the colorful land of Oz had particular significance for gay boys (Horrigan 1999). The theme song from the movie captured their longing and their hope of rescue. Kantrowitz makes use of the metaphor of monochrome/Technicolor in discussing his own struggle and his discovery of the Emerald City in New York's Greenwich Village in the late 1960s.

The decade ended with Judy Garland's death by suicide at the age of forty-seven on June 21, 1969, six days before the Stonewall Inn riot. Ironically, Garland's funeral in New York preceded the Stonewall Inn riot by a mere eight hours. Thousands of gay men lined the streets in front of the funeral chapel, waiting for a chance to say their farewells. Kaiser (1997) notes that Garland had refused to be stereotyped, and that she had had affairs with men and women. Although she tried to make everyone else happy, she herself was miserable; she tried several times to commit suicide through overdosing on sleeping pills or slashing her wrists as Kantrowitz himself was to do in his desperation regarding his sexuality.

Summing up his life in the preface to the second (1996) edition of *Under the Rainbow,* Kantrowitz says (xiv), "What a difference a decade can make. My life turned upside down with the gay liberation movement, and it turned upside down again with the AIDS epidemic, yet I haven't ended up in the same place where I began." In an afterword to that edition, Kantrowitz observes that autobiographical accounts may tell too much about us too soon; it is better that others get to know us in a more evenly paced manner. After all, he observes, "an autobiography is a little more complicated than a calling card" (Kantrowitz 1996, 197). This second edition includes letters from younger admirers who have read his account and recount their own struggle in making a gay identity for themselves. These letters testify to the iconic nature of this account; Kantrowitz's memoir had captured something important about growing up gay in America. His goal was to help other gay men avoid the struggles he had in confronting his own gay identity—of fighting public approbation and conquering his sense of shame. He was particularly ashamed that he was not able to be sexually intimate with two close women friends. He also had feelings of hopelessness as he attempted first to disown and later realize with a sense of terror his sexual orientation. Viewed in terms of Plummer's (1995) classification of gay narratives as modernist stories, Kantrowitz's account is an effort to establish a home, a new identity, a new community, and new politics.

Kantrowitz's story is divided into two parts: one in which he accepts his own gay identity, and another following his epiphany, acknowledging that he is gay and that in the words of fellow social activist Frank Kameny, "gay is good" (Clendinen and Nagourney 1999; Shand-Tucci 2003). Consistent with the perspective on the construction of identity of anthropologist Dorothy Holland and her colleagues (Holland 1997; Holland, Lachicotte, Skinner, and Cain 1998) in which social practice leads to construction of an identity, Kantrowitz acknowledges his own gay identity the moment that he accepted a leaflet promoting a rally in support of patron resistance to the police harassment of the Stonewall Inn. Kantrowitz reports that he had finally found his home through his participation the emerging gay political movement of the early 1970s (The Gay Activists Alliance) in which he became a major figure in the emergent New York gay rights movement.

Growing up Gay in Suburban New Jersey

Kantrowitz's narrative begins in a very different place from his later social activism. Born in a lower-middle-class Jewish family that came apart during his childhood, Kantrowitz was the oldest (by seven years) of two brothers. He was the third generation in a family that, like so many others, had fled from Eastern Europe to the United States, following the pogroms persecuting the Jews at the beginning of the twentieth century. Unlike many other such families, though, his family showed little upward mobility; his father never became the lawyer that his father's family had promised his mother's family when the couple became engaged. An occasional laundry truck driver and munitions plant worker, Kantrowitz's father disappeared for a while when he worked for a carnival. Later he failed in his effort to run a small grocery store. His own father blamed him for failing not only to live up to his early promise but also for a failing marriage. Kantrowitz's parents grew apart emotionally and then separated. Kantrowitz's mother was disappointed and humiliated by her husband's lack of success and escaped into romantic women's magazines and movies. Kantrowitz shared his mother's preoccupation with romance and also her preoccupation with leading men.

Kantrowitz's life story prior to his epiphany, just as that of life-writers born in the 1940s and later, parallels what Plummer (1995) and Corbett

(1997) have portrayed as the master narrative for gay awakening: knowledge of same-sex desire from early childhood, distaste for competitive athletics, accomplishment in studies (in part an effort to overcome feelings of shame and concern that knowledge of homoerotic desire would disappoint family and teachers), and finally, lust for the beautiful boys of the locker room during the school years but gripped by an obsessive fear of being exposed by these boys who, as he observed (Kantrowitz 1996, 33), did not like other boys looking lustfully. He reports that at the age of six he encouraged a fourteen-year-old boy to satisfy his desire to be hugged. At about the same age, he was nearly picked up by the proverbial menacing man in a black sedan. In a world that both Kantrowitz and his mother felt was bereft of beauty, like Dorothy in the depressing black-and-white opening scenes in the *Wizard of Oz*, Kantrowitz spent much of his early life searching for the Technicolor world of Oz that would resolve his same-sex desire.

His mother, anxious about his apparent lack of masculinity, made feeble efforts to usher Kantrowitz into the man's world through hormone shots to help him grow taller, and boxing lessons and summer camp to teach him manly ways. Kantrowitz reports that he was much more interested in the locker room than in the ring, although he was terrified that he might be caught looking at his naked schoolmates. He was much more interested in enticing a camp counselor to wrestle with him than in the baseball game the counselor was supposed to be coaching. The theme throughout his account is centered on his enticing men to become his master and to seduce him in a sadomasochistic encounter.

Kantrowitz began to create his own Technicolor world during his early teenage years when he watched a friend masturbate; he was entranced with the "seemingly endless fountain of pearly semen spurting from the head of his cock" (17). One afternoon when studying with a friend, the two boys began to fool around and engage in mutual fellatio; his mother's untimely arrival home and appraisal of the situation led her to seek medical assistance for her son. The doctor reassured her that her son's sexual activity was simply "normal" teenage horseplay. Thus the illusion that Kantrowitz was "normal" continued, in spite of his mother's awareness that his walk, talk, and laugh all betrayed the fact that he was not like other boys.

Kantrowitz's account of his gayness is the prototype of the life stories in which the protagonist discovers his desire in early childhood but believes that this desire must be hidden both from oneself and others. He notes that he was far from the cheerful and kind classmate portrayed in his high school yearbook, and that having to hide his desire made him feel false. Winnicott (1960) described this experience as a false self, as contrasted with a true self, which is vital and lively, and in which desire may be acknowledged. In an effort to assuage his mother's concerns and gain her affection, he dutifully escorted girls to dances and parties throughout the high school years. In college, he tried to respond to the advances of a woman student with whom he was working. He reports that while he was able to perform sexually he found the experience unpleasant. The girl's father discovered the couple together and demanded that they get married. Kantrowitz escaped only by convincing the girl that he would never make a good husband.

Since athletic success was not possible, Kantrowitz took an alternative route and became a superior student, winning the praise of his mother and his teachers. Still, burdened by a false self, he led his life in monochrome, dutifully but without much personal satisfaction. In his spare time, he worked in a dime store owned by his aunt and uncle and read stories in which realizing same-sex desire led to catastrophe. Color first entered his drab world while attending community college; riding home on the bus one evening, he saw a world outside the window with brilliance, clarity, and beauty that he could feel but couldn't yet understand (Kantrowitz 1996, 32). Kantrowitz was beginning to realize his gay identity. At the same time, he shared the self-loathing of his best friend, also gay, and abruptly broke off their friendship. During Kantrowitz's college years, the complacency of the Eisenhower era was replaced by the excitement of the Kennedy era, and Kantrowitz was soon drawn into the social activism of the nascent civil rights movement. Recognizing his troubled family's displeasure with his social activism, and feeling more and more estranged from his parents, Kantrowitz spent most of his waking hours at school.

Finding the Yellow Brick Road

Following graduation, Kantrowitz began graduate studies in English at New York University. He soon discovered the gay life of New York and Newark. Trying "tearooms" in New York's Port Authority bus terminal and on the West Side wharves, Kantrowitz favored anonymous quick sex in public spaces. On at least one occasion, his cruising led to an encounter with the police; he paid a small bribe and was released. During this time he also attempted psychoanalysis in order to unravel his conflict with his emerging gay identity. However, he found the psychoanalyst self-preoccupied and the consultation unsatisfying.

Kantrowitz accepted a teaching job in an English department at a college in upstate New York. He saw this move as a break with the past and a way to escape his urban sexual adventures and seek solace in the life of the mind. Upstate New York presented few opportunities for sexual contact but led to an encounter with anti-Semitism, which was surprising to a secular Jew having had only the perfunctory Bar Mitzvah. He had been more concerned with his sexual identity than his religious identity. Throughout this period of his life he felt disconnected from himself and that his scholarly interests were only a pretense. He felt ashamed as a scholar, a Jew, and, of equal concern, as an appropriate heterosexual man that society and he still regarded as important. He bungled an affair with a close woman friend and colleague at the college. He felt deepening depression when he was unable to consummate their sexual relationship. He sought the counsel of the psychologist wife of a colleague in his department who confronted him with his homosexuality. Following this confrontation, Kantrowitz decided that he should tell his girlfriend the truth. Feeling humiliated, he tried first to overdose on pills in his medicine chest and then, when he ended up only sick to his stomach, he tried cutting his wrists. This sequence paralleled Judy Garland's own suicide attempt in 1947 when she, too, was in her twenties (Kaiser 1997). Desperate and frightened, he called both his girlfriend and his family. Confessing to them all that he was a homosexual, Kantrowitz returned home for recuperation.

Two weeks later, with bandaged wrists, Kantrowitz returned to the college to finish his grading chores, then returned in ignominy to his father's dingy apartment in a neighborhood rapidly changing from Jewish to African American. His father's household included his sister, his brother, and his dying grandfather. Kantrowitz had the good fortune to find as his analyst another gay man who had lived with his life partner for a quarter of a century. Recognizing what Kohut (1984) would later term an idealizing transference, his analyst's disclosure of his own homosexuality was critical in helping Kantrowitz to confront his sense of self-betrayal and the need to find his true self. Kantrowitz's success in finding an analyst comfortable in disclosing his own gay identity reflects the social changes that were taking place in the 1960s, and is in marked contrast with Martin Duberman's less fortunate experiences with psychiatry in the 1950s. Later, in a chance meeting with his former analyst who was watching the first New York gay pride parade in 1970 from the safety of the sidewalk, he urged his analyst to join the parade. His analyst demurred, muttering "not in my profession" (Kantrowitz 1996, 107). Psychiatry and psychoanalysis had yet to come to terms with its own prejudice (Cohler and Galatzer-Levy 2000; Kutchins and Kirk 1997; Moss 1997).

As Kantrowitz began work with his analyst, he resumed cruising, repeating his effort to seduce other men into controlling him in a sexual act.

He confronted his girlfriend with the paradox that he didn't know how he would turn out, committed to loving men or women. The world became Technicolor again as Kantrowitz was able to admit to himself his desire for more than a fleeting moment of sexual pleasure with another man. From the point of his breakdown and reconstruction of his life, with the aid of his analyst, he realized a new sense of personal integrity, and his world became one of color (at times including the psychedelic colors of the mid- to late sixties). In the summer of 1966, Kantrowitz moved into a Sheridan Square apartment in the midst of New York's Village. He wrote: "As I walked down Christopher Street, everything changed all at once, as if by some miracle I was glimpsing a black-and-white world suddenly gone Technicolor" (Kantrowitz 1996, 72). Kantrowitz had arrived in Oz! Everywhere were men unabashed about their gayness and obviously interested in sex with other men.

Continuing his analysis, he also began a teaching job at Staten Island Community College, where he was to spend the rest of his career. Kantrowitz went about the task of being himself, albeit at first with some personal pain. Introduced by a younger relative to the wonders of marijuana, he discovered that it enhanced his pleasure with other men whom he was able to entice into dominating sexual encounters. As he discovered in his work with his analyst, in his masochistic activity he was expressing his desire to be cared for, rather than be dominated by a strict disciplinarian. While he enjoyed the sexual freedom, he still felt guilty about his homosexual desire. He was afraid that other faculty from the college where he was teaching, some even living in the Village, would learn about his newfound sexual identity. Relations with his parents became strained as Kantrowitz entered into the life of a gay man in the Village.

During this time Kantrowitz (1996, 78) kept busy with work. Although his friends were aware that he was homosexual, he still could not acknowledge this to himself. After a period of trying to be heterosexual with his understanding girlfriend of nearly five years, the couple recognized that the relationship would not work. It took yet an additional failed heterosexual relationship and a subsequent depression, including another suicide attempt, in which he returned to the black-and-white world, followed by a brief psychiatric hospitalization, for Kantrowitz to finally accept his homosexuality and to return again to the Technicolor world as a gay man. Recovering more rapidly from this than from his first suicide attempt, Kantrowitz recalled as he was going home from the hospital in the company of his former girlfriend that "I was amazed at the color that blossomed all over the streets of New York, a city I had always thought drab. I began to appreciate it all over again" (Kantrowitz 1996, 83).

The late 1960s were a time of unusual acceptance of personal freedom; social change following the Stonewall Inn riots reflected larger social
changes taking place in American society. Living once again in Technicolor, Kantrowitz adopted the colorful dress that was a hallmark of personal freedom in those days. Reflecting his colorful grasp on his life, Kantrowitz outfitted himself with yellow-tinted sunglasses. He freed himself
from the strictures of an oppressive academic world. Just as Duberman had
struggled at the same time with the task of making education relevant for
students, Kantrowitz focused his efforts as a teacher on listening to and
appreciating his students' fledgling efforts at writing. Together with colleagues, students, and friends, Kantrowitz organized an artist's collective,
while sorting out his sexual identity and participating in the radical social-
sexual activism of the time.

Problems of pretending and honesty regarding his homosexuality still
posed a paradox for Kantrowitz on that fateful night in June 1969 as he
passed a growing crowd in Sheridan Square, two blocks from his apartment. Unaware of the significance of the crowd and the evening, Kantrowitz managed to walk right past history taking place in front him. Unlike
Martin Duberman, born in the previous decade, aware but avoiding participation in the social change taking place outside his window, Kantrowitz
admits that he was too self-absorbed to recognize what was going on
around him. Entranced by Timothy Leary, the charismatic icon of the late
sixties, the psychedelic color of the drug experience, and the Esalen Institute movement, Kantrowitz joined a group where he announced that he
was both a homosexual and a masochist.

Kantrowitz felt that while five years of analysis had not helped him
understand his sexuality, his experiences in the Esalen group helped clarify
for him what he had missed. Just as Dorothy in the *Wizard of Oz*, Kantrowitz was waiting for his personal tornado to transport him to his psychological Oz and his new gay identity. This cyclone, his epiphany or turning
point (McAdams and Bowman 2001), arrived in the form of the demonstration in Sheridan Square where hundreds of gay men shouted in unison
the words coined by Frank Kameny: "Gay is good." Finishing the Sunday
crossword puzzle in the *New York Times,* he ventured out to Sheridan
Square, where a gay bar had been raided on the previous evening, and
learned that a gay patron had been badly beaten by the police. Leaflets
were being passed out calling homosexual men to rally, and one had been
handed to him.

Questioning his identity—was he a homosexual?—he was drawn to the
demonstration; he had to know for sure if he was gay. Joining a straight

couple, friends from the college, he watched from the far side of the street as five hundred men shouted the slogan "Say it loud: gay is proud." As Kantrowitz comments: "Those words ate into my bones. Don't just say it apologetically, say it loud: demand it" (1996, 94). The next night, following his group therapy session during which the group members encouraged him to speak in a louder voice, he stopped by his friends' apartment to explain that he had asked them to the demonstration the previous day because he was afraid to go alone and was afraid that he would be labeled homosexual. He announced that he was no longer afraid and that he no longer needed to hide his homosexuality. His friends took his announcement in stride, noting that they had lots of gay friends and knew he was gay but never discussed it because they assumed he didn't want to talk about it.

This encounter in Sheridan Square, the decision to take the leaflet handed to him and to attend the demonstration, represented Kantrowitz's final step in his journey to self-acceptance. The day following his acceptance of his gay identity, he saw a poster advertising a rally for the newly formed Gay Liberation Front (GLF), one of the first gay rights groups and the predecessor of the politically visible Gay Activists Alliance (GAA) of the early 1970s (A. Evans 1999). Kantrowitz slipped into the back row of the hall where the GLF was meeting. He was attracted by the electricity in this meeting of activists similar to himself, drawn together by a common need to affirm a gay identity. Kantrowitz volunteered to gather petitions protesting the raid on the Stonewall Inn and the police brutality. Working with another volunteer, a man he found very attractive, Kantrowitz had little difficulty gathering signatures, even getting one from a cousin living in the Village whom he had previously avoided out of concern that she would recognize that he was gay. Neighbors, strangers, and friends from his college all willingly signed the petition. That night, Kantrowitz went to see *The Wizard of Oz* on his friend's new color television, where along with half a dozen other gay men, he watched as Dorothy appeared in Technicolor, determinedly marching down the yellow brick road on her way to the Emerald City to seek help from the Wizard.

Later that same evening, Kantrowitz ventured out to his first gay club where he danced openly with another man, celebrating a world in which people could now freely enjoy their gay identity. He had found the Emerald City. As Kantrowitz observed: "Arms linked, the legions of gays were marching to Oz. We were off to see the Wizard. We were coming out" (Kantrowitz 1996, 109). Having come to terms with his own desire at the age of twenty-nine, and having informed his parents and brother, Kantrowitz finished his individual and group therapy and became instrumental in guiding the gay rights movement. Larry Mass, Kantrowitz's life-partner, reports that at one time or another, he, Kantrowitz, and other friends were all seeing the same analyst who had been educated in the school of psychoanalysis pioneered by Karen Horney, one-time associate of Freud. Kantrowitz consolidated his identity as a social activist within a tightly knit group of close and activist friends.

The Emergence of a Gay Activist

The remainder of the Kantrowitz account portrays his emergence as a major figure in the gay rights movement of the 1970s, and his quest for a lover and partner. He emerged as a natural leader in the GAA, rising to the position of vice-president before the GAA fell victim to the political intrigues that so often befall such radical groups, and which was ultimately eclipsed by the broadly based national gay constituency emerging in the 1970s. As Kantrowitz became more politically active, his own story was joined by that of a cohort of gay activists in New York. As he observes: "I was a homosexual first and anything else second. I was professionally gay" (Kantrowitz 1996, 114). He also notes that he was a gay Jew. Kantrowitz narrates the inevitable dissension characteristic of an organization headed by passionate volunteers with strong egos. At the same time, the efforts of these organizers led to a strong sense of community. Kantrowitz brought his activism into the classroom with what he acknowledged as messianic fervor. He announced his gay sexual identity in all aspects of his life, from the classroom to his friends. Now he was able to search for his sexual ideal, as he observed, some combination of his father and the Wizard of Oz.

Much of Kantrowitz's time was taken up with the GAA; in the exuberant years following the Stonewall Inn riots and the gay rights movement, the GAA sponsored radical political demonstrations together with social events, such as the infamous Saturday night dances at their new headquarters, the Firehouse, which attracted hundreds of men, their half-naked bodies writhing in rhythm with the rock music. Political demonstrations known as "zaps" were organized to bring to the attention of the mayor and city council the need for an antidiscrimination ordinance for the gay community (Evans 1999). Gays embarrassed the mayor by appearing at receptions and agitating for support for this ordinance. In their detailed history of the gay rights movement in the United States from the time of the Stonewall Inn riots through the early 1990s, Clendinen and Nagourney (1999) note the many political obstacles preventing passage of this antidiscrimination bill in the New York City Council—from the first introduction of this ordinance in January 1971 until May 1986 when a terse, narrowly defined version was finally approved by the New York City Council over the objections of both Catholic and Jewish religious leaders.

For Kantrowitz, the GAA offered support for his gay identity, a means of socializing, and a means for meeting sexual partners. Kantrowitz observed that sex was always in the air, spontaneous and enormously pleasurable, the more so in contrast to the secretive search for sex that had marked both his own life and that of his compatriots before the gay rights movement. Revolutionary, liberationist, and confrontational in the spirit of the times of the early seventies, sex and politics made for strange and complex relationships within the movement. As lovers broke up, they sometimes took opposing positions within meetings defining next steps in the organization's agenda. Kantrowitz met his first lover through the GAA. The visibility of this affair made some of the other GAA leadership nervous at a time when such relations were still expected to be clandestine. Demonstrations, confrontations with the police, and the highly visible "zaps" (techniques later to be adopted by ACT-UP in the 1980s in the struggle for government action against AIDS), filled the hours not occupied by his teaching. Kantrowitz was arrested in one such riot. It was during these years of political fervor in the early 1970s that Kantrowitz made a name for himself in the gay rights movement, associating with other significant figures, many of whom were to die of AIDS in the succeeding decade.

In addition to being a center of political activity, New York during the '70s was also a place of fervent, passionate, public sex. The baths, long a feature of gay New York (Chauncey 1994) and an important venue also portrayed by each of the life-writers born in the 1930s, now took on new significance as a gathering place for young men seeking sexual intimacy with other men (P. D. Young 1973). Kantrowitz (133) reports sexual contact with as many as a dozen men in an evening. While the baths have long been controversial as inimical to intimacy and, later, incorrectly condemned as a major site for the spread of HIV (Henrickson 1989; Cohler 2004c; Woods and Binson 2003), the baths, together with such venues as bars and gay porn movie houses, were important in building a sense of a community (Delany 1999).

It is both a reflection of the shame felt by gay men and the Western bourgeois ethos regarding intimacy that has fostered such opprobrium regarding the gay bathhouse. Certainly, during the '70s as gay men began to question this shame, gay baths assumed new visibility within urban culture. There was much discussion of the gay baths in the New York press; it was considered chic for liberal, straight couples to visit the Continental Bath where, on one side of the bar there were men dressed in towels draped around their middle, while on the other side well-dressed men and women listened to the torch songs of Bette Midler. Both Kantrowitz and Martin Duberman were ambivalent about this visibility of the gay community:

We had struggled to become visible, and our very visibility was inviting people to come to see us, to threaten inadvertently with their presence the edges of our own private world, making us feel "different" in our own territory because they were wearing clothes and we were naked. (Kantrowitz 1996, 135)

In addition to the baths, Fire Island assumed new prominence as a space for public gay sex during this decade. Long a gathering place for the community, for Kantrowitz, this beach community was truly over the rainbow. He describes Fire Island in vivid colors, from the flowers sold at the ferry landing to the garish colors of the summer homes with their equally colorful names. The use of psychedelic drugs, also a feature of American culture in the '70s, certainly enhanced the color of both Manhattan clubs and Fire Island.

Kantrowitz's parents' troubled marriage, his distaste for his mother's second husband, together with the pathos of his father, all combined to direct his life away from New Jersey and family. His brother Ira was particularly critical of him. Kantrowitz soon made the GAA and the community of Sheridan Square in New York's Greenwich Village and Fire Island his family. His mother died in 1971; he was notified of her death by his roommate while tripping on acid and in bed with a man he had met at the warehouses and West Side piers.

Kantrowitz's family had difficulty adjusting to the changing times and retreated into lonely isolation, but not so Kantrowitz himself. As the GAA disintegrated, wracked by political dissension and corruption, Kantrowitz took his activism back to his college campus where he broadcast his gay identity and lectured his students on the virtues of "coming out of the closet." His friends chastised him for thinking of little else but the politics of gay liberation, which led him to talk about his beliefs on a nationally broadcast television talk show. Kantrowitz's family resented its exposure to millions of viewers. He reports feeling disappointed that his father expressed little interest in seeing him on national television, speaking for a cause to which he was so passionately committed; later he was disappointed that his father did not read his published memoir (although his sister-in-law commented that his father had at least looked at it). At his father's death, more than a decade after his mother's, the rabbi refused to include Kantrowitz's life-partner among the family mentioned in the eulogy and left him to grieve his father's death without family support.

With Nixon's resignation and the Vietnam buildup, the nation as a whole was maturing. Just as Kantrowitz had resented the straight couples in the bar at the Continental baths, so he resented the tourists peering at the close-knit gay world of Christopher Street. He was disappointed that he had looked over the rainbow to Oz, and that the promise of this Technicolor world had once again faded into the grim monochrome reality of life in the late 1970s; the increased nationwide opposition to the gay rights movement (Clendinen and Nagourney 1999) left him dispirited and disillusioned.

Discovering Writing and Love

Over time, Kantrowitz began to resent his political involvement. The time and effort necessary for this community work was at the cost of finding a lover. A failed affair and the increasing complexity of gay political life led Kantrowitz to abandon New York for Europe. In England he visited the Lake Country, which had inspired the poets he'd once taught to students; in the stillness of this craggy countryside he felt a strange sensation of light and the desire for the strength of a father, a lover. Again, light becomes an important metaphor for his personal quest. Standing on the lakeshore of the lake, he recollected: "The day was charged with a current that passed through everything, making the landscape radiant with light. I no longer saw with the eyes I had seen through that same morning. I had ripped aside a curtain and unveiled the truth. I was no longer lonely . . . I was something new" (Kantrowitz 1996, 166). With this epiphany, he resolved his disappointment over his emotionally distant father. Following this turning point in his life (McAdams and Bowman 2001), Kantrowitz continued his "Grand Tour" through the European capitals before returning to New York and his teaching.

Following a year's sabbatical in San Francisco and missing the frenetic life in New York, Kantrowitz returned and once again became involved in what he had termed "the pornographic gay spaces" such as the baths and the Mineshaft, an infamous gay sex club later closed by the city (Brodsky 1993). It was at one of the baths that Kantrowitz met Lawrence Mass, destined to become his life-partner. They met again at a party some six months later; Mass recalled their first meeting, then disappeared in the crowd. Another meeting at the baths the following summer led to mutually satisfying sex and an exchange of phone numbers. Mass was the Jewish doctor of his mother's dreams, and sexy to boot. It took only a few meetings for each to realize that he had found his mate. Passionately devoted to Judaism and to the work of the anti-Semitic composer Richard Wagner, Mass grew up in a part of the American South that was intolerant toward both homosexuality and Judaism. Kantrowitz urged him to write his account of his well-traveled but troubled life prior to becoming a physician and an author (Mass 1994).

The two men have remained lovers for more than two decades, each influencing the other's life story, although much of Mass's own account is focused on his youth and his love of Wagner, and the men with whom he shared this passion. At the same time, the first years of their relationship endured times of great stress. Mass was present at the beginning of the AIDS crisis, working with Larry Kramer. Kramer was an emotionally volatile social activist whose life and legacy has been preserved by Mass in collections of Kramer's writing (Mass 1990) and a volume reviewing Kramer's social and political contributions (Mass 1997). In addition, Kramer had been among the first to alert the gay community to the specter of AIDS, and together with Mass was an active participant in the Gay Men's Health Crisis (GMHC). Although the mission of the GMHC has become controversial in recent years, it was a nationally recognized resource for exchange of information and for the treatment of AIDS over the first years of the pandemic. The GMHC played a central role in the formation of the socially visible AIDS Coalition to Unleash Power (ACT-UP).

Kantrowitz and Mass also agreed to have an open relationship with each free to find other sexual partners so long as there was no emotional entanglement in these encounters. As Blumstein and Schwartz (1983) and Lee (1991) have suggested, this means for managing sexuality has been common among gay couples for whom the model for an enduring relationship may be described as "best friends." Anticipating the theme for the generation of 1950s life-writers coming to adulthood in the '80s, sex soon stood for death and "safe sex" became the order of the day. As Kantrowitz's friends became ill and died, he reports that he had lost more than two hundred friends to AIDS. Only two of the original eight founding GAA members survived. Among the fallen were his two closest friends from GAA days, each of whom had attained national visibility for political organization on behalf of the gay rights movement. The illness and death of close friends, so well symbolized by the memorial quilt movement created by Cleve Jones (Jones and Dawson 2000), re-energized Kantrowitz's political engagement. However, his own health soon became a concern. Turning fifty, he fell victim to diabetes. Feeling his losses acutely, Kantrowitz observes: "I felt as if I had lost both the Scarecrow and the Tin Man and except for Larry, I was alone on the yellow brick road to nowhere" (Kantrowitz 1996, 214).

His account ends with his recognition of an exhaustion throughout the nation in the wake of the preceding years of the 1960s. He retrieved his tweeds, the collegiate symbol, cut his hair, discarded his jewelry and tinted glasses, and settled into the mundane world of New York's rapidly changing Upper West Side in the 1980s. His account ends before the AIDS epidemic. An afterword accompanying the 1996 reprinting of his memoir details this shift from the dogmatism of the early 1970s to the more tolerant attitude of the present. Reflecting on the stormy activism of that time, Kantrowitz notes that the movement did transform gay life from self-hatred to self-respect. His earlier fascination with the gay world of the baths and bars retreated as he turned to his literary work, which included a biography of the nineteenth-century poet Walt Whitman, whose own homosexuality was obliquely evident in his poetry.

Kantrowitz concludes his afterword with an observation regarding historical change and the experience of realizing a gay identity. He notes that gay and lesbian students no longer feel it necessary to celebrate their sexual identity; they consider his life story dated. At the same time, the shame that he had hoped his generation of gay men would obliterate has returned as a consequence of AIDS. Kantrowitz hopes that future generations of gay people will be able to grow to adulthood without this mantle of shame. Kantrowitz has achieved through his writing what the Wizard was able to do for his four simple petitioners. After all, the magic of the Wizard of Oz was simply a narrative turn. What the Wizard did for his supplicants was to rephrase desire in ways that made sense to each.

The Gay Education of Andrew Tobias

In 1973 Andrew Tobias published *The Best Little Boy in the World* (1973/1993), the story of his youth, shortly after his graduation from Harvard, under the pseudonym John Reid, and with his college disguised as Yale. An enlarged paperback edition was published in 1977. A second volume on his adult life, *The Best Little Boy in the World Grows Up* (Tobias 1998a), was published under his real name at the time that he "came-out" gay in the pages of the Harvard alumni magazine (Tobias 1998b). Tobias notes that the cover picture of the second volume is of the real Andrew Tobias rather than that of a model, which had been used for the cover of his first memoir. Tobias shares with Martin Duberman, born a decade earlier, a childhood spent in comfortable circumstances in the New York suburbs and, like Duberman, attended a private college prep school and a prestigious Ivy League college.

The first of these two volumes comprising Tobias's life story is of a well-socialized boy trying to please his family and community, even as such efforts were at the cost of his own longing. It is the same intention to please that led Tobias to write under a pseudonym so that he might not upset his parents or, presumably, his alma mater. As he observes relatively late in his education:

How could I write a book that might cause my parents so much pain? I am writing it because I want to, because like everyone I want to try to do something meaningful with my life, because I *do* want to be the BLBITW, and because I think they will understand. (Tobias 1973/1993, 174)

Concluding the book, Tobias observes:

I haven't managed to say all that I wanted to say or to say it properly or in a way that would inspire the indignation I wanted you to feel. Throughout the book I have felt like adding footnoted apologies to gay readers for sounding simpleminded, naive, and supercilious. It should go without saying that having tried so hard for years to remain ignorant of it and having been out a relatively short time, I don't know that much about homosexuality. I only know what it was like for me to come to terms—or to begin to, anyway—with my own. (Tobias 1993, 241)

The first of the two books of Tobias's memoir was written when Tobias was twenty-five, just starting on a promising business career, which ultimately led to his becoming a successful entrepreneur and later the treasurer of the Democratic Party. It is a particularly important memoir, not only because it became an icon for later gay self life-writers, but because it is one of the few memoirs written almost contemporaneously with the events portrayed and thus less likely to be subjected to the inevitable reconstruction of a life read backward, influenced by personal and social circumstances—and by the life writing of earlier generations of gay men. The second book, published a quarter of a century later, is a rather straightforward account of gay life in the midst of affluence in New York and Boston in the 1970s, including a brief mention of AIDS. Just as with Kantrowitz's memoir, Tobias acknowledges the impact of AIDS upon his life but does not dwell on it as do life-writers of the generation born in the 1950s.

This first book is a cleverly written story of Tobias's effort to keep secret his homosexuality, even at a time when the expression of this desire was more widely accepted. The second book is a story of the emergence of a community of men for whom gay desire has become acceptable, even fashionable, who speak their desire, and who become activists in the gay rights movement. This account is of being "virtually normal" in the terms used by the writer Andrew Sullivan (1995) in his argument for accept-ance of gay men as different only in terms of their choice of sexual partner. Together, these two volumes chronicle the course of urban gay life over nearly half a century and reflect the changing manner in which gay desire has been portrayed.

Tobias writes so as not to affront any well-educated liberal reader. His friends are gay activists, socially responsible as founders of voluntary asso-ciations devoted to preserving legal rights for the gay community, who sup-port gay teachers, and write about the most positive aspects of gay culture.

It is at first puzzling why Tobias's first book has become an icon of gay self-life writing. The tone is self-indulgent and flip but also self-deprecatory. Robinson (1999) has criticized the first volume of Tobias's memoir in similar terms. He views the book as "slapdash" (Robinson 1999, 318) written in an off-hand, jocular manner, rushed to completion, and not as amusing as Tobias would like us to believe. Robinson criticizes Tobias's continuing attempts to get in touch with his body, which Robinson finds not amusing but simply tiresome and uninteresting. Robinson also com-plains that Tobias seems to be writing less for a gay readership than to fos-ter understanding of gay life among straight readers. Tobias tosses off re-marks in the first book such as "my closest straight friends and my close gay friends tend to be handsome" (Tobias 1993, 205) or "by gay standards I was something of a hot shit . . . a smaller proportion of gay people than straight people are attractive. I had proportionately less competition" (To-bias 1993, 130).

His first book was an overnight success. Tobias's expression of his own gay desire, his bungled efforts to make contact with the gay community, his self-consciousness about his inhibitions, and his concern for the reac-tions of family and friends describe issues for many gay men in contempo-rary society. Even Robinson (1999), hardly a fan of Tobias's writing, admits that Tobias's memoir was the inspiration for his own study of gay lives. As Tobias concludes his second book: "You don't have to be 'somebody' to be somebody. You just have to be true to yourself" (Tobias 1998a, 270).

Tobias doesn't confront such questions as the "cause" of being gay. He observes that homosexuality is a tangle of causes. One boy may become gay because he is meek while another may become meek only as a conse-quence of prejudice and comments that "parents may as well give up on trying to keep their kids from growing up gay. A child's sexuality is too complicated to engineer" (1993, 195). He traces his need to be the best little boy in the world to his competition with his older brother for his parents' attention. While he doubts there is anything random about it, the reasons for being gay are too complex to permit simple answers. What is clear to him is that the effort on the part of the larger society to isolate gay people leads them to lose self-respect and self-confidence. As a result, gay people may adopt the stereotyped, often effeminate identities that society presumes that they must have.

Becoming a "Cowboy"

Tobias's life story begins at age five when, while playing hide-and-seek, he hid in the hall closet; the gay reader (Tierney 2000) will understand this metaphor of hiding in the closet, which pervades Tobias's life through his college years. He introduces himself: "I am five years old. I am the best little boy in the world, told so day after day" (Tobias 1993, 5). This presentation of self continues as the theme for his life. Tobias cannot even bring himself to remove the tag from his new mattress and fears retribution for every "naughty" thought. Highly over-socialized in an upper-middle-class family in the 1950s, with adoring parents whom he refers to as the Supreme Court, and an older brother whom he refers to as Goliath, his sense of guilt is of Freudian proportions. Tobias reports working overtime as a child to please his parents. He was expected to achieve and excelled at an exclusive private school in New York—he gave his parents everything they could wish for and more. The problem was that it led him to feel a false sense of self (Winnicott 1960), always seeking to please others to cover up that secret of the closet. He could not even let himself masturbate until he was in college even though he shared a room with his older brother who regularly masturbated. Needless to say, sex was not among topics of discussion in the Tobias household.

The self-deprecating tone of the narrative reflects Tobias's discomfort with his sexuality and avoids the gender-stereotyped activities expected for boys in middle childhood (Corbett 1997). Tobias traces his first awareness of his same-sex desire to age eleven. By the time he was thirteen, Tobias reports feeling very guilty about this desire and working ever harder to please his parents who, he was sure, would so disapprove that they would no longer regard him as the best little boy in the world. Sent to a sleep-away summer camp, Tobias dreaded team sports, playing right field where he could do the least damage to his baseball team, although he carefully notes that he excelled in tennis and swimming. He reports not being accepted at camp, where he was not considered to be one of the boys. During high school, his determination to achieve academic success required long hours of studying and provided a means for avoiding contact with his classmates. He worked frantically at developing a great body just as he worked frantically at his academic work; he edited the high school newspaper, was a star swimmer and wrestler, and even played soccer. At the same time, Tobias was aware that he was not like other boys.

Being unable to masturbate became the metaphor for not being able to be like his classmates, many of whom talked dirty and had heterosexual encounters, like his college roommate. Recalling that he watched his older brother masturbate, it may be that this experience led to traumatic overstimulation (Phillips 2001, 2003) in which he felt both desire for sexual contact with his brother and a sense of shame regarding this wish, leading to avoidance of a situation in which he might have to acknowledge this wish. Finally, in his sophomore year of college, he was able to let himself masturbate. His favorite fantasy was of wrestling with a boy from camp to whom he had been particularly attracted. This fantasy may have been a displacement from overstimulation during childhood watching his brother masturbate. Tobias euphemistically refers to this "wrestling" as being cowboys: his sole adolescent wet dream centered on his fantasy of being cowboys with this boy. Some years later, talking with an old friend from camp who was visiting him at college, Tobias learned that his friend had messed around with other boys, that the boy of his fantasies had been sexually involved with their counselor, and that many of the camp staff had been gay. However, Tobias was so terrified of his own same-sex desire that he couldn't look about him, either during childhood or even in college when, as he learned later, many of his classmates and indeed his freshman house proctor were gay and regularly socialized together.

One of Tobias's high school teachers, married and a parent, seemed to pay attention to the same good-looking boys to whom he himself was drawn; it was tacitly acknowledged by both, but Tobias resented his teacher's effort to pry his secret out of him and felt uncomfortable with his teacher's all too obvious expression of interest in these boys. On another occasion in high school, working on a report at New York's American Museum of Natural History, he was approached by a man proposing to "do him"; he fled from the room in terror. He was mortified that he didn't know what a blow-job was, but only learned the following summer at camp when the topic came up for discussion with a camp counselor who was obviously attracted to him. Another time, at the movies with a boy whom he desired, a stranger propositioned the pair. Again, he felt disgusted. He dealt with his feelings by working out, swimming, wrestling, and playing soccer. Eventually he realized that his efforts at wrestling were connected with his desire to be "cowboys" with other boys—but by that time he was in college.

Tobias tried hard to show an interest in girls and to date, but he had had only three dates before college, including a double date at summer camp with the boy of his cowboy fantasies. He was repulsed when the girl he was with overpowered him and forced a tongue kiss on him. Another double date was with his cabin counselor and his girl friend, and fellow camper Rita Mae Brown, later the author of the 1973 iconic lesbian autobiographical novel *Rubyfruit Jungle,* published about the same time as his own personal account. By the time he arrived at college, Tobias had learned how to fake an interest in women. His parents expected him to show the usual adolescent interest in girls. Tobias felt increasingly lonely and unable to tell his secret to anyone. He worked at being "straight looking–straight acting," and became reconciled to the impossibility of being cowboys with any of his friends or roommates.

At Harvard, Tobias took an active role in starting a student marketing association that became highly successful and still thrives. Among other things, his student marketing business published a series of "must have" travel books. He played tennis, swam, and did his best to look normal, since all his friends appeared to find gay demeanor disgusting. On holiday in Spain with his roommate and friend Hank, he was caught in a position with one of a pair of girls they had met. Unable to get aroused he begged off. He pretended to Hank that he had a great time. He even took another room so as not to appear to Hank to be the first one back in the evening. It was now the mid-sixties, and "pot" or "grass" was suddenly widely available. When stoned, one of his college friends enjoyed wrestling, apparently never noticing the bulge in Tobias's shorts. He was depressed at the thought that he would end up like one of his prep school bachelor tutors always hunting for boys to seduce. He had been aware of camp counselors and schoolteachers who subtly showed an erotic interest in him; he found this interest disgusting because of the fear that he might turn out to be like them.

While Tobias longed to find other students gay like himself, he wanted to be a "red-blooded American boy" and closed his eyes to the reality of other students dealing with similar desire. Gay parties were held in the basement of his Harvard freshman house as upstairs he was struggling with his secret. Believing he was the only one to harbor these feelings, he was oblivious to Rusty Kothavala, his freshman proctor and popular natural sciences instructor and astronomer, and later the life-partner of Toby Marotta, author of *Sons of Harvard: Gay Men from the Class of 1967* (Marotta 1982). He was also unaware of two gay house tutors (including now-congressman Barney Frank) (Tobias 1998a, 13; 1998b, 4). Tobias notes that even at the time he knew that Rusty, who then lived with his wife and child, was simpatico; depressed and despairing over his inability to act on his gay identity, he tried to talk to Rusty but couldn't bring himself to tell Rusty his secret. Decades later, Rusty remembered Tobias's visit and understood Tobias's effort to talk with him but felt that it would have been intrusive to bring up the subject.

Following Tobias's graduation and a successful career at Harvard, the Vietnam buildup was under way; Tobias was called up for military service. He passed his physical exam. There was just one thing, item 93 on the mental examination, which asked if he was homosexual. He obsessed over item 93, checking yes, erasing and checking no, only to check yes again, then no. What finally kept him out of the service was a varicocele, which led to an enlarged scrotum; he assured the army doctor that it was painful. He was exempted from service. Considering the options of business school or working, he chose to move to New York and continue the marketing company he had started at Harvard. Ever more successful in his business, Tobias reports that at the same time he was lonely outside of work. His older brother had married, and his family began to pressure him about developing a serious relationship. For Tobias, having to go on a date with a woman was like having to go to the dentist!

Tobias's oldest friend from camp had graduated at about the same time. Jim had once confessed an attraction to him, explaining to Tobias that he was sort of gay and sort of straight. Although not reciprocally sharing Jim's wish for a sexual relationship, Tobias decided that his friend would at least be a good roommate and would understand why he never dated women. He maintained contact with some of his old Harvard classmates, learning that a number of his Harvard friends had been gay. Still, he pretended that he was not gay. Walking past Forty-fifth Street and Third Avenue, a hangout for gay hustlers, he carefully avoided looking at the men he so much desired. One time he even exchanged glances with a man at a street corner, waiting for the light to change—a man who was like the man of his fantasies. He felt guilty when their eyes locked before the light turned; they walked on in different directions.

His sometime gay friend Jim married and he was alone once again. That second summer following college, while he was a guest of his old roommate and his roommate's girlfriend, and in the presence of so many beautiful men lounging by the pool, Tobias could no longer bear his secret and told his friend of his gay desire. Tobias says: "This time I told him. I told him because after eleven years of silence, I could stand loneliness no longer, I could stand pretending no longer, and I wanted to tell someone that I loved him" (Tobias 1993, 97). His friend not only accepted this revelation but also was able to tell him that during the college years he himself had occasionally been with other men. Next, Tobias told his other college roommate who, while straight, was open and accepting. This roommate wondered if he had seen a psychiatrist about his condition, but Tobias explained that he could never be changed. As he explained to his roommate, he was sexually just like him, except in reverse, and that change was out of the question.

Having confided to his two best friends from college days that he was gay, Tobias summoned the courage to check the graffiti in men's bathrooms and the personal ads in an alternative newspaper, still coded in the terms necessary prior to the gay rights movement. Just past his twenty-third birthday, with the encouragement of friends and some slackened personal control, Tobias visited an address listed in one of the personal ads for male models available for painting or photographs. Entering a seedy warehouse with filthy makeshift cubicles, one of the models led Tobias into a cubicle where Tobias confessed his story that he still had not had sex with either men or women. The hustler listened to Tobias's story, told him about New York's gay venues, and explained the idea of "coming out." Tobias made a quick getaway but did find his way to Christopher Street a few evenings later. Imagining that everyone in the city was looking at him and would know of his destination, he couldn't ask for directions; he had trouble finding the gay neighborhood that the model had told him about. It was still early in the evening, and many gay bars didn't really get into business until after midnight. Tobias reports that he paced nervously back and forth before a gay bar with plate glass windows but could not summon the courage to enter; the evening ended leaving Tobias feeling defeated.

Tobias's next effort was to answer a personal ad in the alternative newspaper from a man describing himself as a theater student seeking to meet new friends. Tobias wrote to the address given in the ad and soon received a phone call. When he met his correspondent at a Greenwich Village bar, he couldn't allow himself to go home with the theater student. Responding to another ad by a male hustler, he met Dick for a drink in a gay bar in the Village. As with his other respondents, he explained his inhibition and lack of experience. Dick was initially suspicious of Tobias's naïveté and said that he had never before heard such a story. However, the two men got along well, and after several beers, Tobias was able to accept Dick's offer to accompany him to a midtown hotel where, with considerable trepidation, Tobias booked a room for the evening. Twelve years of indecision and turmoil were about to end as Tobias sat next to Dick on the bed in their hotel room.

With Dick's active encouragement, they were soon wrestling and removing each other's clothes and feeling each other's bodies. Although neither had an orgasm, Tobias was pleased and relieved that he was finally able to be a cowboy. Wrestling about excited and naked with another man who enjoyed touching and being touched, he had finally been able to let himself realize his desire. Tobias thought Dick liked him, but Dick appears to have felt overwhelmed by Tobias's psychological struggle. He did complement Tobias on his great body, and urged him to purchase a pair of blue jeans!

An Education in Body and Mind

Tobias decided to return to business school and was cheered to learn that an old college friend had also recently returned to Cambridge. Through friends of friends, he met another gay student. However, when they did have sex, he was still too scared and inhibited to relax and enjoy this sex. Not only did Tobias feel guilty about his gay desire, but now he also worried that he couldn't please his partner. His friend guided him around Boston and introduced him to Sporters, a collegiate gay bar, which had also been patronized by Martin Duberman. Going into Sporters was an epiphany, the turning point in Tobias's realization of a gay sexual identity. Pushing open the door meant accepting that he was gay. A fresh, handsome face, clean-cut, with a great build, Tobias was an instant success. Sporters provided the closed, secretive world that Tobias and other gay men of his generation had sought. Terribly nervous this first time in a gay bar, Tobias couldn't even let himself exchange looks with the many men who showed an interest in him.

Later in the evening, casting glances about while anchored to his barstool, he spotted a man who was of the type he was looking for. He made eye contact with the man of his dreams, and Rob came over and introduced himself. Tobias reported to Rob that he had been out of the closet for a full two hours and willingly accepted Rob's invitation to go home with him. Still naive, Tobias was eager to turn a one-night fling into a lifelong relationship. However, Tobias froze when Rob suggested mutual oral sex and anal intercourse. Still terribly inhibited, Tobias couldn't even let himself think about such things; he observes that even decades later he still finds it difficult to enjoy them.

Finding Rob's intellect less attractive than his physique, Tobias moved on and met other men. He was finally able to have an orgasm, and he even developed a sort of a relationship with Eric. The two shared common interests in economics, and Eric was an organizer of one of the homophile organizations emerging in the years preceding Stonewall. Tobias confessed his fantasy about being cowboys to Eric: cowboys wrestled but did not like being kissed, yet Eric helped him to enjoy kissing for the first time. With a distaste for feminine-acting men (Tobias observes that if he enjoyed femininity he would have gone out with girls), Eric also introduced him to the more masculine of Boston's gay bars and provided Tobias with the gay education that he had been seeking. Eric showed him cruising places where boys could be picked up for a brief paid encounter; he told him about published guides available for learning about gay attractions in most larger cities. However, Eric carefully avoided taking Tobias back to Sporters where he might meet other men.

In the late 1960s, information regarding gay bars was generally passed on through a network of friends. Gay bars, although still without visible outside identification, were becoming popular. It was still necessary for some bar owners to bribe the police in order to avoid the kind of raids to which the Stonewall Inn was continually subject. In time, Tobias tired of his relationship with Eric. However, before the break occurred Eric took Tobias on a summer weekend to Provincetown. Located at the tip of Cape Cod, Provincetown had become a major venue for gay life during the 1960s. By this time, Tobias had become more confident with his own sexual identity. Tobias had made a journey by himself to Provincetown a few weeks earlier but couldn't locate the gay cruising area along the beach. With Eric as his guide, he now realized that he had turned the wrong way on his previous visit, going right to the straight beach rather than left to the gay beach. Much to Eric's dismay, Tobias turned many heads as he walked shirtless down the Provincetown beach. Tobias easily fit into the gay life of the summer season. He began to dance—just a little; experienced the usual longings for beautiful but unattainable men; had brief alliances with men of his dreams, alas less exciting in reality; and realized that anticipation is often more satisfying than attainment.

His gay education continued as Eric introduced Tobias to late 1960s gay activism at a Boston-area student homophile league meeting. At the meeting he discovered many others like himself, students who were in varying stages of going gay and more or less at ease with their newfound identity. Tobias said that he still got points for being a newcomer. Freddie, a southern boy living in Boston for the summer and captivated by Tobias, invited him for a swimming date the following weekend. Freddie was cute and ambitious, liked somewhat older and settled men, and was more than willing to continue Tobias's gay education.

Tobias began a relationship of several months with Chris, also a student at Harvard Business School. They became a couple, which Tobias defined as "two gay men who spend most of their time together and who are supposed to feel guilty if they have sex with someone else" (1993, 178). Even within this first longer-term relationship, Tobias was still squeamish about anal sex, but Chris listened patiently to Tobias's "cowboy" fantasies. Sex between them wasn't satisfying, however, and they gradually drifted apart. Through Chris, Tobias had met another idol of the previous summer at Provincetown and began a short-lived affair. Chris had a one-night stand with a man he met while on a business trip who, as it turned out, had been one of Tobias's Harvard classmates. He was as surprised as Tobias to learn that the other was gay. Tobias was later to meet and become friends with other gay Harvard classmates, usually at Sporters. With Chris he maintained the kind of close friendship not uncommon among former lovers in the gay community.

Tobias became acquainted with the kind of fast living in New York that 1930s-generation life-writer Alan Helms had also described in his memoir. Tobias went to the baths and bars, and realized that relationships lasted longer in Boston than in frenetic New York. Further, Tobias was still too sexually inhibited to participate in the vibrant life of gay New York. Gradually, he was able to overcome his guilt and, instead, became angry about society's failure to accept homosexuality. He was able to tell his employer, his straight friends, and even his brother and sister-in-law that he was gay. Telling his brother was more painful—his brother could not believe that a gay man could lead a happy life, and urged Tobias to see a psychiatrist. This somewhat stereotypically sissified older brother had never been able to achieve Tobias's own athletic success. Reflecting changing views regarding same-sex desire, Tobias assured his brother that he was not unhappy and that he had no need to see a psychiatrist, that many famous contemporaries in politics and athletics were gay (apparently by this point in his life he had direct personal knowledge regarding the sexual identity of some of these famous men), and that straight people were not necessarily happy!

This was all said with a newfound positive self-regard. Tobias adopted the same matter-of-fact approach in telling his straight friends; being gay was not something to be ashamed of but to be discussed in a good-natured way. Tobias's education was nearing its end. The last obvious problem was telling his parents. With the best of intentions, he drove to their country house, preparing to break the news. He had carefully outlined in his mind how he would tell them, and considered reassuring them by telling them of great men in history who had been like him. Concerned that they would be hurt, and that they would no longer look at him as perfect, he was unable to bring himself to break the news.

Gay and Successful

Reprinting his 1973 memoir in 1993, Tobias added the comment "I'm fine, a lot of my friends are not. I think it's time to write another book. I never seem to get around to it, but maybe now I will." With these chilling words, obviously referring to the AIDS pandemic, Tobias presages his second book, *The Best Little Boy in the World Grows Up* (1998a). This volume of his memoirs is divided into two parts, the first concerning life in New York in the 1970s, the fast-paced world, which he was not sure he liked, and the second, which begins with the cryptic comment "Then people started to get sick" (Tobias 1998a, 119). This book is a particularly good chronicle of life before and after the appearance of AIDS, and a strong statement of the impact of AIDS on the expression of desire among gay men. At the same time, his discussion of AIDS is somewhat removed from the pain and over-powering sense of loss characteristic of life-writers born in the 1950s, finding themselves in the midst of the pandemic as they arrived at adulthood.

Tobias begins the second book with disclosure of names and places for which pseudonyms or pen names had been used in the first volume. By this time (1998a), Tobias had become an activist for gay rights, noting the number of his classmates who had thought about or attempted suicide as a means of dealing with their sexuality. Earlier fantasies of wrestling as a cowboy had been transformed into living as a gay man with a life-partner. His only regret about his undergraduate years was that he had been so sexually reticent and so unaware of what was taking place around him. Tobias reflects on the secretive nature of gay desire during the late 1960s and the cost of having to bear this secret. Harvard students were expected to be successful; homosexuality was an illness and therefore these men felt that they could not realize the expectations that Harvard had for them by selecting them in the first place. Conforming during the 1960s, with the onset of student discontent at Harvard and college campuses across the nation in 1969, many of these gay students shed their cover and became gay activists. Tobias's (1998b) account confirms that these men have indeed become successful, although perhaps in ways Harvard had never anticipated. They were leaders in forming gay rights groups, several of which have gained national recognition. Tobias himself became an influential figure in the business community and developed one of the first personal computer programs for the management of family finances.

Contacting former classmates who had publicly acknowledged their gay identity while working on a story for *Harvard Magazine* (Tobias 1998b), Tobias reports their similar experiences trying to cope with their gay identity during their undergraduate days at college (their accounts are consistent with those of Holleran [2004] and Shand-Tucci [2003] describing Harvard's antigay prejudice as recently as the 1960s). Tobias points out that the founder of Harvard, the Reverend Wigglesworth (ca. 1653), reveals in his diary that he had harbored similar desire even while condemning it in others. As Tobias (1998b, 54) aptly observes, "We knew what we were; we knew it was completely unacceptable; and we knew there was no way out." Later, he describes his present crowd of friends as "for the most part, decent, productive tax-paying professionals." Tobias himself was later involved in popular economics and wrote a book on the problems of the insurance industry. Hardly a glamorous life, but one marked by respectability.

The second volume picks up on his life at the point of completing his Harvard MBA, living in New York and commuting to Boston on weekends to visit friends. By 1977 Tobias's first book had become a bestseller in the gay community; his quest to satisfy his desire, while maintaining a straight facade, spoke to the common experiences of a generation of gay men from upper-middle-class households anticipating career success. As he was nearing the age of thirty, coinciding with the publication of the revised paperback of his book, Tobias again decided that he should tell his parents. In an epilogue to this first volume of his memoirs he relates: "I told them. They said that so far as they were concerned, I was still the best little boy in the world" (1973/1977, 243). By now it was the late 1970s, and there had been a dramatic change in social attitudes toward homosexuality, in no small part a consequence of Tobias's own book. He reports calling his mother, blurting out over the phone that he was gay. Her response was simply, "don't tell your father" (1998a, 27). Two years later, with his mother's permission, he did tell his father who expressed little interest and surprise upon hearing the news. However, when Tobias gave his father a copy of his first book, his father responded as other upper-middle-class educated parents of gay sons, expressing chagrin at having unwittingly caused his son so much misery.

The second book is replete with references to gay activism and includes information on a number of prominent gay organizations and coupons for memberships. Much of the first part is devoted to Tobias's description of his search for a boyfriend, together with lengthy discussions on the issue of gay rights and of the problems for gay men in finding sexually and personally compatible partnership. Tobias speculates (1998a, 35) that complete compatibility between men may be more difficult than that between men and women. With the success of his book, and his prominence and visibility of a gay professional, he acquired influence within the larger political community and in the network of other influential gay men in New York. He also began dating and sleeping with the famous and the near famous in order to satisfy an appetite too long stilled.

On city nights and summer weekends on Fire Island, Tobias was quenching his sexual appetite with gusto. There is however a note of foreboding in this discussion; this excess of the seventies is believed responsible for the "gay plague" a decade later (Gagnon 1990; Moore 2004). In ways reminiscent of Long Island in the 1920s as described by F. Scott Fitzgerald, these summer weekends were a time of blissful innocence and delight. Tobias found the baths less enticing; he says that he may have been saved from AIDS by his revulsion at seeing men walking around in towels. More likely, it was his personal distaste for both oral sex and intercourse, particularly being penetrated, which protected him from being infected by HIV. Much of this second account is taken up with effort to find a satisfying relationship with another man, concluding with his current long-term relationship.

In this second volume of his memoirs, Tobias provides a succinct summary of gay life in the late 1970s. Increasing awareness of gay life was evident in the press; Tobias maintains that it was President Clinton's effort to talk about gay rights in the military, more than a decade later, that fostered public discourse regarding gay rights. Tobias is also much more introspective than in his first book (Tobias 1973/1993). He notes that he is not a confrontational person. His life-partner, Charles, was one of nine siblings from an Irish family. Charles has an explosive temper; together they have learned to deal with Charles's occasional outbursts. There was also the problem that, at least at the outset, Tobias was considerably more affluent, and Charles resented not being able to pay his own way. As Blumstein and Schwartz (1983) state, this is potentially divisive for gay and straight couples alike.

Tobias's first partner, Ed, was a young dentist. Tobias was looking for the straight-acting husband he could take home to his parents in the suburbs. Ed was extraordinarily good-looking, had terrible self-esteem problems, and needed continual reassurance. Their relationship was problematic from the outset: Tobias was still uncomfortable with gay sex, which frustrated Ed, who had difficulty committing to the monogamous relationship that Tobias expected. Ed felt he had to compete with Tobias's writing projects for his attention. Then Ed met Todd and began a relationship, which was to last for more than thirteen years, and Tobias was left with a broken heart.

Just past the age of thirty, Tobias met a Yale senior through a mutual friend. An aspiring writer, Scot was then the film critic for the *Yale Daily*

News and traveled to New York to review new films. At first, Tobias was not particularly attracted to Scot. However, Scot fell in love with Tobias. Their sexual relations left both feeling embarrassed for using the other to satisfy what Tobias (Tobias 1998a, 80) portrays as basic animal needs. With Scot, sex ultimately blossomed into a meaningful relationship. Tobias achieved success writing about money; Scot achieved success managing magazines. Scot came from a close-knit family completely accepting of Tobias.

The couple enjoyed the increasingly visible life in New York's gay community with summer weekends spent on Fire Island. As Tobias observes, "We'd do what people *do*—talk about our work, talk about our friends, talk about our hopes" (Tobias 1998a, 92). While they didn't live together, their apartments were close by, and Tobias took particular delight in surprising Scot with trips and good times with friends. He reports that "I was alive and happy. I had made it . . . those summers, those winters. If I was the best little boy in the world, I was also one of the most fortunate—and keenly aware of it" (Tobias 1998a, 97).

Tobias's relationship with Scot was close and caring; they held each other tenderly and loved each other but were not always entirely faithful. Tobias says that he "slipped" less often than Scot who sought sexual activities that were difficult for Tobias to accept. He was still a prude sexually, most often satisfied with "wrestling." Again, problems of sexual compatibility led to the breakup of the relationship. Tobias reports: "I *hate* sex. Not having it—I like having it. But the way it screws everything up . . . because there were some things I couldn't bring myself to do" (1998a, 124–25). One of Tobias's friends sent him a hustler for an evening, but Tobias was unable to perform. He does relate one experience with a beautiful man at a Fire Island party who had fallen in love with him. The joyous first part of this account of his young adulthood ends with recollection of an incredible Miami Beach weekend party and glorious brunches, which he and Scot gave at his beautifully decorated New York apartment.

And then his friends began getting sick. AIDS would eventually claim four of his housemates and about half of his Sunday brunch list. In his late thirties, Tobias was not only losing large numbers of his friends to AIDS, but also his father was dying of lung cancer and his grandmother was dying as well. Then, to make matters worse, he lost Scot to a more sexually compatible lover. Scot died of AIDS as did his friend Peter, who had introduced him to the pleasures of Miami Beach. Tobias narrates the horrible course of the illness among his friends, the inevitable final days, the deathbed vigils, and then the funerals. However, AIDS largely disappears as a topic in the later chapters of Tobias's account. He notes in an epilogue "along the way, our friends stopped dying" (1998a, 267), and reflects advances in treatment of HIV through the discovery of antiretroviral medication in the mid-1990s. In this second volume of memoirs, Tobias appears to be less concerned with the pandemic itself than with the time beyond the pandemic, a "postgay" period of increased gay rights, including recognition of same-sex civil unions.

Tobias's next relationship was with Matt, thirteen years younger, who had arrived to paint his apartment. Matt fell in love with Tobias at once; it took Tobias longer to reciprocate the relationship, which lasted for about two years. Tobias never considered him a grownup. Ultimately, Matt found the sexual side of their relationship less satisfying than he had hoped—a continuing problem for Tobias, always somewhat sexually inhibited, who reports working on the problem. Matt later on went on to live with another Yale graduate for more than ten years. One summer day on Fire Island, about a year after yet another unfortunate relationship had ended, he met Charles, a casual acquaintance who had been to his party over the preceding July Fourth weekend. Charles had lost a great deal of weight and Tobias thought he must also be sick since dramatic weight-loss or wasting was a cardinal sign of AIDS. Feeling compassionate, he suggested dinner. He ran into Charles again in the community store some days later and invited him to a party he was attending that evening. The party was boring, and they returned to Tobias's place, a mutual attraction growing, and soon they were a couple. Charles was in many ways like Scot; he came from a large Irish-Catholic family, which was completely accepting of their relationship. If family is defined by those we have Thanksgiving with (Weston 1991), then Tobias and Charles accumulated a very large family, including Tobias's parents, Charles's large family, and a group of friends in Miami. Christmas in Miami Beach was a repeat of the joy of Thanksgiving.

Tobias writes that he has had the ideal life. His personal finance computer software was a big hit with many early personal computer users in the early days of the 1980s technological revolution. He became a regular participant at the annual Renaissance weekends, which have also become a favorite of his friends Bill and Hillary Clinton. He worked hard on the first presidential campaign for Bill Clinton; when Tobias came out at a Renaissance weekend, the Clintons were completely warm and accepting. Later, his life-partner Charles joined him for these weekends.

By the mid-1990s, the liberal community, including the press, had become comfortable with the word "gay" and with discussing gay issues. Together, Charles and Tobias enjoy more than the usual luxuries of life and have been generous in their support of the gay community. Tobias became involved with the Campaign for Human Rights, a gay lobbying organization. Charles and he also exchanged rings worn on the left hand—after all gay people can have the same meaningful, committed relationships as straight people. His friend and fellow gay activist Richard Socarides, another Clinton staffer, whose father has achieved notoriety for his position that homosexuality was evidence of psychopathology (Socarides 1988), has observed that his own relationship with his gay lover has lasted longer than his father's four marriages. Impassioned about coming out and being visible as successful and gay, Tobias writes about the myriad ways in which he came out, to magazine editors, in his daily Internet column, and to former business school classmates from whom he solicited contributions preceding a reunion. At his Harvard Business School reunion, Charles and he were prominently pictured along with his classmates' husbands and wives.

Interviewing Harvard College alumni for his 1998 report on being gay at Harvard, where he "officially" came out, Tobias (1998b) reports that accompanying the social change of the past three decades, his former classmates had found satisfaction they would never have expected while struggling at Harvard with the opprobrium they were certain would follow upon disclosure of their gay identity. Much of this social change has been documented by Tobias's classmate Toby Marotta's (1982) book *Sons of Harvard: Gay Men from the Class of 1967*. A similar account has been provided by Shand-Tucci (2003) in his report on generation and social change among gay men at Harvard. Generational differences became clear when Harvard graduates from the 1950s and earlier wrote hateful letters to *Harvard* magazine excoriating Tobias's report about being gay at Harvard in the 1960s and generally condemned homosexuality. However, the generation beginning with the 1960s wrote approving letters of support for Tobias's portrayal of his undergraduate experiences.

Concluding his second book, Tobias observes that depression and anxiety, which beset gay men, are likely the consequence of life-long stigma rather than anything intrinsic in being gay. This observation concurs with Meyer's (1995) study of the impact of antigay prejudice on the mental health of sexual minorities. Tobias concludes his two-volume memoir with a plea for tolerance and with an affirmation of the successes of the gay rights movement, a stinging critique of the Religious Right and its stance against loving relationships among gay men, and the importance of liberation from guilt among gay men. Turning fifty, Tobias celebrated in his usual cheerful and somewhat outrageous manner. Viewed in terms of Plummer's (1995) typology of modernist stories, Tobias's account is an account of a journey, a progression through stages and at last finding a new home, that which he shares with his partner in the postgay world of the new millennium.

Getting Ready for the Gay Rights Revolution

The two men whose life writing I have reviewed were born in 1940 and 1946 respectively, and were in their mid- to late twenties at the time of the Stonewall Inn riot. The riot has acquired symbolic meanings for the gay community far beyond its immediate impact. Police raids on gay bars ended almost immediately in the aftermath of this resistance to police harassment (Carter 2004). That gay people could resist such harassment made Stonewall into a symbol that has endured over time. The formation of gay rights groups in the wake of the Stonewall riots is well portrayed in Arnie Kantrowitz's (1977) description of the formation of the Gay Libera-tion Front and, shortly thereafter, the more successful and more controver-sial Gay Activists Alliance, the first gay pride parade in 1970 celebrating the achievements of the Stonewall Inn riots of the previous year, and the emer-gence of a sense of community among gay people in cities across the nation (Marotta 1982; D'Emilio 1983/1998; Clendinen and Nagourney 1999).

Missing in the personal accounts of these men is the torment and pain as a consequence of social oppression, which had propelled the gen-eration born in the 1930s into psychiatric treatment. While Arnie Kantro-witz suffered as he struggled to acknowledge his gay identity, this struggle was more a consequence of personal turmoil than distress from more overt stigma that confronted life-writers of the 1930s generation. Significantly, it was possible for gay men born in the 1940s and coming of age in the 1960s to find a gay or gay-friendly psychiatrist.

Two events particularly characterize the experiences of Tobias and Kantrowitz: (1) the dramatic increase in community tolerance for the ex-pression of same-sex desire, and (2) the devastating emergence of AIDS. Coming from quite different backgrounds, with quite different educational experiences, both men became active in the gay rights movement. Kantro-witz and his fellow activists developed the first political infrastructure within the gay community in the period immediately following Stonewall. Tobias used his considerable political leverage to influence national policy regarding gay men and women.

These two themes are also evident in Toby Marotta's (1982) survey of his fellow Harvard classmates graduating a year prior to Andrew Tobias. A self-described political homosexual, Marotta had the courage to include his gay identity in the tenth Harvard reunion book distributed to his class-mates. He observes that:

older generations of homosexuals have tended to adjust to the world without making a big fuss about the problems they've encountered. What sets my genera-tion apart is our belief that we can make things easier for ourselves, other homo-sexuals, and everyone else by being very open and very honest about our homosex-uality. (1982, 9–10)

Marotta continues:

The term "gay community" was our creation. We wanted to replace what seemed like an almost invisible and often unhealthy subculture with something that would be . . . a symbol and haven for homosexuals. . . . Indeed, we wanted to make it possible for all people with strong homosexual feelings to embrace their own homosexuality and to relate to other homosexuals with our own countercultural values . . . freed from traditional ways of thinking about and dealing with homo-sexual desires. (1982, 12–13)

Seeking to give homosexuality a natural, appropriate, and enriching place within personal and social life, Marotta suggests that it is this commitment that sets his generation apart from older generations.

Marotta's report was written just as the first cases of a strange cancer were being reported among gay men. Kantrowitz and Tobias both report on the impact of AIDS upon their own life and experiences. Each of these life-writers reports losing a number of close friends to the epidemic as it became a menace in the gay community throughout the 1980s and into the first half of the 1990s. In the afterword to the 1996 printing of his memoir, Kantrowitz discusses the illness and death of his closest compatriots during the time of his earliest political activism. However, his memoir was written in the heady days of the gay rights activism, nearly a decade before the ap-pearance of the AIDS epidemic.

The second volume of Tobias's memoirs was written in the aftermath of the worst years of the gay plague, at a time when the antiretroviral med-ication was already prolonging the lives of many gay men with AIDS. Per-haps it is this success in treating the pandemic among gay men that led Tobias to regard AIDS as almost an afterthought, a passing phenomenon within the larger story of gay lives as "virtually normal" (Sullivan 1995). In the next chapters, I discuss the life writing of the generations of gay men coming to adulthood in the years following the Stonewall Inn riots and the emergence and acceptance of gay rights. Attaining political efficacy as gay men was less an issue for these men than dealing with relationships within the family, finding a lover for a long-term relationship, and, particularly within the generation born in the 1950s, coming to adulthood in the 1970s and dealing with the scourge of AIDS, which emerged as the major problem afflicting this generation a decade later.

4

Born in the Fifties
The Gay Revolution

At the center of the internal homophobia of gay men is a kernel of hopelessness invari-
ably first experienced by the gay adolescent: my life will be impossible because of *what*
I am. The epidemic so often feels as if it has brought that hopeless future to adult fru-
ition. Gay sex will be punished, and AIDS is the punishment. . . . AIDS has provided
new unconscious motivations . . . for gay men and their AIDS educators to further
introject the projected self-hatred of homophobes. . . . As adolescents caught in confusing webs of sexual drive, hopelessness, and societal prohibition, many men found sex
itself the only completely convincing, natural, and conflict-free way of being gay . . .
sex has now become as problematic and conflict-ridden as the social complications of
being gay.

Walt Odets, *In the Shadow of the Epidemic*

The epidemic opens out . . . endlessly consuming my generation and the one before
and the one after me, immense bitter wave, the floor beneath us pulling back, pulling
away, a huge gap opening beneath whatever seemed momentarily solid, downward
pull, dizzying absence: multiply, endlessly these human faces.

Mark Doty, *Heaven's Coast*

The Dark Cloud

Psychologist Walt Odets has provided a detailed and painful view of life in
the 1980s when the generation born in the 1950s had been able to attain
some measure of satisfaction with their adult lives as gay men. The '50s
generation may have suffered the most egregious losses from AIDS, and
these men have lived much of their adult life under the shadow so well

depicted by Odets. As they celebrated this revolution that brought increased personal and sexual freedom, a silent killer was stalking gay men. The revolution had indeed turned dark. This chapter portrays the lives and losses of this generation through the life writing of two men who assumed that the "gay plague" must be the inevitable cost of their same-sex desire.

Writing in the midst of the AIDS pandemic, Murphy (1993) suggested that writing about suffering in the pandemic fostered a distinctive form of life writing:

Such writing first creates a record of the lives of the dead . . . describes these persons then and now still . . . and yet writing is no substitute for the dead themselves . . . what can it all mean that these men suffer and die? What can all the beauty and intimacy of men be for if not to live and love in the way that they can? Thus is this writing also a protest of what happens to mortal being. (310–11)

Murphy (1993) also notes that life writing about the loss of a partner to AIDS has a healing function as well—a way of coping with this terrible affliction and of seeking to make sense of this loss. This is clearly reflected in poet Mark Doty's account of his partner's illness and death, and in such memoirs as those of Paul Monette (1988, 1994) and Fenton Johnson (1996) regarding the loss of their partners to AIDS. Yet Murphy worries that this exercise of self-writing may also lead to self-indulgence. There is often an assumption that AIDS is shameful, a punishment, with an expected death penalty as a consequence. He observes that there is a paradox: talking only of AIDS is to essentialize gay lives; on the other hand, *not* talking about AIDS (particularly in the midst of a time when a generation of gay men had become infected and was dying) means to silence this crisis, and especially in this context silence equals death.

America in the 1950s was a time of unparalleled peace and prosperity. The trauma of World War II had led to triumph in both theaters of war, and the nation emerged as a superpower. With shortages and rationing at an end, an ever-expanding labor market, an explosion of consumer goods, and readily affordable housing in the expanding suburbs, Americans settled into a new and unique era of prosperity (Coontz 1992). A high savings rate, rapid increase in wages, and the generous benefits accorded to veterans all contributed to this new prosperity. It was a time in which suburban life became the idyll. Bedroom communities were created almost overnight. From Levittown on Long Island (Gans 1967) to the new westward migration to California, Americans assumed personal and economic comfort as their entitlement. The new medium of television situation comedies reflected this family lifestyle—the suburban husband and father, the "breadwinner," leaves for work in the city on the early morning train and returns home late in the evening. The wife and mother stays at home with the children, tending to cooking and housekeeping. Family historian Stephanie Coontz (1992) suggests that this decade was the foundation for the new nostalgia of an imagined family, one which haunts the present family debate, including the issue of gay and lesbian marriage.

Coontz observes that the decade of the 1950s *was* unique as a time of prosperity and social consensus. National wealth exploded as Americans moved into the middle class. Home and family became the new utopia. There was, however, a dark side to this prosperity and social stability. Overshadowing the era was the threat of nuclear warfare. An overzealous Congress threatened civil liberties, vigilant to the communist (and homosexual) menace. Of particular significance for the present study, the emphasis on conventional family life posed a particular challenge for sexual minorities even though there may have been increased tolerance for diversity in sexual lifeways through the immediate postwar years. In the terrifying hearings of Joseph McCarthy's House Unamerican Activities Committee, communism was equated with homosexuality. Never mind that Roy Cohen, McCarthy's chief prosecutor, was himself a "closeted" homosexual (he later died of AIDS), or that J. Edgar Hoover, the head of the FBI, lived in a long-term relationship with another man. Boys growing up in the 1950s learned early that same-sex desire was viewed as a threat to the social order and would be suppressed at any cost. As a consequence, this epoch spawned a new and particularly virulent self-hatred among gay men.

Men born in the 1950s came of age at the cusp of the gay rights movement and thus flung themselves into the sexual revolution. Emergence of such visible public sexual spaces as gay bars with clear plate glass windows and signage visible from the street replaced the secretive venues of a previous time (Read 1973). The tragic events that befell these men in the 1980s with the emergence of AIDS only affirmed their own lack of self-worth. Without any awareness of the dangers inherent in the overt but casual pursuit of sex during the 1970s (Moore 2004; Sadownick 1996), these men all too often became casualties of AIDS.

The two life-writers born in the 1950s who are discussed in this chapter experienced two linked events: the emergence of the gay rights movement during their young adulthood, which led to unparalleled freedom for gay self-expression in the 1970s, and the tragic and unanticipated effect of the AIDS pandemic in the following decade. As Odets (1995) has suggested, the shadow of the pandemic hangs over the accounts of life-writers born in the 1950s as an ever-present threat to mortality. Each of the two life-writers has confronted the meaning of the pandemic in his own life story. Both authors narrate a typical 1950s childhood, yet they are aware of being different from other boys, swept along into the social change of the late 1960s and early '70s, later to watch their lovers and friends become sick and die in the 1980s and early '90s.

Mark Doty: Poet of the Revolution

Mark Doty shares with 1940s-generation life-writer Paul Monette (1988, 1992, 1994) and fellow 1950s-generation life-writer Fenton Johnson (1996) the experience of caring for a lover who succumbed to AIDS. Doty also shares with Monette a reverse order of life writing. In each instance, the first account narrates the illness and death of a lover, followed by a life story from birth to maturity. In a third, particularly lyrical volume (Doty 2001), Doty provides some additional detail of his childhood and the later grief following his lover's death. Perhaps as Pollock (1989) and Murphy (1993) have suggested, the act of writing about the illness and death of a lover is a creative act fostering mourning and thus working through the loss, which frees greater energy for self-reflection and allows the author to be able to write about his own life. Monette himself had become HIV positive during the years of caring for his partner Roger, and a subsequent partner, both of whom had AIDS and died of its complications. Doty, on the other hand, remained HIV negative, and his life story continues on beyond the death of his parents and his lover Wally to his present relationship with Paul (Doty 2001). My discussion of Doty's life story reverses the order of his own writing and creates a linear narrative of his life, considering first the account of his childhood and youth, and only then his memoir of his adult years, which focuses on Wally's illness and death.

Doty's first book, *Heaven's Coast,* was published in 1996; it was followed in 1999 by his memoir, *Firebird,* which recalled a bleak childhood in a family waiting impatiently for the apocalypse, through the turbulent late 1960s, and his first poetry. Writing has been a healing experience for this internationally recognized poet, and he uses his talent in both books as a means to make sense of adversity. Doty observes in the first pages of his narrative of Wally's illness and death: "All my life I've lived with a future which constantly diminishes, but never vanishes" (Doty 1996, 4). In the prologue Doty wonders, as he anticipates Wally's death, whether there was a future.

The Firebird and the Problem of Perspective

Just as in the work of 1940s life-writer Arnie Kantrowitz, metaphors of color are important in Doty's life story. The title for his memoir of his youth, *Firebird* (1999), is based on an experience in the fourth grade when, following a class excursion to the symphony, his teacher played Stravinsky's *Firebird Suite* while the class was encouraged to paint their responses to the music. Doty remembers the swirls of color that he made on his paper. Some days later, his teacher read the story of the firebird to the class; Doty was captivated by the image of the firebird, awash in flames, rising up radiant once more. Perhaps this became a metaphor for the impending apocalypse, which was central to his life story; Doty was propelled into motion by Stravinsky's music.

Having previously taken dancing lessons, and with his teacher's encouragement, Doty began to dance about the classroom. He reports that the walls of the classroom receded before him as he was overcome by the music, with "the bird in the fullness of its light" (Doty 1999, 82) and rising into the "tower of light" (81) in a crescendo of pleasure and pain almost too painful to bear, similar to ejaculation after discovering masturbation. Doty carried this image through in his memoir recounting Wally's death; he was "no longer in the sky above, but in our bed" (Doty 1996, 4).

Mark Doty was born in 1953, the younger of two children of an impoverished Tennessee family. Doty's older sister Sally disappears and then reappears throughout his life story, less able than he has been to rise above the abuse and chaos that reigned in his family. His father, a government contract worker, shuttled back and forth between assignments in the South and the West. Doty's memoir is that of a searcher, intent on realizing an epiphany or transformation, which he sometimes glimpses through his life and craft. This search becomes more urgent as he considers the misery of the lives of his parents and sister, and his own failed marriage of nine years.

In an introduction to his memoir, Doty describes a visit to Washington's National Gallery of Art prior to receiving a prize for his poetry. Encountering a miniature box by a seventeenth-century Dutch painter, he becomes entranced by this tiny room complete with furnishings. Looking into the box from different angles, he discovers that no matter where he looks, the artist had been able to correct for possible distortion of perspective. Illusion and reality are intertwined in this little room as patterns appear, dissolve, and reappear anew. The box becomes a metaphor for memory itself, which always corrects the past while creating additional illusions, just as the story of his youth must also be distorted and cannot be corrected by such devices as the tricky lens of the peepholes into the Dutch miniature rooms. Alone with his private thoughts and desires but not lonely, Doty was fascinated by illusion ordered as story. He is explicitly aware of illusion and distortions of memory, and is entranced by light, shadow, and color that contribute to illusion. He recalls his childhood pleasure at being able to create the illusion of monsters from the shadows he could cast in front of the light, just as the movie theater was able to create similar illusions on film (Horrigan 1999).

Doty is acutely aware of the role of memory in writing his personal account. As he observes: "Forgetting is a long, deep well, already dark with layers of unrecorded time. Who knows what occasions and relics that seemingly empty shaft contains? I have no conscious awareness of this problem, of course, as children never have terms for what in their lives is truly grave" (Doty 1999, 19). Doty is also aware of his parents' memory of his childhood in forming his recollections. While working on his life story, he revisited a Florida community where he had spent his middle childhood years. He had remembered the community as dull and gray but now found it balmy and colorful:

The horizon of childhood is a little one; the small field at the center of which a child stands seems almost infinitely rich, but it is still a small field. I couldn't see Titusville except through the dimming lens of my parents' point of view until I went back—sheer serendipity—I didn't understand how shadowed their vision of the place had been. (*Firebird*, 87)

Doty (2001) writes of his fascination with still life paintings, particularly those of seventeenth-century artists. There is a striking contrast between the swirling activity of the firebird, and the sexual act, which contrasts with the quiet and stillness of the miniature room and the still-life painting. Doty connects stillness with death, recalling the death of his grandmother when he was five. Just as with Alan Helms's (1995) devout and terrifying grandmother, Doty too had been initiated by his grandmother into the mysteries of death and the afterlife. Even as a child Doty connected "style" with death, a reference to the presumed sense of style among gay men, particularly of his lover Wally, who had been a window and dress designer before he became ill.

He begins his life story anticipating Wally's impending death and his struggle to maintain some sense of a future. The drama and color of the stage, reminiscent of Arnie Kantrowitz's use of color and black and white in his life story, is highlighted from the outset. He recalls his sister's membership in Rainbow Girls, his mother's membership in the Order of the Eastern Star (represented by a little golden symbol on a chain round her neck), and the names Miss Sunbeam and Rainbow for the brands of bread available at home. His early awareness of brightness, beauty, and presentation was later evident in his fascination with dance. He details his drive, also expressed by other life-writers in this study, that he excel in school, perhaps to overcome the shame and low self-esteem connected to his attraction to other men.

Shame was everywhere in Doty's childhood. He saw it in a girl in his class who defecated in her pants, and in his concern that he follow the rules and avoid danger that lurked everywhere—from the playground and the big boys in the safety patrol who might misuse their authority in order to humiliate younger boys, to the menace posed by the mysterious man offering candy in exchange for a ride. On one particularly humiliating occasion he broke a glass; his angry father rushed barefoot into the room, cut his foot on shards of the glass, and was rushed to the hospital emergency room for stitches. This event further confirmed for him the perils lurking everywhere in the world.

Desire in a Troubled Family

Doty experienced uneasy intimacy with his mother. While they might sit together on the porch in the twilight and sing favorite songs from her childhood, she also was able to make it clear to him that he had opportunities that had been denied to her. He was destined to be her delegate in the larger world (Stierlin 1981). His mother grew up the youngest child of a large, impoverished Dutch-Irish family in which his maternal grandfather was often seductive with his mother.

Doty was drawn to his mother, but not, he believes, in the sense that the psychoanalytic literature has sometimes portrayed of the close mother-son relationship believed to be formative in the origin of same-sex desire (Bieber et al. 1962). Rather, his mother appears complex and vulnerable. During the years they were living in Arizona, his mother wanted to become a painter. She shared her son's love of illusion and color as she painted the colors of the desert and sky. In addition, Doty was fascinated by his mother's world of colorful frills and sequins. During this time, his often dispirited and emotionally unavailable mother seemed uniquely approachable and available to him; he recalls being together as a family while slides of the classic art that his mother was studying were projected on the living-room wall. His relationship with her shifted unpredictably: at one moment his mother expressed her love for him, in the next moment she was remote.

Doty found her dangerous yet also enticing. He observes (Doty 1999, 50) that "There's a particular hold love has over you when you're afraid of who you love." Doty recalls, again using the metaphor of opaqueness, a childhood memory of being in a bathtub with his mother, feeling frightened and repelled by his mother's body. He also remembers coming home from school early one day and stumbling in on his parents having sex, and later of his own sexual play with a neighbor girl.

His mother's emotional unreliability may have led Doty to turn to his father for the consistent admiration and support that was too difficult to extract from his mother. This desire for an intimate relationship with his father may have been particularly intense as his mother was both seductive yet emotionally remote and troubled. His father was also unable to provide emotional reliability. Often away on government assignments, his father would disappear and just as suddenly reappear. Doty reports that his effeminate mannerisms appeared upsetting to his father, who may have pulled away from a close relationship, feeling discomfort with his son's sissified manner and (perhaps) erotic attraction to him (Isay 1986, 1987). Even so, his father often made generous gestures of affection; Doty wonders if he himself attempted to pull away from his father. This significant observation is consistent with Phillips's (2001, 2003) conclusion that preschool boys experiencing sexual attraction to their fathers rather than their mothers may encounter traumatic overstimulation, thus leading gay youth to withdraw from emotional closeness with their father.

His father too came from an impoverished southern family. Doty's father lived in fear of his grandfather (who reputedly had murdered a creditor who came to the house to collect a payment). Doty's parents met when his father worked for Roosevelt's Civilian Conservation Corps. Families on both sides still lived on farms; during his childhood he lived for a time with his father's parents where he remembers not only the cherry pies of Sunday dinner but also the chickens destined for that dinner, flopping about beheaded and bloody.

As a schoolboy, Doty decided that he had his father's ears and that his sister had her mother's eyes. In other respects, he could find little family resemblance. His sister, a rebel and a sexually precocious adolescent, also felt different in the family; clearly the two of them did not resemble their parents. Looking through early photographs of his recently married parents, he recalls that his mother seemed fragile even then. Doty speculates on what life would have been like if his older brother had not been stillborn.

His mother was thirty-three and his father thirty-nine when Doty was born. His parents had hoped for a girl, and named him Mark Alan for no apparent reason. Doty does not connect his parents' expectations with his own childhood gender nonconformity. With allusions to the postwar master-narrative of the prototypic gay boys' story of so-called effeminate interests (Corbett 1997), Doty preferred the company of girls to that of boys, and he read the books that the girls in his class found so endearing. Doty hated physical education, preferring instead the shapes and colors he could create out of clay. He recalls that by the second grade he was aware that the world of things such as baseball, marbles, car names, and the exploits of the astronauts all were opaque to him. When he tried to be a "real boy," such as when he asked for a basketball for Christmas, his parents provided him with a purple one. This gift symbolized for him his dilemma— he was simultaneously debased and accepted.

Doty's first awareness of his homoerotic desire was at the age of six, while riding on a motorcycle with his sister's boyfriend. He was instructed to grasp the guy's shirtless waist as they went around corners. He reports that something was touched off in him by this experience, far more exciting than the motorcycle ride itself. Doty was more interested in the experience of desire than in understanding it. For him, the most important questions are the way in which we come to know sexual feelings for other men, how we deal with them, and how we deal with our awareness of differences resulting from this desire. He observes that very young gay boys learn that this thrill of touching or even admiring another boy or man is in some way connected with a sense of shame. Doty wonders if the shame is connected with seeing and knowing what other men cannot see or know; he believes that it is the shame connected with a sense of difference that contributes to a terrible feeling of loneliness among gay boys and men. When his mother caught him and another boy playing out a mock wedding in which he was the bride, he remarks:

I have been ushered into a world where adults live. I have been warned, have been instructed to conceal my longing. And though I will understand, someday, that without longing there's nothing to carry us forward, that without longing we wouldn't be anyone at all, I can't see that now. I'm a child, or I was until (my mother) said, *you're a boy*. I am stunned and silent, caught up in a shame that seems to have no place to come to rest. I have been initiated . . . into an adult world of limit and sorrow. (Doty 1999, 102)

Shame is also connected with enjoying the bare-chested Yul Brenner in *The Ten Commandments* as Pharaoh carrying the body of his son, and with the tragedy of his sister's pregnancy—she wasn't permitted to wear a white dress at her wedding. Getting pregnant meant, for Doty, that his sister was determined to go her own way in the world. Later he felt shame because of his own his pudgy, girlish appearance, which led his high school gym teachers to mock and disparage his lack of expected masculine athletic prowess.

The family moved from Tennessee to Arizona where, at the age of seven or eight, he became aware of a hunger that could not be stilled. At the movies, he particularly enjoyed films featuring shirtless boys. In the fourth grade, he found a wiry and wiggly fellow Cub Scout; after school they played a game in which his friend pretended to be a baby needing care; he took off his shirt and was stroked by a kindly Mark Doty. This was a game played behind closed bedroom doors, and Doty was aware of a mystery in need of translation, just as with the mysterious Egyptian objects, which were so fascinating to him. Earlier he had enjoyed being naked with a junior high school girl some years older than himself. He sums up his childhood (in the third person, perhaps as a means of gaining some distance from his painful childhood) as:

plainly alone . . . he's lived in seven houses in seven years. He's a little pudgy . . . his grandparents are dead or far away; his big sister's a teenage girl with two kids now, in another state, so it's him and his parents, who don't seem to have any friends, who keep moving, disconnecting, and whom he already knows he can't tell about a world of things inside of him . . . maybe that's what it is to be a person, all these dreams and apprehensions and questions you can't say to anybody. Either because you lack a vocabulary for them, or because no one would understand if you did say them, since the interior of each person seems to be a separate place. (Doty 1999, 52)

Doty's experience of the grand movie palaces of his youth were quite different from those of '30s-generation Alan Helms for whom going to the movies taught emotional resilience permitting him to withstand the emotional turmoil in which he lived.

Doty's close friendship with a retarded neighbor boy was lost when, as he recalls, the father killed all his family and then committed suicide (his father later corrected his memory; it was the mother who killed the rest of the family and then herself). Perhaps Doty's distorted memory protected him from the painful experience during his mid-adolescence when his own mother, now an alcoholic, pointed his father's gun at him and threatened to kill him before collapsing in a drunken stupor. Fathers, mothers, danger, and guns become connected in a way all too real when in his teenage years his father, broken in spirit, threatened the life of his wife and son with this same gun.

During his middle childhood and early adolescence, Doty's family continued to move from place to place until his mother became depressed by the inability to put down roots. If the move to Arizona had been the best of their moves, the return to Florida was apparently the worst of these moves. His parents quarreled incessantly, sometimes throwing things at each other. Identifying with his mother's illness, Doty's own depression was lessened by the mood-enhancing diet pills, which mother and son took in order to deal with their weight. Doty took up tap dancing in an effort both to slim down and to gain relief from his own sadness through physical activity, just as he had earlier experienced in dancing to the *Firebird*. Doty was fascinated (as was '40s life-writer Arnie Kantrowitz) by the songs of another depressed and lonely person, Judy Garland, particularly her renditions of "Over the Rainbow" and "Come On Get Happy."

Saved by the Sixties

It was the mid-1960s, and the world of rock and rebellion had made its first inroads in teenage culture. Doty learned, from a boy he was attracted to, that the boy's older brother lived in Los Angeles and had told his younger brother of the new fashions of feather and outrageous costumes. Doty dreamed of the colorful world of the city where he could lose himself in the mystical world of anonymity. Moving back to Arizona, now nearly six feet tall and an angular adolescent, Doty was consumed by sexual desire almost impossible to bear. He was drawn to torsos, perhaps a reflection of his riding with his sister's shirtless boyfriend on the motorcycle. He feared the overstimulation of the locker room and the danger of an unwitting erection in the midst of all those bare chests. He "knew" that he should think about women while masturbating but was drawn to images of the locker room.

As his family life unraveled with his mother's depression and drinking, his sister's delinquencies, and his demented grandfather's residence with the family, Doty found ways to keep himself away from home. One summer while working in a Head Start program, his group took a field trip to a fantastic but sad magic land created by an old man playing the part of a mountain gnome. This trip was a time of wonder for both Doty and his young charges; it was a place of mystery and color that evoked twisted beauty and in which the old man struggled to maintain personal coherence as inevitably this colorful illusion would dissolve back into desert. Drama class, too, with its assortment of idiosyncratic adolescents, provided another escape from the conventionality of high school life. Doty's evolving identity as a "freak" replaced his earlier identity as a "sissy." The social turmoil of the late '60s rescued Doty as he realized that it was safer to be a freak than to be a sissy.

His new lifestyle proved to be too much for his parents. Complaining about his long hair, his father dragged the fourteen-year-old Doty to a barbershop where he was humiliated by his father's attack on his appearance and the demand that the barber cut his hair. When he returned home from this traumatic experience, the embarrassed Doty rushed to his room and hid under the covers. Feeling that his body and integrity had been compromised, he saw little choice but to kill himself. He swallowed enough sleeping pills to provide hallucinations but not to actually kill him. He was rushed to the hospital where he was admitted to the psychiatric unit. He realized that he couldn't die without first touching another man's body; death and desire seemed somehow interconnected. Having discovered some books brought by a friend, a male hospital attendant discerned that Doty was probably gay and suggested that another out gay attendant come to talk with him. This attendant was the first such openly gay person he had met, and Doty was relieved to know that it was indeed possible to be visibly gay. He was afraid, however, to talk to this man and lost the possibility of making a connection with another man harboring similar homoerotic desire.

Still feeling disconnected from his own body, Doty returned home from the hospital and reached a new understanding with his parents: they were to leave him alone, including any issues concerning hair, clothes, friends, and hours. Feeling adrift from his former world, he avoided his parents and their bitter and violent quarrels. Downtown beckoned, especially late at night. Doty was drawn to an alternative bookstore with its enticing, colorful posters of Volkswagen microbuses, its romantic poetry, and its vegetarian food. Just as for fellow '50s-generation Californian Tim Miller, urban counterculture offered an escape. Doty hitchhiked to San Francisco for the 1968 "Summer of Love." Overwhelmed by the Haight, the center of San Francisco's social rebellion, he attended a Buddhist meeting, crashed in a "pad" with a group of hippies, and rummaged through alternative bookstores. Lost and confused by the '60s revolution, he admitted failure and reluctantly called his parents to ask for money for a ticket home.

Back home in Arizona, Doty discovered a gay pornographic novel in the local drug store, and he savored each passage, but carefully hid the book in his room between readings. Of course, his mother found and removed the book, and the next time she got drunk confronted him with it and then told his father that his son was a homosexual. His father, preoccupied with his mother's drinking, was only concerned that his son get out of the house. He gave him money and urged him to stay away. Doty avoided going home; he hung out with other teens, smoked his first joint, and jumped headfirst into the drug culture in the company of another teenager from an affluent family able to afford the purchase of hallucinogenic substances. Adopting counterculture dress, glass beads, and a shoulder bag, Doty lived in a "smoky cloud," participated in high school theater, studied transcendental meditation and Buddhist thought, and sketched his dreams and wrote poetry in his ever-present black notebook. Drugs allowed Doty's escape from his body, and he was once again consumed by the color and dizzying movement of the firebird.

Unable to face high school physical education and the terrors of the locker room, Doty walked unannounced into a doctor's office, and explained to a sympathetic doctor that he was a homosexual and could not face the terror of the locker room. The doctor wrote an excuse exempting him from physical education. Later, while attending drama school, he met a poet who taught at a local university and who recognized Doty's talent as a writer. His mentor put the university's poetry center resources at his disposal and often took him home for dinner where the peaceful family life of this household provided Doty respite from his family's turmoil. Confronted by family discord, Doty and his sister each showed resilience. For Doty, it was his relationship with his idealized mentor who encouraged his talent, led him to his first serious efforts at writing poetry, and offered an alternative to his family's misery and his escape from this misery though drugs.

Perspective and Reflection

In his chronicle, Doty admits that his shame, grief, and sorrow may not have been unique. He suggests that we should read such dark memoirs to diminish the horror and pity that we feel about our own lives. His narrative concludes with the incident in which, when he was seventeen, his mother threatened but was unable to kill him with his father's handgun. From that time on, he lived with the memory that his own mother had tried to kill him while his father only consoled his mother while his son was in mortal danger. Doty never forgave his father's preference for his gun rather than concern with his son's safety. Doty left home soon after this terrifying incident and enrolled at the university, even though he had not finished high school. In college he met other student radicals, protested the draft, and lived with a woman, Ruth (who had the same first name as his mother), a graduate student and also a poet, whom he eventually married. He married young with the hope that he would then be made straight.

Ruth was a carbon copy of Doty's mother in more than name. She was an alcoholic, refusing responsibility and demanding care. Doty, at seventeen, had succeeded in repeating rather than remembering his relationship with his mother (Freud 1914). In his first book, *Heaven's Coast* (1996), Doty describes his youthful marriage and his flight both from his family and "a sexual orientation that scared me half to death" (Doty 1996, 50). He hoped that if he ignored his homoerotic feelings, it would go away.

At twenty-three he watched as his mother, dying from the consequences of her alcoholism, observed at the end: "It's funny how so many things just don't make a difference" (Doty 1999, 187). He grieved his mother's death, insisting that neither his father nor his sister knew his mother as he did. At this point, there is a nine-year unexplained break in the narrative. His sister had married for a second time and remained with her husband. After some years, his father also remarried. Confronting the triple terrors of his mother's ghost, his father's gun, and his own self-loathing, Doty finally managed to abandon his marriage. He admitted his arrogance believing that he might save Ruth from her torment. Although he does not explain how he came to this realization, Doty left his Midwestern college teaching position and moved to New York as did so many gay men seeking to understand and affirm their sexual identity. He was unable to find a job in New York and accepted an offer to teach at a small Vermont college.

Twenty years after his mother's death, his father came across his son's book about his lover's illness and death. By now father and son were reconciled in their lingering grief. At age eighty-three, his father wrote to him, revealing the depths of his own despair following his wife's untimely death. Then, when his father and his second wife were touring New England, they visited with Doty and his partner Paul in Provincetown. His father and his wife got along well with Paul, and everyone was startled by how pleasant the short visit had been. Later on, when Doty and Paul visited Doty's father in Arizona, it became clear that the earlier weekend visit had been an anomaly and that father and son could not be reconciled.

Writing and Reading Grief

Mark Doty's account of Wally's death and his own response is portrayed in his 1997 account, *Heaven's Coast*. Writing in the aftermath of his lover's death, he explains that writing in his diary and composing his memoir of Wally's illness was a way of coming to terms with his loss. The memoir focuses in large measure on his own emotional state as his partner became symptomatic. He alternates between describing his own sorrow and Wally's illness, which was marked by a gradual decline in vitality and the growing weakness that left him bedridden. Over the course of the narrative, Doty pictures Wally as slowly being erased: "The metaphor which came to me was of the outline of his body gradually being filled in with a kind of dark transparency, like ink, slowly spreading to fulfill the outline of him. . . . I began to imagine his body filling with an absence" (Doty 1996, 150).

After Wally's death, Doty muses that "remembering is the work of the living, and the collective project of memory is enormous; it involves the weight of all our dead, the ones we have known ourselves and the ones we know only from stories" (Doty 1996, 7). He also observes that "death requires a new negotiation with memory" (Doty 1996, 40). Death has been omnipresent throughout Doty's life. From his early childhood memory of his grandmother's death, the death of his boyhood friend and his family, and his mother's death, then the discovery of Wally's seroconversion and the opportunistic illnesses taking over Wally's weakened immune system and his subsequent death, Doty's life is one of continued experience of loss and grief.

Death and writing are intimately connected for Doty (2001) as for many life-writers of this epoch of AIDS in the gay community (J. Miller 1993; Murphy 1993). The ideal type of a life story among men confronting loss due to AIDS includes the memoirs of Paul Monette (1988, 1994) who wrote in detail about his partners' deaths even as he himself was becoming symptomatic, Fenton Johnson's (1996) account of his relationship with his dying lover, and James Melson's (1992) posthumous memoir of his own illness, dying in the midst of his friends who were also dying during the catastrophic AIDS pandemic. As Doty observes:

To write was to court overwhelming feeling. Not to write was to avoid, but to avoid was to survive. Though writing was a way of surviving, too: experience was unbearable, looked at head on, but *not* to look was also unbearable. And, so I'd write, when I could, recording what approached like someone in a slow moving but unstoppable accident, who must look and look away at once. (Doty 1996, 205)

In the opening pages of this memoir Doty writes "*My lover of twelve years died just last month* ([italics in original] Doty 1996, 19). With this sentence, he seeks to transform grief into memory. Writing provides solace for him:

Writing, in a way, to save my life, to catch what could be saved of Wally's life, to make a story of us that can be both kept and given away. The story's my truest possession and I burnish and hammer it and wrestle it to make it whole. In return it offers me back to myself, it holds what I cannot, its embrace and memory larger than mine, more permanent. (Doty 1996, 290)

Doty's remarks echo psychoanalyst George Pollock's (1989) observations regarding mourning as the wellspring of creativity and also reflects the manner in which writing offers solace when dealing with loss.

Following Wally's death, while visiting Boston and seeing the hospital where he had so often taken Wally for his medical care during his illness, Doty remembered their first meeting, not too far from the hospital on Boston's Beacon Hill. He stared at the doorway of the apartment where they used to live and reminisced about this house full of gay men in 1981, most of whom were now dead.

When Doty was teaching and living in Vermont, he met a man in a bar; an exchange of glances, a deepening of attraction, and passion, and soon Doty and Wally were living together in Wally's Boston apartment. Wally was one of eight children from a Boston naval family; he had another gay brother (also to die from AIDS) and two straight brothers, and four sisters, two of whom were lesbian and two of whom were straight. Wally had come out to his parents when he was eighteen when he had fallen in love with the manager at a local fast food restaurant. Later, when his lover dumped him, Wally's parents were supportive and comforting.

With grant support for Doty's work as a poet, the couple was able to move into a ramshackle house in rural Hew Hampshire, which they had fixed up. Gardening was a shared pleasure. After Wally's death, Doty was unable to enjoy this activity, which had been a source of delight for the couple. In 1989 Wally and Doty had been together for eight years; they both took the HIV test for the first time. By this time, the test to determine seroconversion to HIV had been thoroughly studied, and the course of the illness well charted. While Doty remained negative, Wally tested positive, was asymptomatic for two years, and then developed the symptoms that hastened his death in 1994.

When an offer materialized to teach at a college in suburban New York, and as Wally's T-cell count began to decline, the couple decided that it would be best to move to Provincetown, located at the tip of Cape Cod, then as now a community with a large number of gay and lesbian persons, as portrayed by Andrew Tobias (1998a), with the social and health supportive services appropriate for such a community. Doty commuted twice weekly to his teaching job and was able to remain at home the rest of the week. For sometime after the move to Provincetown, Wally was able to work as a dress designer, and the couple enjoyed a brief respite before Wally's health took a turn for the worse. Death was all about them, including one of Wally's former lovers, and many of their friends and neighbors.

The time from the winter of 1992 to the winter of 1993 was particularly
difficult for the couple, as it was for the larger gay community with large
numbers of men dying (Odets 1995). Doty lived with a sense of dread and
a feeling of hopelessness as Wally's health declined. Wally's dreams presaged his impending death, while Doty attempted to deal with this looming
loss by writing in his journal. During the autumn of 1993, Wally had suffered an aphasia and could no longer find words to express his ideas. With
increasing pain, morphine provided some relief. Wally died in January
1994, without a fight—he just slipped away. Doty reports that he could feel
Wally's soul released from his body, a leap of the spirit with energy.

Doty viewed Wally's illness as a kind of black light used in museums to
show the colors and surfaces of rocks, and which highlights things as they
really are. He recalls the time when he was four or five years old and living
with his grandparents, prior to his grandmother's death; while picking dan-
delions and greens, he glanced up and saw the sunlight filter through his
grandmother's thin rayon dress. From his grandmother, just as Alan Helms
(1995) did, Doty had heard about the significance of the apocalypse. He
viewed his own life much in this way, having rehearsed his entire life as an
apocalyptic scenario. With Wally's diagnosis, the end of the world was
given new meaning. J. Miller (1993) has noted this use of apocalypse as a
metaphor in accounts of AIDS. Doty often made use of this metaphor—in
which heaven descends to earth in the age of AIDS—in his poetry. As Doty
observes: "Apocalypse is played out now on a personal scale; it is not in the
sky above us but in our bed" (Doty 1996, 4). Doty's use of perspective in describing Wally's death anticipates his discussion in his memoir of his youth
and early adulthood of the problem of perspective in the Dutch miniature
box, as well as his childhood experience while dancing to the music of the
Firebird, looking down from above. Following Wally's death he invokes
once again the matter of perspective as he imagines Wally looking down
upon him from above. Wally's last weeks are viewed from this elevation.

Desire, which later appeared in Doty's (1999) account of his youth, is
central to his narrative of Wally's illness and death. In the last months of
his life, Wally's desire was evident in flirtations, which continued to occupy
his daydreams; Wally's desire led to sexual fascinations with all the men
about him as he gazed out of his window, a reflection of Wally's love of life
itself, his love of beauty, grace, and sensuality. Doty believes that it is the
wanting that matters: "Sex is an acknowledgment of the mystery of flesh,
its dimensionality and weight. In touch and touch, feeling the limits of the
body with our hands, testing its boundaries" (Doty 1996, 297). And it is

the persistence of desire, of still wanting, that offers a feeling of being alive, and this provided Wally with a sense of being alive and desiring even as he came to grips with his own mortality. In the meantime, Doty had taken to quick, consensual erotic encounters as a respite from caregiving; they had long understood that playful encounters did not deter from their relationship (Lee 1991).

Doty writes about desire as an expression of participating in the world; Wally's desire for the men passing by his window symbolizes his effort to remain in the world. Images of light and dark, of shadow above and below, later represented by the vibrant red of the firebird in Doty's account of his childhood, is present in his memoir of his struggle with Wally's illness. While teaching in Vermont, Doty had lived on the fringes of the counterculture revolution, which had found an uneasy home in New England's rural setting. The ubiquitous VW microbus, painted in vibrant colors, became one of the most characteristic icons of this remnant of the 1960s when Doty was exploring his own adolescence and gay sexual identity.

Making use once again of this metaphor of color, conjuring frenetic desire and death, Doty describes the quilt splashed with red that accompanied Wally's body when it was cremated; Doty observes that "mourning contracts the eye, like a camera lens in strong light" (Doty 1996, 7). Periodically overcome by grief, the world seemed smaller and farther away, as if looking through a telescope from the wrong end. He struggles with boundaries, of the living and the dead, and with the movement between the world of the living and the world of the dead. Doty relived this transformation as Wally's body gave up its heat, becoming only embers, turning to polished marble.

Committing Wally into memory just as Freud (1917) had described for the process of mourning, yet resisting remembering and mourning and the reality of loss, Doty sat in their bedroom, holding Wally's cremated remains. He stared at Wally's ashes, considering anew his grief and the margins of life and death, symbolically represented by the Cape Cod coastline with its accumulation of dead animals and plants washed up on shore. To walk the coastline is to walk with death: "Wally's ashes went into the grand expanse of salt marsh at Hatch's Harbor; here was endless mutability, receptivity, change, the wide mirroring water full of sky and clouds" (Doty 2001, 63). He writes that nothing stays there long, "the exact edge where water touches land is never still, constantly revising itself, expanding and contracting" (2001, 62).

During Wally's illness and death, Doty found solace in walking the Provincetown marshes and surrounding coastline at land's end *(Heaven's*

Coast), under starry heavens with the couple's ever-present and understanding dogs. He spent windswept and dreary days laboring to understand the difference between grief, which is sharp and immediate, and sadness, which is ephemeral. He submitted to the sorrow of an interior state, which matched the gray and white dunes of the Cape Cod headlands near Provincetown.

It was a month after Wally's death before he was able to write anything in his journal, formerly a source of solace during times of distress. By the following autumn, he was able to teach and work again, now as a "citizen of grief's country" (Doty 1996, 271), able to move beyond introspection for the first time since Wally's death. By the first-year anniversary of Wally's death, there were days when the grief was overwhelming, and days when the pain seemed to recede. Part of him was shattered by Wally's death, while "memory's double-edged sword at once wounds and offers us company, inheritor companionship which enriches and deepens the dimensions of every day" (Doty 1996, 289).

In the epilogue to this first volume of his memoir, largely concerned with his reflections on the meaning of Wally's illness and death, Doty comments: "Always we were becoming a story. But I didn't understand that fusing my life to the narrative, giving myself to the story's life, would be what would allow me to live" (Doty 1996, 290–91). This portrays the significance of the life story as the means for providing a sense of coherence in our lives; memories are both a narrative of pain and diminishment, but also beautiful. In one particularly haunting sequence, Doty recounts seeing a coyote while walking the dunes of his beloved Cape headlands. He looks up and sees the face of a coyote, standing perfectly still and staring at him. In the coyote's gaze, he believed he could see Wally's look, and he had the sense that the coyote had been with Wally. The dead, he observes, regard us from their perspective as a pure presence, wanting nothing, and looking back at us from a world they can no longer comprehend.

In time, Doty began to imagine himself living and wanting to know how the story of his life would turn out. As we learn from the first pages of his memoir of his youth (Doty 1999) published two years following his account of Wally's illness and death, and in a companion volume published in 2001, Doty found another lover. Death, desire, and writing about desire are connected as Doty works to make sense of his own life and his unique perspective as a poet of this dark revolution. Metaphors of whirlwinds and colors, of the firebird itself, and of light and darkness portray a poet seeking through his craft to find a perspective for viewing desire and loss (Tóibín 2001).

Tim Miller: Performing the New Identity

Born in 1958, Tim Miller came of age just at the cusp of the AIDS pandemic. He talks about friends who were afflicted with AIDS, his own fear of becoming infected, and his work in ACT-UP. However, the pandemic is but a part of his greater frustration with an oppressive government, which ignores not only AIDS, but which has also refused to fund the performance art grant he had been awarded by the National Endowment for the Arts (NEA). Most recently, the government has denied his Australian partner Alistair McCartney permission to obtain a work permit. When Miller is not traveling, performing in his one-man show, he teaches performance art on both coasts.

Miller has had many friends and lovers die of AIDS although neither of his two longtime partners has tested positive for the HIV virus. Just as portrayed by Odets (1995), somehow, almost miraculously, he has remained negative, even as friends became ill, and, as in Odets's account, he is torn by feelings of anxiety and guilt regarding his seronegative status. Presaging the experiences of life-writers born in the 1960s, Miller looks over the crest of the epidemic among gay men, concerned instead with fostering community acceptance of a gay lifeway (Hostetler and Herdt 1998). While apparently concerned with his own acceptance of gayness, much of his sexual search belies a need for intimacy and support.

With a background in performance art, Miller sees himself as a cultural provocateur rather than simply as an activist. During George H. W. Bush's presidency, congressional pressure led the NEA to withdraw grants to gay artists and performers. This decision was appealed to the Supreme Court, which ruled against Miller and three fellow artists on the ground that "standards of decency" *are* material in the decision to make an award in the arts and that these standards do not violate the Constitution's First Amendment.

Most recently, after a long-term relationship with fellow gay activist and writer Doug Sadownick, Miller developed a relationship with another writer and activist, Australian Alistair McCartney, who has been in the United States on a student visa, then a business (teaching) visa. Since immigration policy does not recognize the partners of gay men or lesbians as eligible for residency, as it would for married heterosexual couples, Miller faces the dilemma that he and his partner may be forced to move back to Australia. This situation, together with samples of McCartney's own writing, are featured on Miller's Web site, which also includes instructions for purchasing videos of his performance art.

Miller is among the most reflective of the life-writers in this study. He shares with Arnie Kantrowitz and Mark Doty a view on writing about desire, which informs a particularly lucid narrative regarding the gay community in the 1980s and 1990s. He reports that he has kept a journal each day since the fifth grade. He sees his writing as bound inextricably to being gay. In an essay prepared for the Harvard *Gay and Lesbian Review* (Miller 1999), he discussed the craft of writing and performing stories, emphasizing the significance of a presently remembered past in writing a life story. Miller is explicit about the complex role of memory in life writing:

Every time I try to write down anything from my memory, I am pulling the words out through a shrinking device that makes the feelings and the experience and the joys and the shit seem all vaguely squeezed, like trying to coax the last bit of toothpaste (or KY for that matter!) out of the tube . . . I am in trouble every time I start to write down what has gone on in my life . . . when I tell the stories from my life, I hope I can be at least a tiny bit as authentic and surprising as those tears that creep down my face when I least expect them. . . . I want to find the words that might invite you into this place where I live. . . . Inevitably, the act of writing will distill, edit, change, compress, compact, alter, disguise enhance and reduce the raw mess of living. (*Shirts and Skin,* 36)

In his second book, Miller reports that his life story is that of the men he has loved, his audience, and his own memory. He assumes that the reader will be empathic with his search for affirmation in a relationship, which he believes also mirrors concerns within the gay community, and hopes that his words will lead to social change regarding the gay lifeway (Miller 2002). Miller acknowledges the impact of fellow life-writer Paul Monette's (1992) personal account on his own writing. Monette expressed outrage with the government's failure to acknowledge the extent of the pandemic even as thousands of men were becoming ill and dying. Once again we are confronted with understanding a personal account not only written backward but also in the context of a life-writer born in a previous generation. Miller's life story well portrays the shift in talking about same-sex desire over the period from the emergence of gay rights after 1960 to the present time, and it also chronicles much of that change.

Miller writes for an audience similar to that watching his performance art. His performances are autobiographical and confessional; he narrates his progress toward acceptance of his gay identity, and his transformation from self-preoccupation with his body and sexuality to that of a reciprocal and intimate lover. He views his body as an extension of his activity as a performer, and inevitably, takes off his clothes and wanders naked into the audience, sitting on one man's lap, feeding an orange slice to another. Pictures from his performance are included with each chapter in *Shirts and Skin* (1997) and *Body Blows* (2002).

The photograph facing page one of Miller's first memoir is of Miller, wearing only light bulbs. Performance and picture are intended to shock and make the reader aware of his body, just as he attempts to do in his performances. He maintains that art and performance cannot be separated. It is this same alluring, elusive quality of Miller's performance art and life story that makes it so difficult to understand his memoir apart from his performance. Miller starts his memoir at the beginning, quite literally, with his parents' sexual act that led to his conception. His parents' bed becomes an important symbol. Miller later inherits this bed when his parents buy a new one, and it is the place where, at the age of seventeen, he attempts his own first same-sex act. He observes that "every story has to have a beginning, you just gotta find it" (Miller 1997, 1). He conjectures that when he was conceived, his parents were still young and passionate for each other. His parents have told him that he was a "mistake." In his memoir he has them deliberately deciding to make a queer child. He relates his hazardous trip upstream as a sperm to meet the egg and his gay destiny, on the way avoiding his later chief critic Jesse Helms and bullying straight boys, and is born a quintessential queer boy whose book will be bought someday by all those other queer babies.

Miller picks up his life story when he is five, dressed in a trainman's coverall. The purpose of the photograph is to illustrate his love of uniforms and to show that skin can be changed by putting on a shirt. This theme of being clothed, particularly involving T-shirts versus being naked, pervades both his account and his performance where, at one point, he sheds his clothes and wanders about naked on stage and in the audience. Miller grew up in a repressive and conventional middle-class community, which contrasted with his as yet unnamed desire. Important in this story is Miller's birthplace in Whittier, California, which is the prototypic Southern California suburb and the home of Richard Nixon. He sees Nixon and Whittier as intrinsically connected, symbolizing hypocritical suburban WASP culture.

Using a play on the word "fruit," a slang term for homosexuals, Miller was initially drawn to fruit and the desire that it posed, on one occasion masturbating on the root of the family's orange tree. His first grade teacher already recognized that he was unusual and presented him with two apple seedlings; today those same seedlings have grown into mature trees. The metaphor of the fruit trees is juxtaposed with his story of his attraction at the age of twelve to another boy in his class. He trembled with desire to touch and kiss his friend. He first tongue-kissed another boy at the age of fourteen. When trying to be straight, he tongue-kissed a girl on an amusement park ride; at that moment he caught sight of the boy of his early adolescent desire and knew that his tenure as a heterosexual boy would be brief.

Writing in his disarming, charming way, Miller describes his effort to grow pubic hair and to be like the rest of the boys who had developed more rapidly. He lets us know that he was unusual in other ways as well. By age twelve he was immersed in reading Nietzsche and Dostoevski. By high school in the early '70s, his adolescent growth spurt (which he describes as "the blitzkrieg of puberty ramping through my body " [Miller 1997, 16]) was accompanied by the rapid social change in American society. He excelled in school, particularly in German, in which his lesbian teacher taught him the forms of the verb *to be:* "I am. I was. I will be" (Miller 1997, 29).

When Miller was in his senior year of high school, he realized the implication of liking other boys. In an incident that provided the title for his *Shirts and Skin* and also the basis for his early performance art, he tells how, during physical education class, two teams were selected for a game. In order to distinguish one team from the other, one team would play shirtless. Feeling his body inadequate, Miller always hoped that he would be a shirt, yet he generally ended up as a skin. Huddled to devise a football play, Miller could feel the other boys' heat and their smooth bodies against his own. He realized then that he was "on the skins' team for life. I could cover up and slip into different shirts and disguises, but underneath it all I would always be there with the other boys who were stripped bare. We would always be recognizable as a different team" (Miller 1997, 25). Being bare is a major moment in Miller's performance art: getting out of his clothes and being naked is understood as being genuine and expressing his solidarity with the gay community.

Now that he knew which "team" he was on, he could come out to himself. A woman friend who was already in college introduced Miller to other gay men who might be prospective boyfriends. One of these boys, also a senior in high school and more sexually experienced than Miller, offered the provocation for sex. Miller brought this boy home for the night and slept with him in the bed in which he had been conceived—a mistake who grew into a gay boy. However, his friend demurred at the suggestion of a total sexual encounter, and little more happened than mutual exploration of each other's bodies. Later, in college but still living at home, Miller took up dance; here he met David, a student a few years older than himself. After an intensely erotic evening with David, Miller came home to find his parents still awake, peacefully reading in bed. He told them that he was gay; his mother, familiar with the concept of parents' relationship with their sons as the "cause" of homosexuality (Bieber et al. 1962), proclaimed that it was not her fault. His father, impassive as always, reminded him to put out the garbage before going to bed. The next evening, Miller's eighteenth birthday, he and David enjoyed uninhibited sex on the floor of the darkened dance studio. Miller was smitten by his somewhat older student mentor—it was a totally satisfying experience.

Over the next several months of a stormy relationship, Miller often felt himself engulfed by David at a time when he needed to explore what it was like to be gay. Later, David became the ideal Miller sought in a partner. Miller, like fellow life-writer Mark Doty, decided to leave his Southern California suburb for San Francisco. Miller arrived in San Francisco just as gay councilman Harvey Milk and gay-supportive mayor Moscone were assassinated in a hate crime. Hitchhiking from Southern California to "Land's End," on the Pacific Coast in San Francisco, his first adventure was in a religious, vegetarian commune. This was followed by various erotic experiences while hitchhiking, and an evening with the Moonies.

Disillusioned by San Francisco after the Milk/Moscone assassination, Miller fled to New York. Gay sex was easy to find here following the gay rights revolution, and Miller went from bed to bed. Living in a tenement, Miller decorated and made it his own with salvaged items he found on the streets. An accomplished carpenter since school days when he and his father had found that one interest in common, Miller put his skills to good use in making a living. Exorbitant rents had forced people into the smallest apartments they could afford, and loft beds helped solve the space problem. Miller became adept at building these space-saving beds (beds figure prominently in Miller's narrative from the first page of his memoir describing his conception), and he enjoyed thinking that the loft beds he was constructing were not only places to sleep but also to have sex.

Dressed in a torn Harvey Milk campaign T-shirt and sweat pants, his visage made it clear that he was a quintessential California gay boy looking for anything and everything. After he discovered a dance-movement studio, Miller became entranced with performance art, which combined pleasure and comfort with the body, sex, and social protest. The group he joined created a performance space in which no part of his life or body was off-limits as the group explored the far edges of the outrageous. His parents attended one performance where Miller wandered about the stage naked while reading from the diary written during his adolescence. Just as on the evening when he "came-out" to his parents as they prepared for bed, Tim's parents were not very critical. His mother wondered why it was necessary for him to take all his clothes off while his ever matter-of-fact father asked him if he could make money doing this kind of thing.

Seeking Love, Finding Sex

By the early 1980s Miller had become a queer activist, working as a journeyman carpenter by day, enjoying his friendship with straight men and their tools—and sometimes engaging in oral sex with his fellow construction workers. By night Miller was a performer experimenting with radical theater. Miller's portrait of gay desire at this time was one of inevitable, perhaps even fatal, attraction between two men. Joining John, another gay radical performer he had met, Miller struggled to make the relationship work. Miller and John rushed headlong into a relationship, recognizing however that they could be hurt by yet another love affair gone awry. Over the next year, the pair chronicled their relationship in a series of performance pieces that documented their shared passion, including their enjoyment penetrating each other and swallowing each other's ejaculation. When the relationship ended, their breakup was portrayed on stage with the pair removing their pajamas, announcing that they were going to burn and bury them, and then walking naked off stage.

During the breakup in 1981, after they had burned and buried their performance pajamas (although Miller, always fascinated by shirts, held on to his pajama top from this affair), while they were still occasionally having sex, John's gums began to bleed during a routine dentist appointment. He was admitted to a hospital, an early victim of AIDS. At about the same time, Miller had a brief and stormy sexual experience with his next-door neighbor who was crafting record-cover art for then unknown singer Madonna, and who also became sick.

Believing himself unable to have a committed relationship, Miller sought anonymous sex with men on Lower East Side rooftops. He went to England for a time, and when he returned the pandemic had begun in earnest. Even though he considered himself not fit for long-term relationships, he met his future partner at a Christmas party. Miller turned down John's proposal of a relationship and now found a new love, Doug Sadownick, already a writer of some prominence in the gay community. From very different backgrounds, their relationship became a source of personal and creative inspiration for each; *Shirts and Skins* is dedicated to Doug, although by the time it was published they had broken up.

In 1982, shortly after meeting Doug, Miller observes that:

The early reports in the *New York Native* of gay-related immune deficiency heralded a time when doom was underneath every newspaper headline and turned down bed sheet . . . how did I manage to live in my 24-year-old body, terrified constantly that I might not make it to twenty-five. (Miller 1997, 160)

Sex and death became connected as the pandemic spread within the gay community. It was a very complicated time; one friend even recommended that Miller avoid all sexual intimacies with another man if he was to remain healthy. In Miller's new relationship, Doug felt overwhelmed by Miller's sophistication in both art and love. Doug refused to relax and let Miller penetrate him and couldn't bring himself to penetrate Miller. For Doug this was a way of protecting himself from his feelings of vulnerability and from surrendering his sense of himself in the presence of his sexually adept and charismatic lover.

By the mid-1980s the gay lifeway and AIDS were both in the news. A steady monogamous, close relationship was a means of assuring protection as the epidemic struck all around them. Doug and Tim's courtship was at first tentative, but still they decided to move in together. They shared common intellectual interests, two smart gay men self-consciously building their relationship and working at their careers. As a sign of the permanency of their relationship, the couple decided to get a dog. Miller suggests that in a later time, the couple would have wanted a child, but the dog was a suitable substitute at the time, drawing them closer together. Buddy became integral to their closeness and would, in his doggy way, let the couple know when things were not going well between them. When their relationship reached the three-year mark, one year longer than any of his previous relationships, Miller believed that it might work. Doug gave up on his early plans for an academic career and turned to writing. He provided emotional support following crises in Miller's life, including the unexpected death of his father and mixed audience response to his performance art.

As former boyfriend John's health declined (he died three years later), Miller was reminded of the vast amount of unprotected sex they had each enjoyed in the era before the epidemic struck. He was certain that he, too, must be infected. In fact, his doctor relayed that belief to Doug at a time when the test for seroconversion had not been worked out. They lived through the 1980s haunted by the fear that every bruise, which might later appear as Karposi's sarcoma, would be evidence of a compromised immune system. Miller writes about this time, when:

my body had felt so isolated in a paralyzing fear of AIDS. With the bathroom door locked, I would check the lymph nodes in my groin and armpits each morning to see how my immune system was doing. (Miller 1997, 203)

Later, Miller and Doug faced the terrifying matter of getting tested for AIDS. As Miller so well observes about the meaning of getting tested:

For gay boys who had always felt ourselves "tested" by parents, priests, and our gender, to have to submit our blood to the big pass-or-fail seemed fit for a soap opera, the Old Testament, or a little kid's nightmare. (Miller 1997, 206)

Ultimately, Miller did get tested, was seronegative, and thus began promiscuous sexual experiences, which made up for the time since the specter of AIDS had crimped his sexual explorations. These forays ultimately led to lessened intensity in his relationship with Doug, which ended after eleven years together.

Miller's memoir reflects the dual problem of experiencing and writing about sexual desire in the age of AIDS. Monogamy was considered essential. While Miller had been monogamous during the first three years of their relationship, Doug had sought sex with numerous men in the movie houses and game parlors in Times Square (Delany 1999). Miller felt pressured to be monogamous yet, ignoring the mantra of safer sex, began a guilty, torrid affair with a fellow performance artist. Doug moved out after Miller confessed to this affair, but later agreed to resume their relationship. Things became more complex as the couple entered into a three-way gay affair with one of Miller's attractive friends, and then Doug and this friend had their own affair without Miller's knowledge. Miller and Doug acknowledged to each other that they would have to allow for the possibility of each exploring other men in an "open" relationship but presumably engaging in safer sex.

With friends and former lovers dying all around them, and in the aftermath of the complex three-way relationship, Miller and Doug sought an escape and moved in 1986 to Los Angeles. As the epidemic became national and then global, ACT-UP was organized, and Miller and Doug became active participants in this rapidly growing political movement. Miller used his skills as a performance artist to attract attention to the cause. The assembled group of gay men demonstrating together could share their worries and realize mutual support: it was better to be angry than to be scared. In the late 1980s, when hospitals were still reluctant to deal with AIDS, ACT-UP forced the issue out into the open. The demonstration, only months after John's death, took on a very personal quality for Miller, who still had the memory of John lying in his hospital bed, hooked up to the IV, his body a mass of sores. The demonstration was a media success, and the rally broke up with hugs all around. Sadly, many of the participants would be dead within the year.

Miller returned to New York in 1992 to direct a workshop and decided to establish a gay performance space. In the meantime, the NEA had been pressured into canceling the award it had made to him, and he had become a target of the Religious Right. Congressional speeches carried on C-Span called him a "porno slime jerk," and the Supreme Court ruled that taste was more important than First Amendment guarantees of free speech in awarding government grants in the arts. Later on, a group of gay men gathered to learn Miller's performance art. Among them was Andrew, a dark, handsome, young man with whom Miller enjoyed a passionate night. Andrew confessed to him that he was HIV positive; this news, not from the first HIV-positive man with whom he had sex, increased both his passion and also his fear that he might become infected.

In the eleventh year of the AIDS outbreak, fully aware of the consequences, Miller permitted himself to be penetrated by Andrew, a man who had the courage to tell him that he was HIV positive. Miller's description of their night together, the pleasure of ejaculating into this beautiful man, imagining that he was making Andrew pregnant, implanting a part of himself into his lover, is told as another performance, writing about gay desire in the AIDS epoch (Murphy 1993). The explicit portrayal of this torrid evening conveys the complex nature of desire in the age of AIDS. It is an example of the manner in which a historical event has shaped both the experience of desire and writing about desire.

Shirts and Lovers

Intimacy with Doug grew less as the lovers each pursued sex outside of their relationship. Doug moved out in 1995, although the two remained close friends, enjoying occasional sexual encounters in the manner of many former gay lovers. Miller continued to do Doug's laundry even after he had moved out, using a metaphor of three laundry baskets: his own and those of Doug and Alistair, each containing a special T-shirt. Miller recounts the meaning of these shirts, part of his metaphor of gay desire, which recalled his discovery of his homoerotic desire in the shirts-and-skin episode of his high school gym class. Miller informs the reader that there were two lovers in the laundry basket: the almost-magical sleeveless shirt featuring the cosmologies of a medieval cabala that he had bought Doug while on tour in Australia in 1993, and a nearly identical shirt belonging to his life-partner,

Alistair McCartney, whom Miller first spotted wearing the identical shirt in the audience while on a London lecture-performance tour.

Miller was immediately drawn to the young man in a shirt identical to the shirt that had made Doug so happy. The shirt brought the two of them together. Alistair loved his own shirt with the cabala design. At twenty-two, thirteen years younger than Miller, having finished university and wishing to escape from his Australian Scottish-Catholic family, Alistair readily agreed to Miller's suggestion that he join him for the night. Miller relives his story of their first meeting as he folds the identical shirts of the two boyfriends, one former, one present. Alistair joined Miller in Los Angeles following a long-distance relationship marked by months of phone calls and brief meetings during Miller's performances around the world. Alistair challenged Miller to maintain a monogamous relationship. Doug was still on the fringes of Miller's life, and things were quite tense at the outset. Miller felt torn between the two men in his life; the situation was resolved by all three men going into psychotherapy. Partly as a result of this experience, Doug, in time, became a psychotherapist, but not before becoming suicidal after Alistair read aloud a story based on an intense, erotic sexual encounter (presumably with Miller) at a writer's workshop, which Doug was leading.

Miller's account ends as he folds the shirts of two boyfriends, two laundry baskets, and a third laundry basket, which includes his own high school T-shirts, presumably the same ones he had to take off in gym class, together with the singed pajama top from his relationship with John. These items of clothing represent his important relationships and life experiences. Miller notes at the end of the book that he has recently heard from one-time sex partner Andrew and that his health was improving now that he was on the new antiretroviral drug "cocktail." The book ends with the promise of a new treatment for persons with AIDS, which presages another turn in writing about gay desire. In addition, there is the promise that Miller himself could realize not only the admiration so difficult for him to sustain but also the intimacy he seeks but is not sure will be sufficient to prevent him from seeking sex outside his relationship with Alistair.

Miller reports that he has always had two boyfriends, one real and one imagined. Desire is all the stronger from the imagined partner. He acknowledges that he has long harbored a secret fear of never having enough love or parental attention, which may explain his continuing affairs with men, many of whom were HIV positive, well into the years of the AIDS pandemic. The intensity of Miller's sexuality was likely driven by his search for affirmation, perhaps initiated by his parents' devastating disclosure that he had been a "mistake." Moreover, audience admiration and appreciation add to the intensity of Miller's performance; there are times during a performance that seem as if Miller and the audience have a love affair. The chasm between stage and audience is breached as Miller leaps over the footlights to wander about the audience, continuing his monologue all the while.

Again, Miller considered himself as not good enough to please his parents, who regarded his birth as a mistake. It is likely that he did not receive the admiration he had sought from them. Indeed, he was almost disregarded, as portrayed in his father's lack of response when Miller told his parents he was gay. Intense sexual experiences evoke the emotions missing in his family. At the same time, it is important to realize that Miller has been able to overcome this deficit in parental emotional responsiveness in an adaptive manner, which is reflected in highly positive reviews of his work and in his ability to convey his social concerns to a global community. While continually searching for self-esteem, he lets himself enjoy the admiration of his audience. Following his performance, Miller greets his many admirers in the lobby. He meets old friends with a hug and relishes hearing about their lives. Miller instantly establishes rapport with the crowd, flashing a smile, greeting well-wishers with a hug, and graciously signing autographs. He regales them with the adventures he and Alistair have had with the Immigration and Naturalization Service. He informs his fans that his most recent performance, *1001 Beds* (Miller 2006), may be his last in the United States. Alistair lost his student visa, got a brief reprieve through a business visa for teaching, and is now in the final period of that visa. Unless a university sponsors Alistair for a green card, the couple may be forced to return to Australia where domestic partners are legally acknowledged by the immigration authorities.

Looking Forward

From first realization of the awesome destruction wreaked by the epidemic through the end of the decade, AIDS was a dark presence looming over gay life-writers of this and the previous generation. Men born in the 1950s came to adulthood just as the gay rights movement was underway, a social revolution providing new possibilities for the realization of socio-erotic desire. This cohort-forming event, marked by increasing visibility and public acceptance of homosexuality in the 1980s (Clendinen and Nagourney 1999), was linked to the second cohort-forming event—the widespread emergence, after 1981, of AIDS. Without a doubt, AIDS overshadows all other socio-historical changes for this generation-cohort of gay men. These men, during their young adulthood, their thirties or forties, had faced losses more typically experienced by much older people, those in their seventies or eighties (Borden 1989). With the introduction of anti-retroviral medication in 1996, and the successive refinement of this medical miracle in the intervening years, people with AIDS continue to enjoy good health (Sullivan 1998). AIDS largely disappears as a theme in the life writing of successive generations who are more concerned with civil rights and community acceptance than with the virus. Provincetown, once a community of succor for gay men with AIDS and their caregivers (such as Wally and Mark Doty), has now become a center of celebration as gay and lesbian couples nationwide travel to Provincetown to get married.

This work is concerned with the impact upon writing about same-sex desire among men in the context of particular socio-cultural changes significant through several generations of life-writers. Study of popular memory across successive generation-cohorts has shown that events taking place in early adulthood are particularly significant in determining the worldview of their generation (Conway and Pleydell-Pierce 2000; Schuman, Belli, and Bischoping 1997). For the generation born in the 1950s and growing up in the 1960s, and who attained young adulthood just at the outset of the gay revolution, the gay rights era accompanied America's awakening from an age of innocence to the new realities of social change (Tipton 1982). The assassinations of John F. Kennedy, Robert Kennedy, and Martin Luther King Jr., coupled with the Vietnam conflict, became a prelude to such other social changes as the gay rights movement, which provided a social context in which gay men could explore their sexual identities. This social change and its impact upon the intimate and public lives of gay men is evident in the memoirs of Mark Doty and Tim Miller, as well as the life stories of James Melson (1992), Bernard Cooper (1996), and Fenton Johnson (1996). These gay men all write about living and writing in the midst of the revolution.

Within this generation of men born in the 1950s and self-identifying as gay, there was a "pile-up" of generation-cohort defining events in young adulthood (the gay rights movement and AIDS), which, together, colored their response to subsequent social change. It is striking, though, that there is little discussion in their life stories of the larger social changes taking place during the Vietnam and post-Vietnam era. It is much as if, looking at the world from the back rather than the front of a telescope, the concerns and interests of these life-writers are focused largely on self and sexuality.

Both of these writers are concerned with the working out of desire, and particularly the impact of AIDS on the expression of this desire and search for intimacy. Life writing for the '50s generation was focused on the issue of desire in the time of AIDS (Murphy 1993). These life-writers were forced to realize that their concern with sexual desire had been costly as their friends began to sicken and die. Mark Doty and Tim Miller are particularly explicit both about how sexual desire was experienced in the midst of this crisis and the impact of this desire upon writing their life story.

Miller wonders whether he can avoid the HIV virus. Sex is dangerous; Miller's fantasy of making a part of himself inside his partner is, perhaps, an effort to undo his parents' mistake and re-create himself as a gay man with good self-regard. This symbolic gift of life becomes, however, a gift of death in the age of AIDS. Mingling his own ejaculation with that of his lover, at one time a symbol of intertwined life and love, now becomes life threatening. Miller worries what might happen if a small cut or abrasion comes in contact with his partner's semen and leads to seroconversion. The AIDS test itself becomes a symbol of this fear. Partners often go together to get tested, and the look on the face of a partner emerging from learning the test results becomes a critical moment for the life of each, described so well in Mark Doty's account.

The next chapter focuses on the life stories of men born in the 1960s, arriving at young adulthood after the pandemic. Forewarned about the dangers of AIDS and often well versed from grade school on the importance of "safer" sex, AIDS retreats into the background of their life stories. For this generation, while continually aware of the presence of AIDS, the predominant concern is with recognition for alternative lifestyles and the effort to convince the larger society that gay men can be "virtually normal" (Sullivan 1995) in all respects except selection of sexual partner. This generation is particularly concerned with fitting into the larger society, taking action against antigay prejudice and hate crimes, and having the same opportunities, including military service and attaining legal recognition for committed relationships (Herek, Jobe, and Carney 1996; Sullivan 1995).

5 | Born in the Sixties

Living Easier with Homosexuality

Gay identity . . . is, in the end, nothing if not structured by paradox and conflict. . . . You can be two things at once; you can live in the middle voice. You can, some of us have learned, be "queer" and "mainstream" at the same time, someone equally committed to your family in the suburbs . . . and to the pleasures of random encounters with strange men in the city . . . someone who argues for equal rights but insists on living in an all-gay, all-male enclave; someone who desires love but also loves desire.

Daniel Mendelsohn, *The Elusive Embrace*

I knew then I was never going to be able to rid myself of my homosexuality. It was as much a part of me as the fact that I was my father's son. . . . "I am a gay man," I said out loud. I listened as the sound of my words disappeared into the darkness. . . . My acceptance was my salvation.

Marc Adams, *The Preacher's Son*

Being Gay in Family and Community

The early 1980s was a difficult time for the still fragile gay rights movement. Heavily supported by the Religious Right, Ronald Reagan had just been elected president. Reagan himself had none of Jimmy Carter's ambivalence regarding gay issues. He was a practical man who as governor of California had taken a position against a ballot initiative to deny public school positions to homosexual teachers. However, the affable Reagan had been elected on the strength of the Religious Right, which determinedly opposed homosexuality. As the decade began, despite Anita Bryant's anti-homosexual campaign, Dade County Florida had refused to reconsider its antidiscrimination ordinance; in the course of this campaign it emerged that Bryant herself had a gay son.

The Democratic convention that year included a strong gay rights plank in its platform, and even the Republicans allowed program time for a gay caucus to argue for support of a position banning discrimination on the basis of sexual orientation. The gay community itself was caught between a political movement campaigning for equal rights and a social movement emphasizing sexual freedom. For the generation born in the 1960s, coming to adulthood in the 1980s, AIDS had become a reality and a constant reminder of the need for prudence in the pursuit of sexual fulfillment. Adopting the label "gay," this generation of men was particularly concerned with creating a positive gay identity and confronting antigay prejudice. Perhaps symbolic of this change in dealing with matters of sexual identity, the first bar catering to the gay community (with uncovered plate-glass windows and a sign visible from the street) opened in Chicago in 1979. No longer was there need for furtive meeting places.

A particular emphasis of gay life-writers of this and the subsequent generation was concern with family ties, particularly the father-son relationship, following the disclosure to the family of one's gay identity (Savin-Williams 2001). These men dealt with their feeling about their fathers whose response to "coming out" gay was often initial rejection, later followed by grudging acceptance, and then recognition that father and son could continue to care for each other even while following different lifestyles. Each of the life stories in some ways explores concerns regarding concern for the next generation among fathers and sons (Cohler, Hostetler, and Boxer 1998; Erickson 1958, 1982; McAdams, Hart, and Maruna 1998).

Daniel Mendelsohn: Writing Desire after the Revolution

Brooding, highly self-critical, and caustic regarding his community of pleasure-seeking gay men living in New York, the classics scholar and writer Daniel Mendelsohn lived with the dilemma of searching for community and finding satisfaction of sexual desire in his generation of gay men who were born in the 1960s and came of age in the 1980s. Mendelsohn sought the foundation of a gay identity; the dilemma is that understanding a gay identity reveals its fragile character. His memoir *The Elusive Embrace: Desire and the Riddle of Identity* was published in 1999; the book considers the paradox of increasing outward acceptance of gay sexuality of the 1980s yet encumbered by pervasive sense of shame regarding this desire.

On the one hand, Mendelsohn is an out, visible member of New York's educated cultural elite whose commentary appears in sophisticated coffee-table magazines. On the other hand, Mendelsohn is a participant in a never-ending succession of anonymous sexual encounters, which he finds exciting yet ultimately empty, increasing his self-criticism and shame. Reflecting this ambivalence regarding his gay identity, he describes his apartment as slightly outside of New York's frenetic Chelsea neighborhood. This geographic and social marginality permits him a critical vantage for viewing this trendy, heady world of gay sex. Mendelsohn wavers between determined detachment from his community and a sense of omnipresent desire for the very men whom he also disdains. He vacillates between endorsement and rejection of a gay identity just as he does between appreciation and scorn for men, like himself, who desire love but who compulsively seek sex for its own sake. As he says, "We're always two things at once" (Mendelsohn 1999, 32).

Two themes characterize Mendelsohn's memoir: the role of the gay lover as a twin, completing sense of oneself as personally integrated and vital; and the significance of generativity as a reparative force in a life story characterized by enduring sense of shame. In childhood he had learned to identify beauty and youth with annihilation. The Greek concept of Eros, of desire, was little more than a series of disasters and afflictions. This connection of death and desire is comparable to the experience of the men of his generation who continue to believe that desire for sex with other men is an affliction (Moore 2004). He claims that his generation came to associate homoerotic desire with shame learned from boyhood (Corbett 1997).

Desire, Sameness, and Difference

The first of the two themes of Mendelsohn's memoir is the search for an alter ego who might complement his search for self-completion, someone able to offer a positive identity and sense of being centered in a real community, missing in his own life. Mendelsohn grew up in an ethnic but not very religious Jewish Long Island family caught in the tension between the culture of the shtetl as it existed in Europe prior to the pogroms of the early twentieth century, and assimilation into the East Coast Anglo culture. His grandparents came to the United States following World War I and made sure that his parents, both of whom became teachers, received an education necessary for middle-class status. Mendelsohn struggles with two identities, Jewish and gay, each of which he experiences as a disparaged or negative identity (Greenson 1954).

Mendelsohn attended Princeton. This choice might have puzzled his friends and family because of the so-called quota system in some Ivy League colleges. His choice was prompted by that of a boy in his high school to whom he was attracted and who was attending Princeton. Mendelsohn was particularly drawn to southern-gentry boys who dressed in blue blazers, button-down oxford-cloth shirts, rumpled chinos, and penny-loafers. These classmates came from families whose ancestors had fought in the Civil War and who lived on in proud defeat in small towns where they were a part of the local aristocracy. Mendelsohn characterizes his own ethnic Jewish heritage and his beloved Greeks in much the same ways: traditions that had been vanquished but remained proud in defeat.

Mendelsohn writes about desire in a paradoxical and conflicted manner regarding both his own identity and that of his ethnic family tradition. Desire, just as his life, is on the margin and governed by wish rather than action. His account is replete with memory of desire unrequited, such as for those apparently straight classmates. He tells a story, central to the narrative as a whole, about a great-aunt who, according to family legend, was engaged to a rich relative in exchange for funds for Mendelsohn's family's passage to the New World and who had died young, still a virgin. This passage also presents a paradox: death and desire are connected, a theme elaborated by Mendelsohn in his doctoral dissertation on the allusion presented in Greek tragedy to the "bride of death," girls who sacrificed themselves for family or community. Desire and death are then connected in a contemporary context as well, as Mendelsohn recalls the 1950s-generation poet Mark Doty's (1996) portrayal of his lover Wally dying after suffering the torments of AIDS.

Greek myths focus on the tragedy of beauty leading to death, the source of Mendelsohn's continuing fascination with Sophocles' play *Antigone,* whose protagonist is a bride of death. He finds in the Greek myths the tragedy of unattainable, elusive, pure beauty. It is an "elusive embrace," as is his continuing and inevitably disappointing quest for a lover just like himself, sought in order to provide a missing capacity for personal integrity and self-soothing (Shelby 1994; Tolpin 1997). Unable to find the object of his desire, Mendelsohn experiences this tragedy as personally meaningful as he continues to search for a desired but elusive embrace by another man, which would complete his sense of self-coherence.

Mendelsohn connects themes of beauty and death when he is told that his mother's aunt Ray was expected by her father to marry Sam, a rich cousin, who would then arrange for the family's passage to America. Family legend has it that Ray died of rheumatic fever in America just prior to the marriage she supposedly did not want. Ray's gravestone features a haunting photograph that Mendelsohn experiences in much the same way as he views Greek statues, beautiful but elusive. Mendelsohn discovered that Ray did in fact marry Sam. Meeting the daughter of the woman who became Sam's second wife, Mendelsohn learned that Sam and Ray had been very much in love and that Sam had been a free thinker who befriended the poor, and enjoyed the company of blacks and homosexuals. Since he didn't as a rule follow his family's Orthodox Jewish ways, he married Ray's sister, as expected by Jewish custom.

This story of Ray's untimely death takes Mendelsohn in several directions, including his study of Euripides' plays, and his realization that he will never marry. He tells of taking a former boyfriend, an elusive object of his desire, to visit his great-aunt Ray's gravesite. Again connecting desire and death, Mendelsohn makes a rare reference to AIDS: he recalls the wedding of a former gay boyfriend to a woman who had provided friendship for his circle of gay college boys; these boys were all dead, dying young like Ray. He recounts a frustrated near-sexual adventure with a classmate, met by chance in a graveyard while both worked on a class project. Mendelsohn's association of death and desire is more ethereal than that of the lifewriters in the generation born in the 1950s writing about the illness and death of their lovers from AIDS. His concern with desire and death is allusion and academic rather than a description of grim reality of a generation of gay men witnessing the death of lovers and friends. He observes that desire is "a sense of beautiful hovering just beyond your reach, to be reflected upon and considered. The reflection becomes, in its own way, another kind of possessing . . . a reflection is irresistible because it is a paradox: an opposite that is the same, an other that is also clearly your self" (Mendelsohn 1999, 25).

Reflecting on his sexual experiences, Mendelsohn observes that gay men know both difference and sameness: "If the emotional aim of intercourse is a total *knowing* of the other, gay sex may be, in its way, perfect because in it, a total knowledge of the other's experience is finally, possible" (Mendelsohn 1999, 74). Women are seen as difference and men as sameness. Having also had sex with women, Mendelsohn reports that in his sexual encounters with women he fell *into* his partner, while in sex with other men he fell *through* his partner back into himself over and over again. He tells of his fascination with the gaze, looking at himself in the mirror, which reminded him of the myth of Narcissus. His search for a partner like his desired self was an effort to complete the visage in the mirror and to provide him with the capacity to realize an identity that might provide the personal coherence he feels is missing not just in his own life but also that of the gay community.

The Elusive Embrace, the title of Mendelsohn's memoir, is an allusion to the story of Narcissus—punished by the gods and confined forever in pre-occupation with his own image. Metaphorically, Mendelsohn sees the gay community as similarly preoccupied with sameness rather than difference, a concern that can be understood as a search for a twin who might provide this missing capacity of personal integrity and ability to modulate desire and to sooth oneself (Shelby 2002; Winnicott 1953). Mendelsohn maintains that gay men seek little more than to be desired by other men—narcissism harnessed to sexual satisfaction. They savor the seduction and turn desire into a "willful private narrative" (Mendelsohn 1999, 100). He claims that it is only desire that shapes interactions with other men, a desire that objectifies and distances relations among gay men while, all the time, they seek only sameness, clones of themselves. The mirrored gaze is echoed in their search for a lover who will match their reflected image (Phillips 2001).

Another direction of Mendelsohn's story concerns his family's collusion regarding the nature of the love affair between Sam and Ray, a lie told to family and friends, just as gay men (like himself) whose desire leads them to secretive gay bars where they feel shame as they cruise for prospective partners in this sexual meat market. He recalls a time when, at age fourteen, he spent afternoons masturbating with a classmate in his classmate's dark basement. Feeling ashamed, he returned home as if nothing had happened.

The metaphor of the eye, as well as the gaze, is important for Mendelsohn as with both Sophocles and Freud. He observes that the Greek statues are missing their eyes—the colored stone for the iris and pupil having long since disappeared from these statues. The photograph on Ray's gravestone is of an aloof young woman; it reminds Mendelsohn of prospective gay partners in the bars who maintain an aloof gaze, which makes them all the more desired. The photograph is also similar to those desirable Princeton boys who remained elusive and unavailable. The embrace is made all the more evocative because it can never be realized. He views his desire for other men, or his homosexuality, as he disparagingly uses this term (Mendelsohn 1999, 133), as a kind of fulfillment similar to that felt by his Jewish relatives, involved in nominal Judaism but unable to attain the solace and identity that Judaism and its culture had provided his family in the Old World. Mendelsohn's homosexual world exists in an eternal present, just as with the family life represented in a treasured photo album of long-deceased relatives. Mendelsohn observes that we can't live without stories; however, the photos in the album have no stories and offer little connection with the present time. Partners in a quick sexual encounter resemble photos; these partners have no stories and no past, and exist only as the experience of desire momentarily slacked.

Mendelsohn writes about gay men overwhelmed by the frenetic activity and demands of the gay community. He recalls the desire expressed by so many of his friends to return to where they grew up and where they had real roots. Indeed, this connection with the past is a part of Mendelsohn's search for a positive identity and perhaps explains a part of his attraction to the boys at his college who came from places where their families had lived for generations and where there were solid traditions, together with his fascination with his own family's life in the shtetl where traditions sustained and enhanced one's sense of personal coherence. Homosexual men in the 1930s generation, such as Alan Helms (see chap. 2) or Texas-born life-writer Stanley Ely (1996), had fled the tight-knit rural communities of the American heartland for the excitement and anonymity of New York. The allure of New York for one generation had become the anathema of another generation. One "trick" who Mendelsohn noticed while on the way home from errands in his neighborhood, and who invited him home for sex, reported that it was his last day in New York: he said that he had come to New York to find himself but instead got lost.

Mendelsohn describes his childhood and his same-sex desire in the third person, observing his own life as if he were looking on from the outside at his very traditional family. His father, a mathematician, was "very cerebral, a great problem solver and dogged crossword puzzler" (Mendelsohn 1999, 111) who constructed "Rube Goldberg" devices that somehow didn't work in spite of their scientific foundations; he depended on his wife for advice on what to wear to work. His mother, a former schoolteacher and housewife, decorated the entire house in shades of blue and attended daily housekeeping rituals assisted by a weekly visit from the cleaning lady.

In this neatly ordered world, with three older brothers and a younger sister, harboring desire for other boys, Mendelsohn believes that he failed to please his father. On one occasion during childhood he told his father about a "perfect friend" he had met. Apparently understanding all too well the true nature of Mendelsohn's desire, his father, usually a quiet and mild-mannered man, replied in anger that boys didn't have such perfect friends. His preadolescent years are recounted in the familiar manner of the gay master narrative for his generation (Corbett 1997; Plummer 1995). He repeats his mother's story that while he sometimes played with trucks and cars, he also played with the girl next door, his best friend, enjoying her Barbie doll and playhouse. He felt different from other boys his age who engaged in "rough-and-tumble play" (Friedman 1997) and feared being beaten up by his classmates. He speculates that the preoccupation so many gay men have with their bodies may be a response to having been taunted as boys for being too skinny, weak, or clumsy. He describes how he was humiliated when he was unable to lift the yard tool his father had asked for. Later, finding an advertisement for weight training, he began working out at night in secret. Echoing the concern among gay men regarding their possible erotic desire for their fathers (Isay 1986, 1987; Phillips 2001, 2003) he concludes that gay men don't want to feel ashamed of their bodies in front of their fathers.

Consistent with Phillips's (2001, 2003) discussion of the gay boy's fear of being overstimulated, Mendelsohn's boyhood preoccupation with the study of language and classical civilizations supports Phillips's observation that the gay boy's avoidance of "rough-and-tumble" play may be less evidence of gender nonconformity than a means for avoiding the stimulation emerging in contact sports, perhaps also a means of avoiding painful, possibly overstimulating locker room experiences, elusive desire felt in the presence of boys undressed and in the shower. Mendelsohn knew that his youthful desire for other boys could not be fulfilled. He watched, enjoying fantasies while feeling shame by his desire for the classmate whose selection of Princeton determined his own college choice and whom he sought to be like in an effort to attract this classmate. Masturbation was the fulfillment of the memory of desire.

His fascination with the tales of shtetl life told by both grandfathers—his mother's father who lived with the family for a part of his childhood, and his father's father, a frequent visitor—led to his intrigue with archaeology and with languages. His mother's father, clearly preoccupied with himself, had an Old World charm; he was a gadabout who had had many wives, a snappy dresser who recognized the power of desire. His grandparents spoke and read several European languages and language became important for Mendelsohn. Classical languages were particularly important, for they represented longing conveyed so powerfully in the work of both Sappho and Ovid. Classical languages provided Mendelsohn a private world. Classical languages were the stuff of serious scholarship, conferring true intellectual authenticity, languages not spoken, frozen in time and begging for contemplation. As a preadolescent, he kept a diary in Egyptian hieroglyphics. In his diary he could write about his secret loves.

In college Mendelsohn became fascinated with the German language. This was the language of his ancestors and that used in Freud's own discussion of desire, as well as in the stories and plays of Arthur Schnitzler, writing about fin-de-siècle Vienna, Isherwood's account of the Berlin cabarets between the two world wars, and *Death in Venice,* Thomas Mann's (1912) novella of an older man preoccupied with a young adolescent boy he observed while on holiday. This elusive desire is repeated in Mendelsohn's preoccupation with those Princetonians observed across the lecture hall, the elusive blond college classmates with rumpled khakis, ties askew. Again, Mendelsohn notes that he experiences desire as memory:

In my desire for men there is always repetition, the hunger for a return to something I first saw and wanted, which was itself a reminder of something earlier; this is how it is with boys who want other boys . . . the illusion of multiplicity and choice and, finally, of difference. (Mendelsohn 1999, 65)

Mendelsohn returns to the first person voice when he narrates his first sexual act at the age of twenty-one. His chosen partner was a southern preppy of his fantasies who enticed Mendelsohn to come with him back to his dormitory room for a night of humiliating sex. His lover's friends also treated Mendelsohn with derision, adding to his feeling that he was very much the outsider. With some satisfaction he notes that the southern boy is now dead, a veiled allusion to the AIDS pandemic. Subsequently, when he was a graduate student in classics at Princeton, he began a relationship with an undergraduate. His boyfriend returned to his southern hometown over the Christmas break, and their difference dissolved into sameness when he stayed in his boyfriend's college dorm room, sleeping in his younger lover's bed, surrounded by his lover's possessions. His lover sent him a boyhood snapshot. Years later he came across a similar picture of himself at the same age and observed that their boyhood snapshots were amazingly alike. Again, some years later, enjoying life on a gay beach during a lazy summer, he noted that differences between these gay boys dissolved into sameness in the gathering shadows of the late afternoon.

Writing about sameness, difference, and desire and his participation in Internet chat rooms and personal ads, Mendelsohn reports that the list goes on and on; he portrays sex among men as flat, repetitive, almost boring, merely a means for "getting off" and relieving tension states. Mendelsohn claims that this disconnect between sexual gratification and intimacy has been hastened by the Internet with its chat rooms, providing easy recruitment among men looking for sex. Thousands of gay Web sites offer up men Mendelsohn sees as little different from the statues of classical civilizations, and ponders once again the meaning of the elusive embrace in which, like these statues of antiquity, men pose as perfect but are ultimately empty.

Generativity and the Gay Life Story

Generativity is the second of the themes that concern Mendelsohn. Increased interest within the gay community regarding parenthood and care for the next generation became possible for the gay community as a result of significant social changes in the 1980s as the 1960s generation came of age. This interest in parenthood among gay men is evident in Jesse Green's (1999) description of his partner's success in adopting two children of mixed ethnicity. Mendelsohn's own concern for care of the next generation is reflected in the courses he teaches on classical civilization at Princeton where he became an adjunct faculty member. Students have praised his ability to lead class discussions, his helpful comments on papers, and his willingness to talk with them in person or through e-mail.

It has become common for gay and lesbian couples to adopt or to arrange to have children of their own. Some single women seeking to become parents approach gay men to father their children. When he was still in graduate school, Mendelsohn refused such a proposal. Some years later when a single, pregnant friend proposed that he be the man in her child's life, Mendelsohn accepted her offer. He devotes a long chapter of his memoir to his relationship with his friend Rose and her son Nicholas. The depth of his involvement in Nicholas's life was a surprise to him. Mendelsohn observes:

Children are the secret weapon of straight culture: they have the potential to rescue men from inconsequentiality. Fatherhood has the power to confer authority on men; it can be what saves them from eternally being boys themselves. (Mendelsohn 1999, 105)

While he wanted to possess boys who became sexual partners, he loves Nicholas in a way that was new and entirely different. Reflecting on this difference, he states: "To be a lover, to be a desirer . . . is to be self-obsessed, for your desire is ultimately about yourself. But to be a parent is to efface yourself—your *self*" (Mendelsohn 1999, 152).

Mendelsohn has participated in Nicholas's life from his birth to the present. He says that even as he was considering his role of father, fatherhood made him aware of his own mortality and the next generation growing to adulthood. Mendelsohn met Rose while he was on a temporary assignment with a company where Rose was employed. Having her first child somewhat late in life after she had attained some success in her career, Rose was able to devote loving attention to Nicholas. The tone of Mendelsohn's account changes as he narrates his life with Rose and Nicholas. He delights in Nicholas's pleasure in his own body and the ease with which Nicholas gleefully urinates on him as Mendelsohn is changing his diaper. However, he feels uncomfortable with any physical proximity to Rose, such as when she is nursing Nicholas.

Parenthood demands evaluation of what is really important in life. Over time, Mendelsohn spends much of his free time with Rose and Nicholas, even feeling that he is Nicholas's father. He takes great delight in being Nicholas's godfather; he even purchased an elegant baptismal gown and supervised arrangements for the ceremony. Coming home from Nicholas's baptism reception, Mendelsohn met an irresistibly cute boy with whom he had to have sex. The conflict between Mendelsohn's quest for immortality through generativity and his desire for sex with other men, which he finds alien and a source of self criticism, is symbolized by this contrast between the elegant baptism and reception, and the sleazy (albeit safe) sex with this man met on the street and whose lesions showed his infection with AIDS. Mendelsohn juxtaposes these incidents to point out the compulsive, repetitive nature of gay desire and the sexual release that he seeks but abhors at the same time. He searches for resolution of this fragmented identity. On the one hand, he is like his grandfather: a man of culture and taste whose reviews of the arts and literature are sought after by the media, a much-admired college instructor in the classics, and Nicholas's caring godfather. On the other hand, he is driven by overwhelming desire, reflected in this encounter with the boy met on the street.

Mendelsohn's life story portrays his same-sex desire as elusive, insatiable, and disavowed, desire that once even drove him to the brink of suicide. On the occasion when he took a former boyfriend to visit his great-aunt's grave and to see her photograph, he reflected, while standing next to his friend, on how difficult it was to become close after the sex is over. He can only become friends with former lovers many months later, embarrassed with the knowledge that their bodies had been intertwined and as his memory of their sexual relationship has faded. His own negative identity (Erickson 1958; Greenson 1954) is reflected in his desire for gentile boys from decadent southern families, who represent his own decadent family reflected in the myth of his great-aunt's life and death. This negative identity is also reflected in his decision to live socially and geographically on the margins of the gay community, which offers satisfaction of sexual desire, an elusive embrace that does not offer intimacy.

What eludes Mendelsohn is not only the embrace but also the satisfaction of a passionate and loving relationship with another man, parallel to the one that his great-aunt had realized with her caring husband. This relationship had been deliberately misrepresented in family myth as cruel, and as desire disavowed. The object of his elusive embrace is the ethnic other; as a Jewish man he believes in the need to be buried by a son. His godson who might perform this task is ethnically Italian, as is his friend Rose, who is proud of her Italian heritage. In the end, his own sense of shame and self-hatred eludes resolution. This leads to a continuing, restless tension; he is unable to integrate his disavowed homosexual desire with his concern for Rose and Nicholas and his work as a scholar, teacher, and writer.

Marc Adams: Growing Up in the Shadow of the Religious Right

Marc Adams was born in 1968. His memoir, *The Preacher's Son,* was published in 1996. The account begins with Marc's failed attempt as a teenager to kill himself by slashing his wrists with a razor blade. The pain of his desire for sex with another man was so great, and the prohibition against this expression so strong, that the resulting feelings of shame were unbearable. Adams's father was a Baptist minister in a small town in Pennsylvania; he expected his children to be exemplars for the community. Adams's family believed that the Old and New Testaments were the *actual* words of the Lord. The book of Leviticus makes it clear that it is a cardinal sin for a man to sleep with another man (White 1994). The Bible also demanded harsh physical punishment for any infraction against parents, and so Adams and his sisters all suffered at the hands of their unforgiving and demanding father. Punishment was so severe that the children often suffered physical abuse at their father's angry hands.

Adams reports that images of hell, so much a part of the family's conversations, haunted him in his dreams. Brought up in this fundamentalist Christian faith, Adams assumed without question that his parents' religion was the true way. Since the world beyond the family was dangerous and polluted, the family kept very much to itself, which only intensified the terrifying impact of his parents' teachings. Over time other families drifted away from the church presided over by Adams's father, a stern and unforgiving pastor. He chose to continue preaching on Sunday to a church empty with the exception of his own family, rather than accept an appointment to a church in a nearby community that might require that he compromise his principles.

This view of the world outside the family circle as a source of temptation proved all too true for Adams who, at the age of nine, had developed a crush on a fellow classmate. When his teacher informed Adams's mother that the friendship had a strangely erotic cast, his mother made it clear that two boys could not be intimate. Puzzled, and seeing nothing wrong with his feelings toward Stephen, Adams acknowledged to his mother that he wanted to hold hands with Stephen and to kiss him. His parents sent him to a Christian school where discipline was harsh and punishment meted out by a wooden paddle. Adams realized that he had erred in confessing his love for Stephen. The only virtue of this new school was that students were permitted to work at their own pace, and he could finish school and be ready for college sooner than if he had been in a regular school.

Any recognition of desire, particularly gay desire, was connected with sin and Satan; when he was fourteen, he attended a special service for missionaries at another church in a nearby community. There, Adams first learned about AIDS—a disease sent by God as vengeance on sinners. The preacher lashed out at homosexuals who would stop at nothing to molest children. Adams reports that:

I had never felt an inclination to molest children, and I wasn't sure of the definition of a sexual deviant. But I felt a deep ache within my chest. I knew I must be a homosexual because of my attraction to men. (Adams 1996, 24)

Adams felt intense pain following this service, felt keenly his sin, and believed that he would be consigned to hell for something he had never consciously determined to do. Gay desire was something that happened regardless of individual willpower. One afternoon shortly after this terrifying sermon, in the woods near his house Adams discovered a garbage bag that contained a larger number of men's magazines. Knowing the sin purportedly attached to pornography, Adams nevertheless hoped that pictures of naked women could excite him; when he looked at the pictures he felt little desire, just as when he tried to imagine asking a girl out on a date.

Discovering that he had writing talent when his first short story was readily accepted for publication, and intrigued by the radio programs he had heard occasionally, Adams decided on a career in communications. His sister was attending Jerry Falwell's Liberty University, and Adams decided that he too would like to attend Liberty; he was immediately accepted for admission with a scholarship provided for children of preachers. Falwell was a firm crusader against homosexual rights, and over the preceding year Adams had listened to Falwell's broadcasts. While Falwell was hateful toward homosexual men, he also believed that one could change sexual orientation. It was clear to Adams that Liberty University would be the ideal place for him. He needed to escape from his abusive father; following one particularly violent attack, he warned his father never to hit him again. Adams reports that what was left between father and son was anger, coldness, and his father's imprecation that he would fail in life (Adams 1996, 37). Just as among many of the other life-writers of this generation, the father-son relationship is among the most central concerns in Adams's account; he could make little sense of his father's abuse and constant criticism of his personality and interests. Adams tried to accept his father's unforgiving and punitive rejection, even as his talent was increasingly recognized in school and in the community.

Life at Liberty was restrictive in ways expected of a fundamentalist college. Students were required to live on campus and to listen only to approved Christian radio stations. All public display of affection between men and women was forbidden, dormitory rooms were routinely searched for contraband (including magazines and books not explicitly permitted), and students were not permitted to attend off-campus movies. Student residence assistants checked all community venues where students might be found, and those who broke the law were subject to expulsion. Homosexuality was completely unacceptable, and students suspected of same-sex intimacy were immediately expelled. For Adams, though, even this highly restrictive environment was a relief from the unremitting abuse of his home.

Adams often found himself overcome with desire. He was attracted to other men in his dormitory and was particularly attracted to Brad, his resident assistant. Offering to work on the yearbook, the editor came to his dormitory room to talk with him. As he met Todd, he "was paralyzed by a burning sensation that shot through my body" (Adams 1996, 43). Tall, blond, handsome, and gentle, Todd was the man of his dreams. While he tried to concentrate on his studies and his work on the yearbook, he was overcome by his desire to touch Todd. Adams knew that such an overture would be reported to the administration and would lead to his immediate expulsion. Adams and Todd shared common interests and had an unspoken understanding; the two young men began spending increasing amounts of time together studying and working on the yearbook.

One day Todd asked Adams if he had ever looked at a "dirty" magazine; Adams related the story of finding the magazines in the woods but he had prayed to God to help him overcome any desire. As the two friends parted for the night, Adams sensed the strong erotic tension between them. At about the same time, his older sister became pregnant by a black man with a criminal record who worked in the college cafeteria. Adams needed to talk with someone about his sister's dilemma; after professing his trust in Todd, Todd reached over and embraced him. With Todd's arms around his neck, Adams asked Todd if he had ever felt different from other men, and they each confessed their desire for sex with other men. Each became nervous as they realized they had crossed a divide unacceptable at Liberty. Todd reminded Adams that they must not give in to their desire and commit a sin. However, Adams felt increasing conflict between his gay desire and his Christian commitment.

Dreading to return home over the holidays during his first year, Adams decided to remain on campus. The dorms were nearly deserted as the break approached, and both Todd and he had been busy preparing for their final exams. One evening Todd invited Adams to study with him in his room; the two of them planned to stay up together until they had finished preparing for their exams. As they studied together Adams felt a burning sensation in his chest moving to his groin; the sexual pressure between the two boys was again palpable. Fooling around with a pen that had landed on Todd's bed, the two boys moved on the bed to retrieve it. As Adams lay face up on the bed, Todd rolled on top of him. Adams unfastened Todd's belt; both were soon naked and locked in an embrace. Todd had an orgasm, but Adams was yet to have his orgasm when Todd, apparently frightened of what had just happened, broke away from their embrace and screamed at Adams to get out of his room. Todd moaned that he would never be able to become a minister after that evening and blamed Adams for what had happened. Adams made it clear that Todd had invited him to study together and had made the first move. He was unwilling to accept all the responsibility for what had just happened but was also terrified by the certain consequence, sure that God's vengeance would result in AIDS. He, too, felt that he had failed, had let down his father, the college, and his church, but he also realized that he loved Todd.

Todd left for the Christmas holidays, refusing to even look at Adams, who keenly felt Todd's rejection. Over the holiday, he worked on the yearbook and spent countless hours in the public library reading about AIDS. His reading reported on means for contracting AIDS, which he and Todd had not done; it contradicted the claim of the college ministers who maintained that AIDS was the result of loving another man. Adams felt betrayed again: the ministers had in fact lied about AIDS. He believed in the doctors rather than the preachers, and once again he was at odds with his religious beliefs. His quandary reflects the experience of many lifewriters of his generation coming to adulthood in the mid-1980s, a time when AIDS was omnipresent in the media, conflated with gay sexual identity. The condemning rhetoric of the Christian Right further added to Adams's conflict, as his narrative clearly shows. His quandary was even greater when Todd returned after Christmas, offering to make amends and telling him how much their friendship meant.

Both tried dating women but Adams continued to feel a strong attraction to other men, including Brad and Todd. Adams confessed to Todd how much he had wanted to have sex with him, and the two boys once again fell into a passionate sex leading to a mutual orgasm. The two would-be ministers were confused by their feelings for each other. What they were doing was supposed to be wrong, yet they loved each other and they had been told that their religion was one of love. Adams wondered how it could be that something that felt so right, so natural, could also be wrong. He was puzzled when a friend of his sister told him that she had a gay brother and was worried that her brother would inevitably contract AIDS as a result of his gay identity. It made no sense. Todd proposed that they quit school and live together, but Adams, more ambitious, was determined to stay at Liberty and become a pastor. Feeling guilty, yet desiring each other, they continued their sexual relationship, mostly in the yearbook darkroom. One particularly lusty but dangerous encounter took place in the woods near Liberty in the moonlit warmth of the late spring night. Over the spring break, the two lovers, staying at Todd's house, were finally able to sleep together naked in the same bed. Unfortunately, one evening that same week, they fell asleep cuddled together while watching television. They were discovered by Todd's mother who demanded that Adams leave at once. Todd confessed their relationship to his mother; she declared him sick and dragged him off for conversion therapy with a Christian minister and psychologist.

Adams was devastated when he learned that Todd and his family had decided that he would not return to Liberty for the spring term. His resident assistant, Brad, inquired why Todd hadn't returned to Liberty. When Adams acknowledged that he missed Todd, he felt that Brad understood all too well. On this, as on other occasions, Adams sensed the sexual tension between them. The term ended and Brad graduated; Jerry Falwell himself had been impressed with the yearbook that was largely Adams's creation. Again, unwilling to face his family, Adams remained at Liberty over the summer, working as a student recruiter and designing recruiting information. With his increasing media skills, he accepted an offer from the Liberty extension division to produce instructional videos. Adams lived off-campus between his first and second year of college, longing for Todd. Falwell was pleased with Adams's work and told him how much he admired what he had been doing for Liberty.

The following autumn, while serving as a prayer leader for his dormitory, Adams met two freshmen who had found each other just as he had found Todd. Only three weeks into the semester, the roommate of one of the boys became suspicious and reported them to the administration; the two were expelled from Liberty that same day. Adams had tried to befriend Peter and Kent but was afraid that he would also be found out. He could do little more than listen sympathetically when Kent told him of the punishment likely to follow at the hands of his temperamental, fundamentalist father. Since Adams had access to student addresses, Kent asked him for Peter's address, but Adams was afraid to accede to even this simple request. Later, he received a letter from Kent, telling him that he had found a way to deal with his own desire and asked Adams to call a number, which he had given in his letter. Adams called the number. It was Kent's home, and he learned from Kent's brother that two days earlier, Kent had shot himself in the head with one of his father's guns. Shocked at the news of Kent's suicide, Adams wondered how he could go on with his life, knowing that Kent had suffered to such an extent that he had ended his life while Adams himself had been so distant from Kent's distress.

A year later, when Todd returned for a visit to Liberty, he told Adams that he had in fact gained victory over his desire through Christian conversion, which had changed his life. Adams was sure that Todd felt the same desire as himself when they were together. Adams was confused: if Todd was right, there must be something wrong with the way in which he was managing his own spiritual life. He wept at the thought that Todd had gotten over him. He reorganized his prayer group to include a number of students who might be gay and who he wished to protect from Kent's fate. He discovered that he could mask his feelings by heterosexual dating, which was always relatively formal since Liberty forbade any kind of physical contact. However, when he double-dated, he was often more attracted to the other guy than to either of the women. Furtive sexual encounters with other gay students were painful; orgasm was followed by torment and shame. Gay students were caught by vigilant resident assistants or reported on by their fellow students. Determined to root out any homosexual students, the Dean of Students broke down the door of an apartment in a building off campus where, as reported by their roommate, he discovered two boys showering together.

The summer between his sophomore and junior year, answering the recruiting phone, Adams received a disturbing call from a gay priest in Cleveland who was dying of AIDS and had just lost his lover. The priest wondered how Falwell, a Christian minister, could continue to blame gay men for AIDS while men all about him were dying. He wondered what kind of a loving God would permit such misery. He noted that being gay was hardly a choice and that he had never consciously decided that he would be attracted to men. The caller asked Adams if he had ever been in love. While acknowledging that he had, he couldn't reply that he was still in love and that, yes, it was also a man.

Adams began buying gay men's magazines, now readily available. He panicked when he realized that his roommate had probably seen one of the magazines, which he had hidden in the sofa. He was terrified at the possibility of being found out and reported to the Liberty administration. Feeling depressed and anxious, he walked to a nearby convenience store where he exchanged knowing looks with the clerk, who agreed to meet him after work. In spite of all efforts at conversion, he still found men attractive, including his roommate. Thinking of his conversation with the priest who had called the previous day, Adams determined that he would accept and love himself as he was, a homosexual man. He walked back to the convenience store, met the clerk, and had a quick tryst in the back of the clerk's van. While he enjoyed the sex, he didn't feel the love that he had felt for Todd. His roommate called him a "fag" and soon moved out, although he did not report Adams to the administration.

By the third year, most of the other students Adams knew to be gay had already quit Liberty. New students confessed in chapel that while they formerly had homosexual yearnings, they had been saved and were determined to be heterosexual. Adams's prayers for these boys was not that they succeed in their supposed conversion but that they would come to their senses and accept their homosexuality. As his own self-acceptance continued, Adams experienced renewed doubt about his Christian evangelical faith. After studying and learning that the Bible had been rewritten and interpreted numerous times, he now decided that the Bible was not literally true. He began to mistrust this close-knit evangelical world, which deemed love between two men to be Satan's curse.

The freedom, which at first had seemed so promising when Adams started Liberty, had become an atmosphere of oppression. Sermons preached hate rather than love, particularly toward homosexuals, and Adams began to question his decision to become an evangelical minister. He realized that if he left Liberty he could live freely as a gay man, proud and content, instead of troubled and ashamed. In the middle of his junior year, Adams packed his things and left Liberty. At about the same time, his older sister was having difficulty in the abusive relationship with her boyfriend and her daughter's father. Returning home, Adams wrote to the *Advocate* to see if they would publish his experiences as a gay man at Liberty. However, he put off acceptance when he realized that the magazine's sole interest was to publish "dirt" on Jerry Falwell, long an enemy of the gay rights movement, and whose antigay activism has also been chronicled by 1940s-generation life-writer Mel White (1994). White, too, had been raised in a Fundamentalist family and, even as he was struggling with his own gayness, worked as Jerry Falwell's ghostwriter.

Adams, now living at home, took a job in a local store where he met Ryan, an older man, toward whom he felt a strong attraction. Ryan was just recovering from his lover's death in an auto accident, and as they embraced, his new friend fell over dead from a heart attack. Stricken by this experience, he threw himself into his work at a restaurant. Two weeks into the job he met Richard. Again, there was the now familiar spark of desire in their mutual recognition. Richard gave him his phone number, and they met the same evening at a local hotel after Adams had finished work. Sex with Richard was wonderful, but there was little else between them; Richard would only meet him for furtive late evening encounters. Later he discovered that Richard's family was affluent and influential in state politics and that he risked being disowned by his family unless he remained closeted. Adams was overcome with feelings of emptiness and loneliness living with his family and therefore decided to move to California.

Shortly after making this decision, he got a phone call from Todd. His heart raced as he heard Todd's voice and listened to Todd's apology and his wish to see his friend. They decided to go together to California, and Adams made airline reservations. The two lovers met at the airport, wearing virtually identical clothes, reflecting the extent to which they had become important for each other as alter egos or psychological twins, which fostered their own sense of completion of sense of self and enhanced personal vitality (Kohut 1984). They spent the flight getting reacquainted after having been apart for two years. While they avoided discussion of sexuality, Adams could feel the pressure of Todd's leg against his. At the hotel, Adams was disappointed to learn that Todd had requested a room with double beds. Still troubled about his sexuality, Todd had originally intended not to have sex with Adams, but the sight of his former lover emerging naked from the shower was too much for Todd, and he gave in to his desire. Adams reports that nothing could compare to this joining together of their two souls. Adams looked at his lover, reflected in the pale light of a full moon streaming in through the hotel window, and felt the scars of the past dissolve in the moonlight.

The remainder of the trip was everything that the two young men had ever hoped for. Todd told Adams that he was the missing ingredient in his life, and with a mutual expression of deep and tender love, they agreed that they would spend their life together. They planned to move to Los Angeles where Todd could get a job as an illustrator and where Adams could pursue a writing career. It was difficult for them to part after their holiday even as they went their separate ways to prepare for the move. Adams was deeply in love with Todd again, yet also angry with himself for falling for him so completely. A few days later Todd called to say that he couldn't wait until they saw one another again and pleaded for Adams to come to Florida where he was living. Adams quit his job. On his last day of work, Richard told him that he had come out to his parents and was now free to begin a relationship with Adams. While it was tempting to have sex with Richard one more time, he recalled his feelings for Todd and refused Richard's request.

Todd told Adams that the minister who was supposed to cure him of his homosexuality had instead propositioned him, that the minister's own son was also gay, and that the minister had been molesting other boys in the church. When Todd had informed the church deacons, they had covered up the incident and spread rumors about Todd's homosexuality. Todd acknowledged that his earlier conflicts about wanting to be with Adams were caused by his confusing feelings about the minister. Each of the two had been seeking a close bond with a father figure; they felt that their own stern and emotionally distant fathers had denied them this kind of relationship. Todd acknowledged that he had needed someone to care about him, a need that the minister at first had appeared to meet; Adams acknowledged a similar need for a caring father.

This concern for a relationship with a caring father is an important theme among life-writers of this generation. Their focus shifts from concern with their sexuality within a society little able to tolerate same-sex desire to issues of expression of this desire within the context of family and community. While, as Isay (1986, 1987) has suggested, fathers of these gay men may have been uncomfortable with their son's homoerotic desire (and in Adams's life story this is palpable in his father's condemnation of his childhood expression of closeness with his classmate), emotional distance between father and son for both Adams and Todd was not only a consequence of the family's Fundamentalism but also of the father's awareness and flight from his son's erotic desire for him.

Neither family offered any support for Todd's and Adams's decision. Todd's mother barely tolerated his relationship with Adams. At first she believed that Adams was responsible for her son's homosexuality. However, as problems increased in her relationship with Todd's father, eventually leading to divorce, Todd tried to patch things up with his mother. She readily accepted Todd's invitation to visit with them in California; upon her arrival at the airport, she enthusiastically embraced both her son and his lover. She noted how much more comfortable with each other the couple had become. Things were more difficult with Adams's own family where his younger sister said that she could not let him near her own son for fear of what he might do. When Adams's older sister was left by her boyfriend after yet more crime, violence, and imprisonment, Adams and Todd financed her relocation to Arizona. Adams ends his memoir expressing the hope that he can once more have a close relationship with his lover's mother, which he had enjoyed before she discovered that he was sleeping with her son.

The New Gay Identity

By the time that the generation of gay men born in the 1960s reached young adulthood, the gay rights movement had taken a firm hold. With basic civil rights for gay men increasingly acknowledged, there was less social activism within this generation, but too, there was less need than in previous generations for gay men to hide their lifeways from their family. As gay men increasingly decided to come out to their parents, supported by a society growing more tolerant of gay lifeways, focus shifted from the larger political agenda to relations within the family of gay men and their parents and siblings, and to an inward quest for the meaning of a gay identity (Sullivan 1998).

Essentialist academic and popular accounts regarding purported stages in the realization of a gay identity within family and community were widely discussed in this decade (Cohler and Hammack 2006; Herdt and Boxer 1996). Daniel Mendelsohn's (1999) memoir illustrates this concern with an affirming gay identity. He is often ambivalent as he attempts to come to terms with his gay lifeway. He finds a parallel in his family's denial of the desire in his great-aunt's marriage and his own efforts to come to terms with his own desire and accept his gay identity.

Formation of parent support groups such as Parents and Friends of Lesbians and Gays (PFLAG), the development of student support groups in high schools, and attainment of civil rights protection within many cities presaged a new discourse within families in which gay men sought an increased sense of personal integration through acknowledging their gay identities to parents and friends. As Savin-Williams (2001) has shown, gay youth often disclose their identity first to friends and brothers and sisters, and then to mothers. Mothers were viewed as much more likely than fathers to accept their son's gay lifeway. Mothers and sons shared together the dilemma of whether and how to disclose the son's gayness to the young person's father. Fathers are most often viewed by other family members as emotionally closed off and intolerant of deviation from heterosexual expectations for their sons. Indeed, fathers often appear to be threatened by this disclosure, perhaps because of some discomfort with their sense of their son's homoerotic attraction toward them (Isay 1986, 1987). Much of this struggle between parents and offspring has been shown by Dew (1994) in her portrayal of her family's response to her oldest son's revelation that he was gay.

Adams's account doesn't discuss whether or how he disclosed his gay lifeway to his parents, but apparently they came to this realization after he returned home from Liberty University. Instead, he focuses much more directly on his effort to make sense of his homosexuality and the journey to acceptance of a gay sexual identity.

The Religious Right, or the so-called Moral Majority, attained prominence by the 1980s, both supporting and supported by the politically conservative Reagan administration. During the time '40s-generation life-writer Mel White (1994) was coming to adulthood, it had been difficult to imagine a clearly defined life course for homosexual men. White was forced to deal both with the internal demons imposed by his family's Fundamentalism and also a society in which expression of same-sex desire was still covert and highly stigmatized. On the other hand, '60s life-writer Marc Adams, from a similarly Fundamentalist family, came to adulthood at a time when homosexuality was at least tolerated, if not always supported by the larger society. Adams never considered conversion therapy, while Todd was forced to undergo this destructive treatment and was subjected to continuing abuse by his family and his therapist.

Life-writers born in the 1960s, coming of age in the 1980s, were able to take advantage of the successes of the gay rights movement. For many members of this generation, by the time they became sexually active in mid- to late adolescence, the specter of AIDS had been well publicized, and means of transmission had been empirically traced. Members of this generation were informed regarding safer sex, even though they grew up in a climate of fear expressed within both family and community, which all too often linked gay sexual identity with the inevitability of AIDS. With a changing political climate less connected with AIDS than that of their counterparts born a decade earlier, these gay men managed to obtain respect from family and community for their gay lifeways and, with the process of attaining a positive gay identity, realized enhanced morale and personal coherence.

The generation of the 1970s and '80s came to adulthood at a time when to be gay was to be "virtually normal" (Sullivan 1995), a time when AIDS was regarded as a chronic illness held in check by a parade of ever more effective antiretroviral medications, and when the issue was less whether it was acceptable to be gay than to have a gay relationship that would be legally recognized, perhaps even called "marriage" as the Massachusetts Supreme Court made possible. Many gay men followed in the path of Daniel Mendelsohn, seeking to express their concern for the next generation by adopting or arranging to have children, and becoming active as mentors and leaders within gay communities across the nation.

6|

Born in the Seventies and Eighties

Postmodern Memoirs

The '90s showed themselves to be a decade not much of new developments or new social revolutions but a new synthesis of the events characterizing the previous twenty-
five years.

Douglas Sadownick, *Sex between Men*

It is not possible today for most men to view public sex (or any sex for that matter) except through the viral veil of safety and risk . . . for us younger men . . . who *cannot* re-
treat to the backrooms of 1976—because we were in grade school, or even diapers at the
time . . . today's public sex renewal does not represent a step backward in gay men's sexual development-either *to* the days of liberation or *from* the horrors of the epidemic—
but rather a step ahead in time toward a new kind of sexual and political expression.

Eric Rofes, *Dry Bones Breathe*

Into the Millennium

It has never been clear why Bill Clinton chose to make the issue of gays
being able to serve in the military one of his first priorities upon assuming
office in 1991. What is clear is that the controversy regarding gay life was
brought to national attention. Gay life-writer Scott Peck, author of *All
American Boy,* described in chapter 5 his father's testimony before the Sen-
ate Armed Forces Committee. For men born in the 1970s, coming to adulthood in the 1990s, debates such as those regarding gay men and women
serving in the military showed that alternative sexualities had become a
recognized part of contemporary society. By the 1990s the two postwar
cohort-defining events for the gay community were well understood; the

gay rights revolution had taken hold. Even with such cataclysmic events as the assassination of San Francisco mayor Moscone and city councilman Harvey Milk, and the Anita Bryant antigay campaign, gay identity had entered the national political debate. When a group in Miami Beach sought once again in 2002 to repeal the antidiscrimination ban associated with Anita Bryant's 1977 successful campaign, the national media acknowledged that gay rights had come too far for such campaigns to have any success.

Andrew Sullivan (1995) has argued that at least within urban life homosexuality had become "virtually normal." Others maintained that the time of the "postgay" movement had arrived, suggesting that the issue of sexual identity was no longer a salient issue in urban American life. Only a few holdouts such as Michael Warner (1999) were left to complain that this new visibility for gay and lesbian lifestyles was compromising traditional gay culture. Others complained that gay men still were not normal enough. Gay critic Michael Signorile (1998) continued to chide gay men for their fetishistic interests in public sex, pornography, and wastrel circuit parties fostering "crystal meth" and other substance abuse.

An alternative perspective regarding the gay lifestyle of these recent generations of gay men, which contradicts Signorile's (1998) portrayal of gay life, is reflected in the work of such out gay writers as Dan Savage (1999) and Jesse Green (1999), who describe their satisfaction adopting children and being fathers who also happen to be gay. Even sometime gay escort and gay porn producer Aaron Lawrence looks forward to the time when he and his husband, Jeff, can settle down in their suburban New Jersey home and become parents. Indeed, if the generations born in the postwar era were concerned with finding fathers in the ideology promulgated by misguided psychiatrists that their own fathers had been emotionally distant (Bieber et al. 1962), men born in the generations of the 1970s and 1980s were more concerned with becoming fathers themselves through adoption or cooperation with a woman friend. In these more recent accounts, such as that of 1970s-generation Kirk Read and 1980s-generation BrYaN Phillips, fathers are often portrayed as close, supportive, and indeed role models to emulate in becoming parents.

The major mental health professions had long since removed same-gender desire from diagnostic manuals of psychopathology. By the end of the decade even the American Psychoanalytic Association, the last of the mental health professional holdouts, had acceded to the view that homosexuality was, as Freud (1935) had put it, not necessarily a virtue but certainly not a vice. The American Psychoanalytic Association (APA), long dominated by a group of recalcitrant New York analysts under the leadership of

Charles Socarides, had insisted that same-gender desire reflected fixation at primitive levels of psychological development as a consequence of deficits in the family environment long after the other mental health professions had abandoned that view. Finally, even this venerable association endorsed the view that same-gender sexual orientation was in itself irrelevant in considering persons for psychoanalytic education or for promotion to the ranks of training and supervising analyst. Sessions at the annual APA meetings across the second half of the decade of the 1990s featured clinical case reports by analysts out in the community. Indeed, by the end of the decade the APA had joined the other major mental health professions in endorsing same-gender unions and gay and lesbian parenthood in the aftermath of a spate of studies all testifying to the reality that children of gay and lesbian parents showed few adjustment problems or sexual identity conflicts (Cohler and Galatzer-Levy 2000).

In Chicago, the first "streetscape," or improved urban commercial street equipped with broad sidewalks, decorative lighting and signage, and artifacts portraying the ethnic character of the neighborhood, was completed in the late 1990s in "Boystown," an area with a heavy population of gay men. The city-planning department wanted to erect neon rainbows, but even the gay community protested this splashy representation. Instead, lighted pylons portrayed the colors of the gay rainbow flag, which had been designed in 1978 by San Francisco artist Gilbert Baker. At the dedication ceremony for the streetscape—attended by the mayor, several aldermen, and the chief of police, among other city notables—one onlooker observed that if he had been loitering on that same street corner twenty years before, he would have been arrested; now the mayor was praising the contributions of the gay community to a vibrant urban life! While there was clear regional variation, with southern states clearly less supportive, even in the South these traditional barriers began to break down (Sears 2001).

The epidemic of AIDS continued to ravage the gay community, particularly through the first half of the decade, but the mechanism used by the HIV virus to destroy the immune system had been carefully explored, and means of transmission of the HIV virus was clear. Gay men were cautioned to practice safer sex and to "wear their rubbers," and many men admitted with a sense of shame that they had at one time or another "fallen from grace." As Rofes (1998) has observed, young men coming of age in the 1990s knew means of transmission; from the fifth grade, students in many schools had been explicitly taught about the AIDS virus in health education classes, perhaps to the extent that desire was once again accompanied by fear. Then in 1996, first reports of a new treatment for AIDS—this time promising significant symptom relief and life extension, based on well-supervised clinical trials—further changed the experience of sexuality within the gay community. While safer sex was still important in order to curtail the spread of AIDS, the antiviral "cocktail" provided a new lease on life for many gay men. There was even some evidence that this rather harsh medication regime could be effective in preventing infection if begun soon after engaging in unsafe sex. By the end of the decade, the medication regime had become less arduous; gay news magazines featured pictures of HIV-positive men in the bloom of health—although no one could be sure that the ingenious protease inhibitors could continue to hold the infection at bay.

The result of increasing public acceptance of homosexuality as simply another lifestyle, facilitated by the protease medication that removed the visible stigma of AIDS, once again changed the discourse regarding the experience of gay desire. Douglas Sadownick, gay dramatist and activist, and sometime-boyfriend of 1950s-generation life-writer and performance artist Tim Miller, has suggested that the 1990s represented a second sexual revolution parallel to the 1970s. Equipped with latex condoms, dental dams for oral sex, and gloves for fisting, and following safer sex guidelines, gay men felt it was once again permissible to enjoy their sexuality.

Two factors stand out in this new sexual decade: first, particularly across the second half of the 1990s, younger men coming to adulthood had never experienced the sorrow of watching a lover or friend die of AIDS. The illness had either attained mystical properties or had receded into the background as something happening to gay men in another era.

The second event of this decade was the emergence of the Internet. It provided chat rooms and websites where men could post their "personal" ads complete with pictures, which facilitated finding a sexual partner or simply provided a convenient shortcut to cruising and finding a man to have sex with. Prospective partners, even gay escorts and their prospective clients, met over the net, exchanged information regarding what they were looking for, and, if in the same city, arranged a personal meeting often leading to a sexual encounter. Since men could find other men with similar interests, men meeting for the first time knew more about each other than in previous generations when men had sought partners in a park or public bathroom. Thus, a man coming to another man's apartment might exchange information about preferred sexual activities and HIV status; additional cases of AIDS and other sexually transmitted disease arose when one or both men either did not know their HIV status or dissimulated. Bathhouses sponsored safer sex demonstrations in which men could watch as other men demonstrated how to have anal intercourse with condoms and how to enhance enjoyment of gay sex.

Sadownick (1996) also observed that pornography, and gay sexual experience more generally, has been enhanced by the technology that arrived in the 1990s, particularly the development of the World Wide Web and the cell phone. The emergence of the Internet and the development of gay Web sites facilitated discussion of the gay experience, provided not only a means for meeting other gay men but a seemingly endless source for gay porn—from sites specializing in particular forms of erotic stimulation to first-person accounts of gay sexual life. Streaming videos and downloadable pictures provided a new opportunity for younger gay men to learn about the expression of gay sexuality. Exchange of e-mail and photos facilitated the process of finding a partner and arranging to get together, while both personal and commercial gay Web sites publicized such services as escorting and pornographic videos that appealed to every kind of gay sexual appetite.

Many of the videos made before the late 1980s featured men having unprotected sex and implicitly endorsed such activities. Since many gay men first learned about gay sexuality through male magazine and videos (Burger 1995), these videos not only structured the expectable sexual encounter moving from kissing to foreplay to fellatio and penetration but also endorsed the idea of pleasurable sexual fulfillment. Indeed, 1960s-generation Scott O'Hara's personal goal was to convince other gay men of the pleasures of gay sex: he was filmed obviously enjoying explicit encounters. Gay porn stars realized celebrity status, appearing in gay entertainment venues and demonstrating their sexual prowess. Harris (1997) has observed that

the entire history of gay self-acceptance since Stonewall can be discerned in the changes that have occurred to the brilliant, clinical lighting of present-day films, which take the place in spaces free of guilt, of the erotics of sin. Contemporary pornography is anchored in the here and now, in real bedrooms and real cars, rather than in indeterminate fantasy realms whose flickering light and dramatic chiaroscuro provide an almost allegorical representation of the stealthy conditions under which homosexuals were once forced to meet and cruise. (119)

Harris added that

gay liberation ultimately relocated intercourse from the murky, surreptitious darkness of the proverbial "twilight world" featured in pornography from the 1960s to brightly lit spaces in which there was no need to swaddle sex in thick veils for euphemisms, to shield the reader's eyes like a watchful mother at the crucial moment. (144)

Video reflects the reality of the Internet as a place to meet and arrange a liaison in the privacy of one's own home, replacing the uncomfortable and dangerous cruising for sex of other times and places. Amateur videos often featured men just learning how to have gay sex. These unedited videos sensitively show men beginning their first sexual encounter. Improved video technology made it possible to film in natural light in the comfort of an apartment borrowed for the occasion (aaronlawrence.com; Cohler 2004b).

Together with increasing acceptance of the gay sexual lifeway (Hostetler and Herdt 1998), coming out gay in the 1990s was a very different experience from that in previous decades. Herdt and Boxer (1996) have described the manner in which, in the late 1980s, gay urban youth created their own identity as out, proud, and gay, visibly identified as gay and lesbian in their high schools, encouraging each other through their weekly support groups, and creating safe spaces such as dances and coffeehouses. This activism prompted many high schools to support gay/straight alliances. The GLSEN and PFLAG associations supported new activism in support of gay youth on the part of teachers and parents. Some school districts mandated showing of videos such as "It's Elementary," which portrays both gay and lesbian students out at school, and gay and lesbian adults talking with children in both lower and middle grades. While many teenagers were still subject to antigay harassment, many urban and suburban school districts took a strong stance against this harassment. The tragic 1998 murder of gay college student Matthew Shepard in Laramie, Wyoming, not only reflected the controversy surrounding an out gay lifestyle but also galvanized civil rights groups. This senseless and brutal murder was felt powerfully across the nation, and it fostered new awareness of the cost for young people of being subjected to expressions of hatred by others intolerant of diverse lifestyles (Kaufman 2001; Loffreda 2000).

It is in the context of these social changes that we consider the memoirs of two young men born in the 1970s, coming of age in the 1990s, and the personal accounts of a number of high school and college students born in the 1980s and writing about their experiences growing up gay. These writers are necessarily younger when they begin writing their story than those gay writers, born in earlier decades, who have most often written from the vantage point of midlife. Indeed, only Andrew Tobias and Aaron Fricke from earlier generations composed their memoirs in young adulthood close to the time when events that they narrate had taken place. Writing a life story close in time to events narrated necessarily changes the narrative from one in which the present account is reshaped by a variety of subsequent experiences and events throughout the years of adulthood. However, with these kinds of narratives, such as those of Kirk Read and Aaron Lawrence, we have less evidence regarding subsequent turns and life outcomes. Even these more recent narratives, written in young adulthood, are influenced by stories by gay men who provide accounts of their lives and loves.

Kirk Read: Coming Out and Being Out

Kirk Read's (2001) memoir is significant in several respects. It was written when he was a young adult. Only Andrew Tobias (1973/1993) and Aaron Fricke (1981) have written memoirs so close in time to the events portrayed as does Kirk Read's memoir of growing up gay in the South. Read has in common with Tobias a career as a journalist. Although his early career goals concerned acting, much of Read's present freelance writing is focused on issues in the gay community where he is an activist in such areas as support for gay and lesbian youth, and providing free care for sex workers. His columns appear regularly in the gay press and share the same humorous tone as his memoir. In addition, he shares with fellow '70s author Aaron Lawrence an unabashed awareness of the market. His memoir, *How I Learned to Snap* (2001), was initially published by a small independent press specializing in books about the South (reprinted as a Penguin paperback in 2003), and Read has been successful in promoting his memoir through book tours and media presentations.

Read's memoir is written in part as a source of inspiration and support for queer youth struggling to find their way in a straight world. He traces his concern for gay and lesbian youth to his childhood wish for an older brother who would rescue him from his feelings of self-defeat. In part, this wish is reflected in Read's adolescent attraction to older men, including a college student who befriended him and introduced him to gay sex just as he was beginning high school, and two middle aged men working in the theater, one of whom became his lover while Read was in high school. Just as expressed by Scott O'Hara (1997), who, while a high school student, seduced his sister's young adult gay friend, Read sees nothing wrong with intergenerational sexual intimacy as long as it is consensually desired by members of each generation.

Born in 1973 and growing up in Virginia, Read shares much in common with '60s-generation authors Scott Peck (1995) and Marc Adams (1996). All three had stern fathers who had served in the military, maintaining their military perspective in civilian life. Read and Peck also share, along with '40s-generation author Alan Helms (1995) and '50s-generation author Mel White (1994), the experience of growing up in a traditional Christian family. By the mid-1980s, however, when Read began to deal with his gay sexual desire as a junior high school student, the winds of social change were being felt even in the South (Sears 2001). The South had long been the most conservative region of the nation, heavily influenced by Southern Baptist and other fundamentalist traditions, which even today emphasize the biblical prohibition upon homosexuality.

Biographer James "John" Sears (1991) has suggested that growing up gay in the South was shaped by four distinctive characteristics:

1. Fundamental Christian values whose continued strength is enhanced by a lack of cultural diversity. From recital of prayer in public schools to reliance upon the Bible as a guide informing social policy, gay boys growing up in this culture would feel a particular sense of being different and defective.
2. A rigid understanding of both gender identity and sexual identity has been enhanced by specific prejudice portraying black men as sexually virile, white men as gentlemen and protectors, and white women as innocent and defenseless.
3. Family and family ties are particularly pronounced. Especially in the small southern towns so treasured by Daniel Mendelsohn (1999), family name and standing in the community is significant for polite gentile boys growing up and destined to become the next generation of the town's leading citizens. Being gay poses a particular threat to family standing in the community.
4. Boys and girls attending traditional southern schools, whether private Christian schools or public schools, are expected to be well-mannered and polite, and to accept traditional gender roles. It may be particularly difficult for boys struggling with their same-gender sexual desire to come to terms with this desire within the rigid definitions of gender and sexuality that are part of growing up in traditional, southern communities.

These four factors all lead to a particularly hazardous route from childhood to adolescence for the prospectively gay boy. As Sears observes regarding gay adolescents:

Stymied by fear and shame, these teens' psychological growth and development languishes. In lunchrooms, adolescent gossip and crude comic stereotypes violate their human dignity. In classrooms, the exceptional teacher expresses concern about their hurt and hardship. With not-so-hidden expectations, the school institutionalizes heterosexism while homophobia extracts a heavy psychological prize . . . the pervasiveness of fundamental religious beliefs, the acceptance of racial, gender, and class community boundaries, the importance of family name and honor, the unbending view of appropriate childhood behaviors, and the intensity of adolescent culture constitute the Southern psychic landscape. (Sears 1991, 16)

Kirk Read was his father's son by his third marriage; by that time, with three older brothers, one of whom had also shunned the provisional appointment granted at birth to his father's beloved Virginia Military Institute (known through the South simply as VMI), his father had lost some of his enthusiasm for military discipline at home. Colonel Read was disappointed that his youngest son would not partake of the three-generation tradition of Read men attending the fiercely gender-stereotyped and highly disciplined lifestyle of VMI. (The last preserve of traditional masculine gender definition, it was only in 1991 that a Supreme Court decision forced VMI to accept women cadets.)

Consistent with Sears's (1991) portrayal of southern family life, Read wrote that his father valued VMI, the army, God, and family, in that order. While his older children had felt the sting of physical punishment, Read reports that his father never hit him. In contrast to the memoirs of both Scott Peck and Marc Adams, each of whom suffered from an abusive father toward whom forgiveness was a long and painful process, Kirk Read believes that it is important to maintain a close father-son tie. Indeed, even more than Scott Peck, Read is protective of his stern father, whose vulnerability is also evident. Read's father was fifty-three, eighteen years older than his mother, when he was born. Read's mother had been married before and had had two children from her first marriage to a man who deserted her while the children were still toddlers. These two halfsiblings were entering high school when Read was born. He remembers them better than he remembers his father's children by his previous marriages, all of whom were young adults and living on their own when Read was young.

In many ways, Read's account of his youth is consistent with the master narrative of enjoying activities such as reading and theater, which ran counter to the expected gender-stereotyped norms of southern boyhood. His is the story less of a journey to acceptance of a gay identity than a story of trying to find a home where gay kids could feel safe and realize their sexuality. His memoir is organized as a series of short chapters or essays telling a humorous linear story of growing up gay. These chapters are written to require just a brief attention span, perhaps designed for reading by questioning youth in a generation raised on television.

Attracted to the glamour of the theater from elementary school, and with a strong sense of style, Read traces his interest in fashion to his mother. Shopping for clothes provided Read an opportunity to assemble a creative wardrobe that further separated him from his classmates—and from his father. His father was clearly troubled by the prospect of a future VMI man taking such interest in his clothing. Read suggests that his mother already guessed he was gay and began gently to correct his father's accusations that his son was a "faggot." Early on, Read was aware of his own attraction to other boys in his school. He was inspired in recognizing his own gay identity by Jesse, a boy a few grades ahead of him who was both a talented and flamboyant dancer . . . and also an obviously queer boy. Jesse could dance like no other boy or girl in his school, and he was also the subject of continual ridicule. Read took note of that fact as well. When Jesse graduated from high school, four years Read's senior, still dressing in an outrageous style, his fellow students cheered him as he walked across the stage to receive his diploma. Read himself was later to enjoy a similar accolade in his senior English class: one of his classmates read aloud an essay praising Read as the Authentic Man while his classmates applauded in approval. Jesse once remarked to him in response to Read's inquiry about how he resisted the taunts of his classmates: "I am *not* afraid . . . Three circles and a snap . . . snap on the word *not*. I am *not* afraid" (Read 2001, 56–57). The title of Read's memoir, *How I Learned to Snap,* refers to this ability to resist the impact of antigay taunts and prejudice.

Read went to summer camp at the age of ten. When other boys began to tease Kirk as a "fag," meaning a boy who was weak and failed to conform to the obvious stereotype of athletic prowess, Read was sufficiently provoked that he took on one of his chief accusers and would have pounded him into the ground had he not been stopped by a counselor. He reports that after that time, he was shown greater deference. Jesse too had been violently assaulted in school by his classmates, with no attention paid to these attacks by school authorities. Read later became a competent soccer player and a Little League soccer coach with some success both in winning games and insuring that all the boys had a chance to play; he also earned a green belt in Tae Kwan Do.

Read reports that throughout his high school years and at arts camp, his best friends were girls. They enjoyed his sexually unthreatening company and good humor, and they showered him with attention. What he most wanted, however, was the attention of his physical education teacher, and a poetry teacher from his arts camp! Some of his teachers made antigay remarks in the classroom that were directed at no one in particular but that stung Read. Just as his sometime-ideal Jesse, Read reports that he was also taunted by his classmates. On one occasion, during a soccer game, he sacked an opponent from a Christian Right high school particularly hard as a reprisal for injuring a teammate. His teachers not only failed to intervene when he was physically assaulted in a queer bashing but believed that boys must hurt other boys, a reflection of the natural order of the world.

He also reports the problems faced by gay boys in high school locker rooms. Afraid that he would have an erection while watching his classmates naked and in the showers, he comments that "when you're in the moment, the prospect of showering alongside rapidly developing boys sparks acute terror" (Read 2001, 85). He also reports falling in love with one of his physical education teachers and sending the teacher a series of love poems.

When Read moved into his older brother's room during junior high school, he began to stash his treasures under the floorboards and in the closets. His treasures included packages of cigarettes, condoms and jock straps pilfered from his father's dresser, and an envelope full of ads for Jockey underwear featuring handsome and nearly naked baseball players. He even stashed away his older sister's bra and panties in order to experiment with what girls might wear. It is less clear that he was interested in fetishistic cross-dressing than that he was trying to understand for himself what it meant to be a boy. However, at age twelve he was most interested in finding an older man who would befriend him and teach him the ways of gay sex.

One of the significant aspects of '70s-generation life-writers coming into mid-adolescence in the '80s and early '90s was the emergence of the counterculture within mainstream American adolescence. Read reports little difficulty meeting other students contesting traditional southern values, even in his conservative high school at a time when the emergence of the Christian Right as a powerful force in national elective politics came to the fore. Read's father was in the same high school class as Religious Right leader Pat Robertson, which only added to Read's burden in dealing with his father's own militant stance toward the evils of homosexuality. Read traces his attraction to older men to the desire for an older brother missing in his own life since his older brothers were already in or near adulthood when he was still a toddler. One older brother had become a county prosecutor before he was removed from office for malfeasance, another had a family, while a third had become a born-again Christian.

Read met his first lover, Rich, when he was in the eighth grade attending a rock concert at the local university. A student at the university, Rich soon became his constant companion. The two would attend rock concerts together, even missing school days to follow the rock band R.E.M. They spent evenings drinking beer, talking about literature, and listening to music while Read had an erection all too evident to both of them. After several months, the inevitable happened: at the age of fourteen, Read enjoyed his first gay experience with Rich. He observes regarding this evening of intense sexual pleasure: "That embrace was the most mutual consensual

sexual act I've had in my entire life. Everything since has felt less pure"
(Read 2001, 44).

He particularly enjoyed being penetrated by Rich and reported that
there was no pain when Rich first entered him. He was fascinated by the
semen collecting in the tip of Rich's condom. Read pleaded with Rich not
to use condoms but Rich insisted that it was necessary, for, as Read soon
learned, AIDS was just becoming a pandemic within the gay community.
Read goes on to observe, echoing sentiments also expressed by Scott
O'Hara, that

intergenerational sex saved my life. When I started having sex as a teenager, the
daunting questions that ricocheted inside my skull ceased to be rhetorical. If
it hadn't been for sex at such a young age, my questioning phase could have
stretched on for years, and that would have gotten *really* tedious. Sex with an older
man probably sped up my coming-out process by years. (Read 2001, 58)

Read does acknowledge that he put Rich into a potentially dangerous position by having sex with a teenager but does not discuss Rich's own reason
for seeking an intergenerational relationship, and comments that he never
learned very much about Rich's own life. Consistent with Kohut's (1979)
comment about the problem posed when a mentoring relationship between two men becomes sexual, once Rich and Kirk began having sex together on a regular basis, their former friendship waned. Friendship would
have required discussion of their sexual activities and neither was ready for
that conversation. Read also wrote responses to personal ads appearing in
the *Village Voice,* hungry for contact with other gay men and not aware
that he was placing these men in the position of being arrested. A few of
his correspondents became and have remained pen pals and friends. At one
point Read consulted a therapist to see if there was a problem in being attracted to older men. His therapist heard of his infatuations and wisely observed that there are some things that just can't be figured out. Therapists
he subsequently consulted agreed with this wise first therapist who encouraged Read to be himself and enjoy his infatuations. Times had clearly
changed since life-writers of the '30s generation such as Martin Duberman
(1991c) had been chastised by their therapists for their gay desire.

Read observes that adolescent boys are replete with a sexual energy that
burns wild and that they should have the opportunity to discover their sexuality during puberty, with support from teachers and others, so that these
adolescents won't feel isolated as they struggle with their desire. He has put
this theory into practice by becoming an active mentor within the queer
youth community. As he comments:

Adults have a responsibility to be visible and available to young gay people. Access to adult worlds, especially those of gay adults, kept me from becoming a suicide statistic. We're separated by cultural terror. . . . Young people desperately need mentors apart from the airbrushed celebutantes they're fed by TV. Sexual awareness *must* be a natural part of puberty. (Read 2001, 91)

Read sees his own memoir as a contribution that might help queer adolescents make sense of their sexuality in much the same way as did Aaron Fricke writing a brief memoir of coming out and taking another boy to his senior prom. As a teenager, unaware of Fricke's memoir (he says that he later read Fricke's account), Read thought of taking Rich to his junior prom. He does report that Rich, already having graduated from college by that time, would have been embarrassed by attending Read's senior prom as his date.

Continuing his sexual relationship with his would-be older brother and mentor, Read also found other older men with whom to have sex. Once he obtained his driver's license, he was able to roam about, finding adult magazine shops where he could buy gay pornography, particularly magazines showing real daddies—the brothers and fathers who were the objects of his desire, perhaps as a substitute for the affection he longed for from the father and brothers in his own family. As a young teenager, he was fascinated by two recent college graduates who owned an alternative record store. These men became additional substitutes for the absent older brothers and took responsibility for his aesthetic education, although there was not the sexual attraction that persisted in Read's relationship with Rich. Read observes he was probably more "out" then were his older friends.

He still did not think of himself as gay, but only as someone who enjoyed sex with other men. He reports that while attracted to other boys his own age, the few sexual experiences he had with them as they fumbled about together always left him unsatisfied. On the other hand, he reports that sex with older men was beautiful and life changing. The psychoanalyst Richard Isay (1986, 1989) has suggested that at least some gay men, for reasons unexplained, develop early in childhood an often-unrequited attraction to their father rather than their mother, as is generally the case. Read's attraction to older men can be understood both as the desire for a sense of psychological completion, realized through experiencing the strength of an admired older brother, and also the search for satisfaction of those erotic wishes initially directed at his father rather than his mother.

During his high school years, Read became involved in the theater. He first starred in a children's show and was soon apprenticed to regional theater. There an older man, aware of his attraction to gay theater men, warned him to be careful. One of these theater gurus was particularly supportive of Read's fledgling efforts and invited him home. Undressed and realizing this man's intentions, Read rebuffed him and left; some months later, by chance, he went again to this man's house. The two of them undressed and fondled each other, but his older friend demurred from a full sexual encounter and pulled away.

Having seen copies of gay movement magazines bought by another classmate, now out and living in New York, Read was inspired to read a number of the gay books discussed in these magazines. He spent hours at the local public library, even pilfering the popular and sexually explicit book, *The Joy of Gay Sex*. At about this time, now a high school junior, Read wrote his first play, with a gay theme, clearly his public coming-out statement, as an independent study project. The play later won an award in a young playwrights' competition and was widely publicized throughout the state. Soon news of his success and his sexuality spread through his community; Read was now truly out, including to the Little League soccer team he coached and out as well to his young players' families.

Read's parents seemed to have been little perturbed by his emerging gay sexual identity. His mother understood and even implicitly supported Read's explorations in the alternative adult world. Raised in an upper-class family, she too had been a teenage rebel, sneaking out of her elite woman's finishing school whose hypocrisy she despised. Later, she eloped with Read's father, so many years older than she was and disapproved of by her parents. In his attraction to older men, Read not only sought the brother-father mentors he felt he had missed in his own life but may also have been repeating his mother's desire for older men. Reflecting psychoanalyst Selma Freiberg's concept of "ghosts in the nursery" (Fraiberg with Adelson and Shapiro 1975), Read's mother replayed her own life history and her rebellion against her parents with her second son and the only child of her marriage to Read's father. His father did initially fuss about the bad influence on him from his gay theater friends, claimed that he'd get AIDS, and ranted about what would become of him. However, his mother pacified his father, and he even gave his support as Read set off for the University of Virginia in Richmond where his play was to be staged.

While struggling to rewrite a critical scene of his play, sitting in a coffee shop, Read met an older man, Walker, with whom he immediately clicked. The two soon became inseparable, and Read confessed his desire for sexual intimacy with this supportive older man. Walker and Read became lovers, and over the next several years, Walker was a fixture in Read's life and a welcome addition to the family: his father liked Walker, who listened patiently for hours on end while the elder Read regaled him with his war stories. Read's mother was supportive, understanding, and even encouraging of the relationship (when Read finally turned eighteen, she sent Walker a card, joking that her son was finally legal). On the other hand, Read does not indicate what happened to his early relationship with Rich. In his memoir, Rich seems to have disappeared from his life.

Time and again the couple made love in Read's house in his room next to his parents' bedroom; Read stole condoms from his father's drawer, one by one, so as not to arouse suspicions. Walker was troubled both by the idea of having sex with a still underage youth and about having sex in his younger lover's own home; he was afraid that Read's father would discover their relationship and have him prosecuted. However, Read observes: "I, on the other hand, got an illicit thrill from having *very quiet* orgasms ten feet above my sleeping parents" (185). This thrill may indeed reflect a displacement from his desire for his father (Isay 1986; Phillips 2003).

Read and his older lover spent weekends at isolated beachfront cabins during inclement weather, reading plays to each other and making love. Walker feared that Read would grow up, move on, and leave him behind; Read swore his undying love. Except for one occasion, enthusiastically celebrating News Year's Eve in New York, the couple used condoms. Walker had long been sexually active, yet it was nearly a year into their relationship before the two men got tested—they learned that each of them was HIV negative. They fought, only to make up and continue their relationship.

Read alternated between nights of making love with Walker and the usual beer parties of high school seniors, including a party after his senior prom (which Walker felt awkward attending). At the party, Read confessed his love to a straight classmate. Read notes that nearly every queer teenager develops a crush on a straight classmate, experiencing inevitable embarrassment following the discovery that the classmate is straight. Read's memoir ends with his high school graduation. He does note that the thought of going away to college and being apart from Walker was too painful to contemplate. He confessed his love for Walker to his brother Dwight, who proceeded to quiz him endlessly and with fascination regarding the details of gay sex (187). He told his brother of the pain of even being two hours away at college in Richmond. Together with Walker, Read heard Allen Ginsburg read from "Howl," in part a story of two middle-aged gay men.

In an epilogue, Read reports that he was blessed to have indulgent parents, older when he was born, and perhaps more understanding than younger parents. He believes that he had an easier time than many gay boys who suffered even greater torment and lack of parental support or even tolerance. He traces his parents' tolerance to the fact that he benefited from the mistakes that each believed had been made with their other children. Even his other siblings accepted his relationship with Walker as long as he didn't mention the nature of this relationship. Walker had always been a patient listener as Read's father reminisced about his life, and his father was pleased with this attention. Now Walker was a constant companion at his father's bedside during those difficult final days prior to his death. (During Read's senior year in high school, his father had a stroke and died of a brain tumor the following year.) Read clearly felt the loss of his father.

Ten years elapsed between the events recounted in Read's memoir and his present position as a young adult activist in the San Francisco community. Read has found his home in the gay community there and within what Kath Weston (1991) has portrayed as a family by choice. At the same time, he can comfortably return back to his southern roots and enjoy the company of his former classmates toward whom he harbors lasting affection. Read also believes that it is important to return to his community, now as an out gay man, and to show that it is possible to be gay and happy and well adjusted. As he says, gay men must not disappear from their hometowns where they have the greatest influence.

Just as he sought closeness to his father, Read retains an almost nostalgic fondness for the conservative southern community in which he grew up. His memoir was designed in larger part to provide a supportive message for gay youth facing antigay prejudice at school and in the community. His lesson, learned from Jesse, to snap, to say "I am *not* afraid," is one that he seeks to pass on to the next generation. At the same time, Read's account is one framed very much within the generation of gay men born in the 1970s. In Read's case, early aware of his gay sexual desire and his ability to enlist older men as lovers, Read benefited from this mentorship. He writes of his gay desire without hesitation and expresses pleasure in quenching his desire for sex with other men. He even earned the begrudging admiration from his classmates for being himself and not hiding his gay identity. He had learned Jesse's message well!

Out on the Internet

The advent of the Internet has dramatically changed gay self-life writing. Younger life-writers have taken advantage of the Internet as a means for telling their ongoing life story as a series of journal entries known as a Weblog or "blog." Reporting on the emergence of the blog as an opportunity for self-life writing, the *New York Times* (November 25, 2002) reports that there are hundreds of thousands of such blogs, fostered by development of software that makes management of a website easy, even for those with little knowledge of programming. The *Times* (sec. E1) observes that "the allure of blogging lies in the thrill of circumventing the establishment, of being able to publish worldwide without having to be a . . . famous writer. Blogs can be nurtured at all hours of the day and night." For gay men, the advantages provided by the blog or Web journal are enormous. Often feeling isolated in small communities or unable to be publicly "out," the Web-based journal provides an opportunity to portray these concerns and to read about the means other men have used to overcome issues of stigma and antigay prejudice, and to come out to their family. These gay life-writers sometimes form a "web-ring" of fellow gay life-writers, which provides links to several home pages. Gay journal writers linked to this web-ring often refer in their own journals to the writing of other members of their web-ring, thus creating shared reading and writing that spans countries and even continents.

While much of the life writing of men in earlier generations had been in the form of memoirs written backwards, most often by men approaching midlife, the Internet has encouraged writing about the present in the form of often near daily accounts. The '40s-generation life-writers Arnie Kantrowitz and Andrew Tobias along with '60s-generation Aaron Fricke wrote their memoirs in some proximity to the experiences that they narrate. It is only with '70s-generation life-writers Aaron Lawrence and Kirk Read that life writing once again follows close upon the events narrated. The "blog" or online journal creates new opportunities in writing about same-gender desire since the experience of desire and writing about it follow close upon each other. While autobiography, and the memoir as a contemporary representation of autobiography, is able to offer some overviews and perspective on the course of life as a whole, the journal has the disadvantage of being closely linked with current events of the same or preceding few days. On the other hand, the journal has the advantage of immediacy: the events portrayed and the writer's own feelings are less likely to be subjected to the inevitable revisions of the life story.

Writing about the impact of the Internet on relationships, Bargh, McKenna, and Fitzsimons (2002) show that corresponding with others on the Net leads to enhanced communication of one's self to others and the formation of new and significant acquaintances. Kraut et al. (2002) have shown that this communication with others may facilitate morale. With the advent of the Internet and the technology of the home page, the nature of gay self-life writing has changed. For men struggling to accept their own sexual desire, arriving at a gay identity, or men experiencing stigma and antigay community prejudice, the Net provides a means for sharing these feelings and reduces the sense of loneliness. Nowhere is this more evident than among gay adolescents; such Web sites as oasismag.com offer accounts by other gay teens of their own experiences in school, at home, and in the community.

There are thousands of Web sites providing gay content. Dawson (2000) has listed some of the more prominent sites, and there are plenty of Web sites listing the home pages of gay men. In this study I have used Dawson's guide, together with two Web sites listing more than 1,500 home-pages of self-identified gay men (www.geocities.com and http://search.cybersocket.com). Following the links provided by these two comprehensive lists, I searched the home pages for men born in the 1970s with posted journals. While there are some home pages of men born in earlier decades, I selected only those home pages of men born in the 1970s and later. Consistent with the goal of focusing on the impact of social change on writing about desire and self, I again selected only the home pages of men who had grown up in the United States. This search provided three characteristic home pages from men born in the 1970s. I located an additional four home pages, which included journals by men born in the 1980s. (To date, I have not located any published memoirs from men born in the 1980s. The Internet may provide an alternate and more rapid means of first publication of the gay life story than the more traditional book employed by life-writers of previous generations).

Several gay '80s-generation life-writers, located through the search of home pages, have written memoirs or kept journals focusing on the meaning for them of gay desire. Two of the men discussed here are college students associated with an Internet youth group (oasismag.com), which is visited by large numbers of gay teenagers and young adults, often from communities where there are no gay role models, and where they are able to find affirmation of their gay desire. One particularly detailed account of an '80s-generation life-writer comes from the Web site of BrYaN, a twenty-two-year-old graduate student and gifted writer, who has written what may be the most complete account of the lived experience of a gay young man. BrYaN's journal reflects an absence of concern with issues of shame regarding his sexual identity; he is comfortably out at school and at work, and lives a "virtually normal" (Sullivan 1995) life with his partner Matt.

BrYaN is a Microsoft and Oracle certified software specialist and a graduate student in English literature, whose journal from 1999 to the present is more than five hundred pages. His account is perhaps the "ideal type" of the Internet journal and provides a wealth of information regarding the life and experiences of self-identified gay young men currently coming into adulthood. BrYaN's account is also ideal for this comparative study regarding the interplay of historical and social change in the construction of the life story among gay men. In his study of youth and sexual identity, Savin-Williams (2005) has reported that many youth resist labeling their sexuality or defining themselves as different from their peers. Savin-Williams reports a great deal of diversity in sexual experiences among the youth in his study, and these varied experiences have little impact on friendships and intimacy. BrYaN's account well portrays the new teenager and young adult as reported by Savin-Williams.

The Life of BrYaN

BrYaN's detailed journal spans more than four years, starting with his first year in college. A recent honors graduate of the University of Missouri–Kansas City, afterwards enrolled in the university's graduate English department, BrYaN also works full time in the university's computer center. His software skills are evident in his sophisticated and elaborate Web site, which includes a detailed, indexed archive of his journal from 1999 to its conclusion. Bryan reports that he adopted the unusual capitalization in his first name when a seventh-grade teacher refused to recognize that he spelled Bryan with a "Y" rather than an "I." Even though she deducted points from his essays for this capitalization, he insisted that she learn to spell his name correctly by capitalizing the Y, and then added the capital N on a dare to see if she would subtract even more points (she didn't). Keeping a journal is a central part of BrYaN's life.

Being able to talk to other people in the online gay community has been important for BrYaN when he is not sure about taking next steps in his life. BrYaN is part of a web-ring that includes several other gay self life-writers although none of these other life-writers approach their journal with the detail and self-reflection that is characteristic of BrYaN's journal, which details the life of a gay young man at the millennium. The most important thing in BrYaN's life is his three-year relationship with his partner, Matt. Nearly every journal entry includes discussions of Matt—something they have done together, something Matt has said. The couple shares an apartment together with two straight men. The couple maintains a joint bank account and shares ownership, together with BrYaN's father, of a treasured cabin on a lake in the nearby Ozark hills; to BrYaN, this is evidence of a lifelong commitment between two young men who are deeply in love with each other. Most recently, BrYaN's straight friend Jeff and his lawyer father, together with BrYaN's father, arranged for BrYaN, Matt, and BrYaN's father to be a limited liability company or LLC; the lake property is tangible evidence of a way around refusal by the state of Missouri to legally recognize gay commitments, and this too symbolizes their loving relationship.

BrYaN has titled his elegantly designed Web site "the populace" and views it as an opportunity to be an individual in mass society. However, this title is also a reflection of his belief, realized in his own experiences, that while he is a gay man, he is also a part of the population as a whole and entitled to all the good things of life in the same measure as his straight friends, including being able to get married to Matt. His journal entry for January 20, 2002, states:

Why is it so wrong for Matt and I to want successful careers, an expensive house, and to be like any other married couple out there? . . . The only time I feel defeated in reaching for these goals is when some narrow-minded writers of a corny second-rate show turn the burners up on stupid contrived situations.

The "Gay as Blazes" session that they stuck in the middle of [*Queer as Folk*] wasn't campy, funny, or entertaining in the least. To me, it sounded like the writers of QAF were trying to say that a gay couple striving for a life among the entire population was impossible and that those who try are only trying to fool themselves.

In this statement, BrYaN summarizes the concern of so many gay young men coming of age at the millennium; the issue is no longer simply that of being "virtually normal" but rather totally normal, wherein expression of same-gender desire is but one aspect of lived experience (Savin-Williams 2005). For example, a typical weekend evening finds BrYaN down at the local sports bar, enjoying beer and shooting pool with Matt and their close-knit circle of gay and straight friends.

BrYaN has also reported on his taste in music (the Broadway shows *Evita* and *Sunset Boulevard,* most jazz, swing, and "Matt singing to himself when he doesn't know I'm listening"), literature (Willa Cather, John Cheever, and the literary critic Stanley Fish), and where he hangs out (their bedroom and their apartment, the computer center). His current classwork includes American culture and the American novel, and his master's project, an extension of his undergraduate honors paper. This is the quintessential gay man of the '80s generation, and BrYaN believes that he is in no way different from his straight counterparts—with the exception of his sexuality. His interests range from sports to computers to his study of twentieth-century American literature.

BrYaN's father is an affluent accountant in Kansas City; his mother is a homemaker. During the course of BrYaN's journaling, his parents divorced, and his mother, together with BrYaN's older brother Adam, and Adam's wife, moved back to Iowa to be near her relatives. Matt's father is a successful lawyer in Kansas City whose divorce from his mother took place just as Matt met BrYaN. Matt's father has been very supportive of BrYaN and Matt's relationship. Indeed, both fathers, who have become good friends, have been supportive and have welcomed the two men into their lives with enthusiasm.

BrYaN's journal is influenced by journals kept by other gay life-writers of his generation He is indeed the ideal exponent of the new genre of gay journal writing. His journal is divided into years beginning with 1999, and is complete with a table of contents. He has been a faithful contributor, weekly summarizing his life and his thoughts. Organized chronologically, his first entry describes his life from high school to the time he began his journal. His very first entry well summarizes his outlook on his own sexuality: "What's the big deal about being gay . . . it is only one facet of my life, and there are many things in my life that are important." He notes that his gay desire has caused him guilt, grief, and worry—but not because he has had difficulty accepting his sexuality. Rather, he is concerned about the response of his friends and, particularly, his own family; he believes that his coming out, and his father's continuing support of BrYaN's gay sexual identity, was the cause of his parents' divorce.

BrYaN's first gay relationship, with Kyle, began during the summer between his junior and senior year of high school. He was already aware of his attraction to other boys; at the time he felt alone with his secret because there was no one to talk with about his gay desire and also, he was terrified that his parents might suspect that he was gay. Defying the stereotype of the prospectively gay boy as sissy—so often presumed in earlier generations to presage homosexuality in adulthood—BrYaN and Kyle met on the tennis court where Kyle was looking for a partner for a doubles game. The two boys soon became inseparable, and what began as hugging soon became a sexual relationship. As they faced graduation and attending separate colleges, they began spending less time together since each was working hard at school to earn a scholarship. A major problem arose one evening: while wrestling about and kissing in front of the television in BrYaN's family room, BrYaN's older brother unexpectedly came home from college, and the boys were certain that they had been observed. Even though Adam apparently had not seen the two boys in their erotic play, they became frightened that they had been discovered, and Kyle fled to his own house.

The effort to hide their relationship from family and friends was becoming too much to bear, and the relationship gradually faded. (BrYaN's mother had repeatedly criticized BrYaN for spending too much time with Kyle and was clearly relieved that their intense relationship had dissolved. BrYaN believes that his mother suspected the significance of his closeness with Kyle.) BrYaN periodically kept in touch with Kyle during their freshman year at college, but it became clear to BrYaN over the spring break of his first year that his relationship with Kyle had ended. Kyle had begun a relationship with another student at his college; BrYaN had enjoyed a brief relationship with Doug, another student at the university. It was this first gay college relationship that led his roommate Tyler to ask BrYaN if he was gay. BrYaN admitted that he was, and while Tyler had little problem with this disclosure, their other roommate was more troubled and moved out at the end of the school year. It was clear from the outset that Tyler was not in the least concerned that his roommate, soon to be a best friend, was gay. Tyler, his girlfriend Kristi, some of her sorority sisters, and a classmate with whom he worked in the computer center and also a member of Tyler's fraternity have all become fast friends, together with another student working at the computer center, a gay foreign exchange student BrYaN met while tutoring him, and several members of Tyler and Jeff's fraternity. The group has little problem with BrYaN's gay sexuality. They regard Matt as BrYaN's boyfriend and a member of their "family" just as they are paired up together. Jokes about the sexuality of the couples, gay or straight, are often exchanged and when they are all at the cabin by the lake, they joke with each other about sounds coming from the several adjoining rooms.

Over the Christmas break of BrYaN's first year at college, his brother Adam brought home a handsome friend. BrYaN couldn't keep his eyes off this young man. Adam was quick to spot BrYaN's attention to his friend. Adam recalled that BrYaN hadn't responded to his efforts to fix BrYaN up with girls and asked BrYaN directly if he was gay. When BrYaN acknowledged that he was, his brother's said that it was OK with him, but he asked BrYaN not to come out to their parents. He then asked about Kyle and admitted that he had suspected something of that sort was taking place between BrYaN and his ever-present friend. Adam said that he would have preferred BrYaN not be gay and was certain that there would be problems when BrYaN decided to tell their parents about his gay identity. Later,

Adam moved from cool indifference to outright hostility regarding BrYaN's gay identity and his relationship with Matt.

At the end of his first year of college, BrYaN reports that he felt lonely; all of his friends were out on dates, and he was by himself. He had enjoyed a sometime relationship with Doug, but Doug was uncomfortable with his sexuality and the two of them drifted apart, although Doug still hoped they might get back together. That situation of feeling alone was soon to change. Attending a summer school literature class, BrYaN noticed an incredibly cute boy who asked if the seat next to him was taken. The next day the two boys ran into each other at the student union and began to talk. Matt had just transferred from a community college and lived one floor above in the same dorm as BrYaN. Matt, like BrYaN, had been on his high school cross-country track team and shared BrYaN's passion for running. BrYaN notes that Matt was very much like himself, serious about his studies but also enjoying athletics. In addition, the two of them had a number of literature classes in common (both earned A's in the class, with BrYaN often just edging out Matt in his overall class score). Over the next few days, Matt asked to sit with BrYaN at lunch. His roommate Tyler, and Tyler's girlfriend Kristi, also joined the two boys for lunch and both told him how much they liked Matt. BrYaN and Matt discovered that they shared similar interests in literature, and BrYaN decided to invite Matt to his room to study together for a test.

The next weekend BrYaN invited Matt, Tyler, Kristi, his friend Jeff who worked at the computer center, and Jeff's girlfriend Laurie to join him at his family's cabin in the Ozarks. As things ended up, BrYaN and Matt were to share a room together. Tyler, of course, already knew that BrYaN was gay, and soon Kristi knew as well. That evening the conversation shifted to the Matthew Shepard case because one of Jeff's friends was writing about the murder for a class. As Jeff described the reactions of the class to the saga of Matthew Shepard's murder, the conversation turned to the campus gay support group. Kristi asked BrYaN, not aware that she was "outing" him, if he had attended the group. Of course, Jeff and Laurie didn't yet know that BrYaN was gay. Further, this issue had never explicitly come up between BrYaN and Matt. Matt then volunteered that he had attended a few meetings of the gay support group at his junior college. Terrified and confused, all BrYaN could do was reach for another beer! The group fell silent; Kristi rescued the situation by asking Matt about the group, and the conversation continued on to other topics.

Later, the group ventured over to the nearby resort where local college students gathered for beer and conversation. As the evening ended, the group headed back to the cabin. Matt began undressing for bed; the sight of this nearly naked boy was too much for BrYaN, who soon had an embarrassing erection but was saved by turning off the lights and quickly crawling into bed. Matt leaned over and gave him a kiss. Needless to say, BrYaN didn't get much sleep that night. His leg and Matt's leg kept touching, and he had an overpowering erection!

Over the summer, the group of six grew closer in friendship. They often shared lunch at the student union. It was at about this time, just as the two young men were getting to know each other, that Matt's parents separated and divorced. Matt often left for the weekend to help his mother, now living alone, with household chores, while BrYaN worked on his computer, talked with fellow gay life-writers in his web-ring, or watched old moves on television. He observes about his relationship with Matt: "I can't believe I have become so attached to him so fast. It's crazy the way he makes me feel when I'm around him. His smile and laugh is so incredible." BrYaN found himself very sexually attracted to his newfound friend. When the couple was together over a weekend, they would go shopping in the malls near campus (Matt is a neat dresser and prefers preppy clothes, while BrYaN prefers baggy clothes and feels most comfortable in a T-shirt and jeans). During the summer between BrYaN's first and second year, his mother would call, somewhat anxiously inquiring if BrYaN was dating someone. He notes that he felt guilty about liking men instead of women and disappointing his mother. He reports that his insides were in turmoil. He thought about coming out to his parents but recalled that his brother Adam had stopped talking to him since learning that he was gay.

Later that summer, while at the lake with Matt and his other friends, he and Matt once again shared a bedroom. That night, as BrYaN undressed and got into bed totally naked, Matt could not take his eyes off him. Once in bed together they caressed and held each other; BrYaN notes that they really weren't ready for anything more. The weekend was spent cuddling and caressing each other as they sat on the cabin porch with their friends watching the sunset. Later that summer, annoyed that Matt had to go home to help his mother on so many weekends, he talked with his roommate Tyler about his feelings. Following this conversation, BrYaN decided that Matt needed more space for himself and that the next steps in their relationship would have to be at Matt's initiative.

Striking in this account is the extent to which BrYaN's straight friends and their fraternity brothers were at ease with BrYaN's sexuality. On one occasion, while BrYaN and Matt were visiting Tyler's home in Omaha, Tyler assumed that the boys would share a bedroom. Other friends asked

BrYaN about the ins and outs of gay sex and whether it was like their (straight) sex. Jeff asked him point-blank if he had "done it" yet with Matt, and BrYaN told him that they had only slept together. This was the beginning of what became characteristic of this circle of close friends—mutual respect and appreciation for the intense relationship BrYaN was developing with Matt. When Matt was at home helping his mother on school weekends, BrYaN would hang out at the sports bar with the group of friends.

One night shortly after the beginning of BrYaN's second year, following a night at the sports bar and in the midst of good fellowship, BrYaN invited Matt to his room for beer. Tyler was spending the night with Kristi, so BrYaN found himself alone with Matt. Sitting together in BrYaN's beanbag chair while they watched an old movie, they began once again to caress and kiss, but this time they didn't stop. BrYaN reports that the clothes flew off and for the rest of the night there was precious little sleep. In a vignette that characterizes the attitude of their friends regarding BrYaN and Matt's sexuality, BrYaN reports that about noon the next day Tyler knocked on the door to their room saying that he had to get his things to take a shower. As Tyler came into the room, Matt pulled the covers over himself. Tyler said good morning to him with a giggle, at which point Matt whispered good morning back to him; embarrassed but also somewhat amused, Matt fled to his own room to get dressed. Tyler was totally comfortable finding BrYaN and Matt together in bed. The group asked if he and Matt had enjoyed their night together and were full of praise for Matt and their love for each other. Soon it became general knowledge that BrYaN and Matt were an item; one of Matt's classmates, also gay, was cheered that it was possible for two gay guys to have an open relationship. Other dorm residents began to look at BrYaN in a different way when they were together, not critical, just different. BrYaN notes that people in general just did not care one way or the other.

BrYaN and Matt began spending all their spare time together. BrYaN reports that they got to know each other so well that each could tell what the other was thinking without a word passing between them. BrYaN looked forward to spending evenings together with Matt, snuggling under the covers while watching television. He is always discreet in describing his physical intimacy with Matt (clearly all the members of his circle, including Matt, read his journal as it is posted. With an audience that includes both other gay journal writers in his web-ring and his own circle of friends, BrYaN makes it clear that there are things he can't write about for fear of embarrassing Matt or one of his friends).

As BrYaN's relationship with Matt became more intense, BrYaN realized he was going to have to tell his parents. His mother kept pestering him about whether he was dating and he recalled that she had always complained that he spent too much time in high school with Kyle. This was all the more painful since, from the outset, Matt's dad and his girlfriend were both completely supportive of their relationship. Indeed, when the couple first spent a weekend with Matt's father in his newly furnished condo, it was assumed that Matt and BrYaN would share the spare bedroom. BrYaN approached his mother for permission to bring Matt home for Thanksgiving. As usual, his mother fussed that he saw Matt enough at school, and why did he have to bring Matt home as well. She had hoped that he would bring home a nice young lady. Driving the short distance between the university and BrYaN's house the Wednesday before Thanksgiving, Matt and BrYaN were both nervous about meeting BrYaN's parents.

BrYaN and Matt arrived home just as BrYaN's mother emerged from the garage laden with groceries for the Thanksgiving meal. BrYaN's mother greeted Matt cheerfully, but BrYaN noted that she seemed irritated and preoccupied. When BrYaN's brother came in the door, having driven in from college with his roommate, he said to BrYaN, "so that's the boyfriend," but before he could say more BrYaN's father appeared home from work. At dinner that night the tension was evident to all. BrYaN says he was ready to "come out" right then and there. Matt and BrYaN decided to go out and find BrYaN's friends from high school. Matt hit it off with BrYaN's friends, finding several with whom to talk about cross-country and other sports. Later in the evening, as they returned home, BrYaN encountered Adam in the kitchen. Adam accused him of being a pervert and said that two guys "doing it" together made him sick.

BrYaN reports a feeling of dread as he awoke on Thanksgiving morning. Coming upstairs to the kitchen, he encountered his mother who told him that she had overheard his argument with Adam the previous evening and thought that he had stopped that "stuff" when his relationship with Kyle ended. She blamed him for "destroying his own life and that of the family." BrYaN retreated to a shocked silence as his mother repeated her feeling that what BrYaN was doing was wrong and was fearful of what people would say when they heard of his tie to Matt. She insisted that he not say a word to anyone about his relationship with Matt, particularly not his father. BrYaN writes:

I was so pissed I didn't know what to do. Is this some kind of torture on her part to keep putting things off? HELL it's out NOW. I'm a QUEER . . . I'm GAY . . . I have sex with men . . . I should have stood there and just said that to her. . . . How could she allow me to go on feeling bad about something she already knew about? Well it's out now and she will just have to deal with it. (November 24–December 5, 1999)

Coming back downstairs, BrYaN reported his confrontation with his mother to Matt and began crying. Matt hugged him and assured him that he would always be there for him. Matt went upstairs first, said a cheerful good morning and began conversing about sports with BrYaN's father, who appeared to be completely oblivious to Matt's special relationship with BrYaN. The Thanksgiving dinner went along without further upset, although BrYaN's mother completely avoided him throughout the day. Heading downstairs with Matt after the guests had departed, BrYaN reports that he felt a mixture of fear and shame—fear of what the next day might bring, and shame from not being what his parents had expected of him. He also felt angry for being made to feel that he had done something wrong in having a loving relationship. As he describes his relationship with Matt:

There are times when I feel that there is absolutely no way I can function without Matt. It's almost as if he completes my being. I care for him very much. I love to look at him and love to hear his voice. He is a kind and gentle person with a kind of rare sensitivity. I hate it when he's gone. It's as if a part of me is missing. I even keep his favorite tee shirt to wear when he is gone. . . . (November 24–December 5, 1999)

The following day everyone else was out of the house, and BrYaN and Matt had the opportunity of being together. BrYaN drove Matt around his neighborhood and showed him his old school, which seemed smaller than he had remembered it. They then made the inevitable day-after-Thanksgiving shopping trip to the malls. Although the day was peaceful, and the two even hung out for a while with BrYaN's old friends from high school, BrYaN felt an impending cataclysm with his family. Alone and out of his father's presence, his mother once again threatened him that their conversation was far from over and that he had to change his abnormal behavior and "dirty" habits. BrYaN stood his ground, although he realized that the cost would be that he would just not be able to come home in the future.

Returning to school following the Thanksgiving break, BrYaN felt depressed; his friends were all supportive, which helped to ease the pain, and he decided he had best tell his father. He wrote his father a long letter of explanation and sent it to his father's office. He notes that he and his father had never been very close; his father was much closer to his brother, and BrYaN feared that his father would end up agreeing with Adam's assessment of BrYaN's life as a perversion. He explained in his letter the reason for the tension at home over Thanksgiving, his arguments with his brother, and his mother's hostility. He told his father how it had been particularly painful to hear his brother's scathing criticism since the two of them used to be so close. BrYaN was surprised when his father called him and told him not to worry, that his home was still very much there for him, and that he should stick to his guns. This was totally out of character for his father, who seemed more concerned than disapproving. BrYaN called his father and suggested getting together to talk about the situation. Sharing sandwiches at his father's office, his father told BrYaN how proud he was of BrYaN's accomplishments and confessed that he was much more worried about Adam's future since Adam had little initiative. BrYaN could tell that his father wanted to know about the "gay thing" but found it difficult to ask. Finally, he asked BrYaN about one of the junior members of his staff who was out as gay. He then acknowledged that he had suspected that BrYaN was gay and, while he didn't understand how a man would be attracted to another man, he didn't see anything wrong with it. BrYaN felt that his father was puzzled but sincerely trying to understand his situation. As their conversation ended, his father asked, "Are you with Matt?" Speechless, all BrYaN could do was nod his head. His father, also embarrassed, muttered that Matt seemed like a real nice person. He admitted that he was unhappy hearing that BrYaN was gay, but didn't criticize him, and assured him that he would take care of BrYaN's mother, and that of course it was still his home and family. BrYaN left his father's office feeling less worried but still concerned that somehow he had disappointed his father and his family.

With finals over, BrYaN's group had a chance to celebrate the Christmas season with an elegant dinner. He reported that even though his friends Tyler and Kristi and Jeff and Laurie could share their affection in front of the group, he and Matt still felt uncomfortable doing so. Finally alone before the Christmas break of BrYaN's sophomore year, the two exchanged presents. BrYaN was particularly pleased that Matt's father had sent along a present for him. Matt had also arranged a fancy dinner and overnight stay for them at one of Kansas City's finest hotels, and presented BrYaN with a gold tennis bracelet. Standing at the hotel registration counter, BrYaN was sure he was going to get a lecture from the manager. In the morning, ordering breakfast from room service, BrYaN was sure the waiter noticed there were two men and only one unmade bed.

Although they enjoyed their friends, the two of them delighted in spending the day together, ice-skating and looking in the nearby shops. Heading back to campus, BrYaN helped Matt bring his things down to his father's car. Matt's father greeted them warmly and told BrYaN he was pleased that he and Matt were so close. BrYaN felt depressed about being home for Christmas and about the emotional distance that he felt between himself and his family. Even his cousin Keith, with whom he had always been close, noticed the tension and asked him about it. BrYaN told him the whole story and Keith shrugged. It wasn't a big deal that BrYaN was gay. In fact, he figured that might be the case since he noticed that BrYaN never talked about girls. Keith shared his room, ignoring the objections of BrYaN's mother who protested that Keith shouldn't have to share a room with someone who had BrYaN's interests. BrYaN reports that Keith slept soundly and was no more troubled by BrYaN's revelation than his other friends. On Christmas Eve, BrYaN's father gave him a generous check and asked with concern how BrYaN was doing with his feelings. BrYaN confessed that he was a mess inside, that he felt like he was dirty and doing something wrong in loving Matt. His father again assured him that even though he didn't understand everything yet, he was working on it. His father gave him a hug and urged him to stand his ground with his mother and brother.

Over the weeks following Christmas, BrYaN's father kept his promise. His parents took BrYaN out for dinner on his birthday. The dinner was tense but without further bitterness. BrYaN's mother prattled on about Adam and his girlfriend, but his father was supportive and gave him another check for spending money. Returning BrYaN to the dorm after dinner, while his mother hardly spoke to him, his father gave him a warm hug. Finally, BrYaN's group arranged a large birthday bash, attended by all his friends—except Matt, who was still skiing at Vail on holiday with his father.

Turning twenty, BrYaN had succeeded, albeit with great pain, coming out to his parents; he had found a boyfriend whose very presence inspired him; he had earned a nearly perfect academic record; and had been encouraged by his academic advisor to enroll in graduate English department courses. In addition, BrYaN's comments about writers and writing in his journal during his college years reveal an impressive depth of understanding regarding both American fiction and contemporary literary criticism. Above all, it was Matt who brightened his life. When Matt returned from Vail, the two headed out for a private celebration, and BrYaN told Matt for the first time that he loved him. He muses: "I thought about what happened that night while trying to go to sleep. I felt really great telling Matt I loved him, because I do. Ya know there is an awful lot of power behind those three words" (January 9, 2000).

Much of BrYaN's diary during the winter and spring of his second year at college is devoted to descriptions of classes, problems at work at the computer center, his nights out with Matt and his friends, and the ever-closer tie with Matt. Matt's roommate was accepting but somewhat puzzled about Matt's relationship with BrYaN. Since Tyler often spent the night with Kristi at her apartment, BrYaN and Matt were able to be together in BrYaN's room. Matt still got embarrassed on those occasions when the two of them were together and Tyler showed up, even if they were fully dressed and just watching television. Tyler and Jeff, who also worked with BrYaN in the computer center, both became close friends with Matt. Jeff even convinced Matt to switch into the pre-law program.

BrYaN's instructors were full of praise for his work. BrYaN is a perfectionist: his success at his job and in his studies reflects both his native wit and also very hard work. This combination of intelligence and hard work was important for him as an undergraduate taking particularly difficult courses, some of which were at the graduate level, even as he was saddled with significant responsibilities at the university's computer center. Again, this perfectionism is reflected in his Web site and journal—the Web site is extremely well designed, and his journal is perhaps the most complete and detailed of any journal in his web-ring.

On one occasion, BrYaN's father joined the group for their regular lunch at the student union. Even though it was in the midst of the tax season, his father made a point of keeping in touch with BrYaN and his life. His father talked with Matt during lunch, asking him about his ski trip and showing that he really liked him.

BrYaN and Matt discovered the gay dance clubs. BrYaN loved being able to dance close to Matt in a public place; even though both of them were bothered by the attitude of so many other guys with "attitude." BrYaN was annoyed that strange men approached them and tried to pick up one or the other even though it was clear that they were together. On another occasion, while at a gay club frequented by somewhat older men, Todd, their waiter, turned out to be another gay student from campus whom they knew from having had classes together. Todd was clearly glad to meet other gay students; it was also clear from what Todd said that BrYaN and Matt were recognized on campus as being a gay couple and that their relationship was accepted by other students.

On a few isolated occasions, while hanging out at the sports bar with Tyler and Jeff's fraternity friends, someone would make a casual slur about "faggots," unaware that this antigay remark might hurt BrYaN or Matt. Their friends immediately criticized the one making this reference, stating that such slurs were unacceptable. At the same time, BrYaN was always somewhat on his guard and a bit touchy about the response of other students to their relationship. When one of his roommate's fraternity brothers asked BrYaN about gay dance clubs in town, BrYaN mentioned this to Tyler who pointed out to him that everyone was totally accepting of his relationship with Matt, and that he needed to "chill out" about his sensitivity to questions about gay issues. BrYaN observed that he could talk with Tyler and others in his circle of friends about Matt and the gay scene but that he felt uncomfortable talking with others he knew less well. Again, it is clear that this is more BrYaN's issue than that of Tyler or his friends.

Throughout the spring of BrYaN's junior year, his relationship with Matt grew deeper. Admired and appreciated by faculty and employer, BrYaN's life appeared to be on track. The one constant worry was his mother and brother's continuing rejection of his sexuality and of his relationship with Matt. On one occasion, when BrYaN's mother made a critical comment, his father rushed to BrYaN's defense, telling her that he was tired of her relentless criticism that BrYaN was gay. On another occasion, after his mother had once again been hypercritical, BrYaN's father went out of the way to console him and to assure him that he loved him. BrYaN's father was clearly supportive of his relationship with Matt, as was Matt's father, who regarded BrYaN as another son. On a vacation with Matt's father, who had thoughtfully provided them with their own room and a double bed, BrYaN was embarrassed when Matt's father knocked on their bedroom door one morning. Matt's father asked him if they had slept well, and BrYaN reports that he blushed. In turn, BrYaN's father enjoyed his conversations with Matt, who kept up on sports. BrYaN notes that he still feels kind of uneasy sitting close to Matt in the presence of either father. Again, BrYaN appears to feel in some way that their relationship was not quite right while Matt had little such concern. BrYaN was far more sensitive to what the two fathers thought of his relationship with Matt than the fathers were. This support from the fathers of the two young men is in contrast with the literature on "coming-out" to the family (Cohler 2004a; Galatzer-Levy and Cohler 2002; Savin-Williams 2001), which shows that it is generally the mother who is supportive and the father who is critical of his son's gay sexual identity.

BrYaN makes it clear in his journaling that he and Matt are totally smitten with each other's bodies. BrYaN reports being attracted to Matt's smell. Indeed, when Matt would leave for the weekend to visit his mother, BrYaN would fetch a shirt and shorts from Matt's laundry. This led him to feel Matt's presence and reminded him of the pleasure he found in exploring Matt's body. BrYaN observes about their relationship:

As I lay on my bed trying to read, [Matt] kept popping to my mind. One thing I think is funny is how we have both changed over the course of the past 10 months. It's as if we are beginning to melt together. I've often said that Matt is way too anal about how neatly he keeps his room . . . well as of late, I've noticed that he's loosened up a little bit . . . I guess I've been a good influence. On the other hand, Tyler has made the recent observation that I'm no longer only in my jeans and tee shirts and that I'm dressing more and more like Matt all the time. (March 16, 2000)

He also observed that "Matt is such a joy to be around and every minute that I can find to be with him makes my life so much more fulfilled" (March 26, 2000). Their friends also comment on how much the two had grown together and are even a bit envious of the closeness that he and Matt have. With the end of the semester, students left the dormitory, and Matt moved into a room across the hall from BrYaN and Tyler.

The summer between BrYaN's sophomore and junior years marked the first anniversary of his relationship with Matt. They spent whatever free time they had between classes at the lake. BrYaN treasured this time alone with Matt, Matt's keen sense of the world about them, and their growing intimacy. Matt told BrYaN how important their relationship was for him and how much he feels at one with BrYaN. On their anniversary, Matt purchased identical rings, each with a small jewel. Alone together after their friends had thrown them a party, Matt asked BrYaN to put his ring on his finger; then Matt placed BrYaN's ring on his finger. Matt told him how much he loved him and said that the rings were his way of expressing how he felt. BrYaN reports that:

It feels so completely strange to have a ring on my left hand. I mean physically strange. Inside, it feels totally wonderful. It makes me feel warm, wanted, and a part of something irreplaceable. (June 11, 2000)

He did worry about the reactions of his family, particularly his mother, and, as expected, relations with his mother and brother became more unpleasant. BrYaN's father took his side in these family disputes, and BrYaN began to feel even greater guilt that somehow he had caused a rift in the family. He blamed the obvious marital difficulties between his parents on himself and wondered if he should have kept his private life to himself. BrYaN confronted his mother that she and Adam were preoccupied with the fact that he and Matt had sex together and that she thought him a dirty person. Reflecting on his relationship with his father, BrYaN observed:

I've spent the better part of this year feeling a considerable amount of pain and hurt towards my family. I've also spent a fair amount of time feeling sorry for myself. Now that I look back at it, I really have made some progress in my life, especially with my dad. Mom and my brother may still be the same, but dad is really trying and he shows it by not just lecturing on one facet of my life . . . I know I've mentioned this several times before, but I'm gonna say it again: I really wish things with my dad were like this a long time ago. I really feel that I've missed out on part of my life. (August 12, 2000)

For both BrYaN and Matt, their coming out gay and their relationship clearly had enhanced their relationship with their own fathers. Discussing these issues online with his fellow gay life-writers was also a help to BrYaN as he dealt with his feelings about his family.

BrYaN and Matt enjoyed having their friends join them in the cabin at the lake. The group now included Lee, a foreign exchange student who had come on to BrYaN while BrYaN was tutoring him. The group was pleased when Lee met a bartender at the resort on the lake and soon was spending the night with his new boyfriend. BrYaN still blushed when his friends made jokes about the sex between Matt and himself, but these jokes were no different from those his friends made about each other, straight couples. Over the course of the summer and early autumn, the circle of friends began to talk about moving in together in an apartment. BrYaN was concerned that while none of his straight friends and their girlfriends intended to share a room together, he wished to have a room together with Matt. The idea of waking up next to Matt every morning was particularly enticing.

As the autumn progressed and the group became more serious about moving in together, the others did not see that there was any problem with BrYaN and Matt sharing a room while Jeff and Tyler shared the other room (their girlfriends already had an apartment and the two boys often slept over with Kristi and Laurie). Once again, BrYaN was more sensitive than any of his friends about his relationship with Matt. On one occasion, while shopping with Jeff, BrYaN needed to get some more KY lubricant jelly and invited Jeff into the gay-themed, somewhat raunchy, bookstore while he did his errand. Jeff was clearly embarrassed, particularly as other young men "cruising" in the store tried to make eye contact, but Jeff handled the situation with aplomb. BrYaN reports in his diary that he thanks Jeff (after much begging) to include this humorous anecdote in his journal.

Once the group had moved into together, it was inevitable in these close living conditions that they would see each other naked and hear the sounds of sexual encounters from gay and straight bedrooms alike. For example, one night at the lake, their friends Tyler and Kristi had come down for a visit and as both couples were having sex, BrYaN giggled about the noises coming from the adjoining room and Matt called out in a voice loud enough for the whole cabin to hear: "And they say that all gay men do is have sex, yea, right!" There was a brisk wave of laughter from all parts of the cabin, then quiet, then the moans and squeaks and groans started again (June 16, 2002). BrYaN reports that one morning, with the usual problem of a morning erection, he walked naked to the showers and encountered an equally naked Kristi coming from the shower. Each giggled and throughout the day exchanged sexual innuendos to the amusement of their roommates. On another occasion, Tyler barged into their room just as they were getting to sleep and asked if they had any condoms. BrYaN reports:

Matt and I stopped giggling long enough to remind Tyler that we hadn't used a condom in well over two years and that we didn't have a single one laying [*sic*] around the place. Tyler had the most tortured look on his face. After making a few comments to Tyler about how he should have a cold shower or use a glad bag, I finally confided in him that I knew where some were . . . I climbed out of bed and walked into the living room. I told Tyler that I happened to know there was a box of condoms in Jeff's computer desk. What surprised me was that the last time I saw the box (only a few days ago), it was unopened. Now I found the cellophane gone and three little packages gone. . . . Anyway I grabbed one and tossed it to Tyler who by this time was looking most impatient and frustrated. One wasn't good enough for our manly Tyler, he told me to toss him another one. Horny little devil isn't he. . . . Naturally, I couldn't resist sticking my head in Tyler's room and saying good night to Kristi. After ducking a flying pillow, I made my way back to my own room and to bed. (January 23, 2002)

On another occasion at the lake with their circle of friends, BrYaN discovered that his economy sized bottle of WET was missing as he and Matt became passionate with each other:

Talk about utter frustration! Here we were completely worked up, passions flowing . . . and the very thing we need to continue is missing! Do you know how utterly embarrassing it is to have to attempt to put on a pair of pants that hide your obvious condition, walk out of the back door to your two best friends' room, bang on the door while they are engaging in a little morning passion of their own and ask for your bottle back . . . I don't know who were more embarrassed, Tyler and Kristi, or me and Matt. (June 20, 2002)

Another time BrYaN told Tyler about an escapade with Matt in which they had tried peanut butter and jelly without a sandwich and it was a source of general good humor in the apartment. From time to time, Matt would tease Tyler that in his absence they had tried out his bed. He enjoyed Tyler's discomfort. Once, when the group was discussing lesbian sex, one of the girls said that it didn't repulse her but she liked getting penetrated. BrYaN couldn't let this go by and responded that he too liked getting penetrated. He reports that Tyler nearly dropped his beer bottle, and Matt turned first beet red and then nearly purple while Kristi broke up laughing. These vignettes reflect the ease of these gay and straight close friends with their own and each other's sexuality. BrYaN and Matt found it intriguing to live with straight men friends. On one occasion, when an ice storm caused power outages and some of Tyler's friends camped out in their apartment, BrYaN reports:

After spending two nights and two days with an apartment full of straight guys, I have raised one question. Is it me (and Matt) who has noticed that straight guys seem to go out of their way to show themselves off to other guys? I'm serious. It's all most [sic] as if they wanted us to "see it." Quite frankly, Matt and I didn't mind looking either. Tyler, who always feels considerably nervous in discussions such as this actually agreed . . . (and) said that although gay guys might have a slightly different reason for checking out another guy, straight guys do it as well. He seemed to think it has its roots in the old thought that bigger is manlier, more aggressive, and more powerful. He also added that it just comes down to curiosity. I had to laugh when Tyler said that straight guys are better at checking out other guys and not being noticed. "Guys who say that they don't look," he said, "are full of it." (February 1, 2002)

Watching the straight guys parade naked by his room on the way to the shower, BrYaN mused that perhaps he should move all the towels out in the hall. He also commented that there was nothing better than living in a locker room and watching all the boys get ready for the day. As he says: "How often do you get three guys you hardly know walking around in front of you in the buff?" (May 25, 2002). Tyler found BrYaN's obvious fascination with straight boys quite amusing and was not at all perturbed by BrYaN's fascination with the parade of naked boys on their way to and from the shower.

On weekends when Matt was not helping his mother settle into her new apartment, the circle of friends would hit the mall, checking out the stores and enjoying lunch together, or getting together for beer and pool at the local sports bar, often with Tyler and Jeff's fraternity brothers or Kristi and Laurie's sorority sisters. Over one Thanksgiving, Tyler invited BrYaN and Matt, along with Kristi, to go home with him in Omaha where he put BrYaN and Matt in his room and slept on the living room sofa. BrYaN recalled how different this Thanksgiving was from the last one when his mother and brother had confronted him with their disapproval about his being gay.

In all these ways, the circle of friends was just a typical group of young adults serious about their studies, enjoying their free time together, and appreciating each other's friendship. BrYaN and Matt were just another couple. However, BrYaN and Matt had little sense of camaraderie with other gay students on campus. One day, while sitting at lunch, they were approached by a representative of the gay and lesbian campus group. BrYaN observes:

We have a very good group of friends that we hang out with. They are both gay and straight. Matt and I have a really great relationship with all types of people, neither one of us really saw the need to go to a support group. Matt said that he had gone to a similar group before he came to school here and he just didn't feel right about being there. Matt and I are both very busy with other clubs, interests, friends, and stuff . . . I don't see where I really need to join a group to advertise the fact that I'm gay . . . if somebody wants to know that I'm gay, fine I will tell them. I really don't see the point of going to an organization that seems to be always trying to tell the world "hey, I'm gay." (April, 5, 2001)

He also notes that:

It is not that Matt and myself "choose not to be involved with the gay community" we choose to be members of a much larger community. That being, everything! We both feel that if we narrowed our lives to just the gay community, we would be missing out on or blinded to so many other things. We do not wish to be separatists . . . we also do not wish to be assimilated into anything . . . Our idea . . . is to be members of a huge community sharing, experiencing, and learning about all the differences and similarities between individuals. Rather than flying a rainbow flag that says "Hey, I'm gay" I would rather fly a flag that says, "Hey, I'm me and I'm part of it all!" And on that flag, a smaller rainbow patch is more than welcome. (May 23, 2001)

BrYaN observed that since he was a close friend of Tyler, he was able to meet and become friends with Tyler's fraternity brothers, who ultimately invited Matt and him to join their fraternity. He says that if he *had* joined a frat, the

gay community would have assumed that he was a "wannabe heterosexual."
With both gay and straight friends, he and Matt don't arrange their lives to
be with any particular community on an exclusive basis.

BrYaN's enjoyment of his daily round was interrupted when he broke
his ankle while running one morning with Matt. The two of them enjoyed
their morning runs in the quiet of the shaded running path (and also the
opportunity for sexual intimacy while showering upon their return from
their running). From that time onward, BrYaN's ankle, and the permanent
weakness that it caused, became a regular annoyance in his life. For a long
time he was in a cast and on crutches. Later he wore a leg brace and took
physical therapy. No longer could he go running with Matt or get around
easily. His ankle and the continuing pain had become a constant issue in
his life. Matt was, of course, an ever-present source of care, fetching BrYaN
the diet cola and cranberry juice, which was always the staple of BrYaN's
diet.

BrYaN reports that his father did mention to the doctor tending his
ankle that BrYaN was gay. BrYaN was hurt by that and wondered if his
father thought he had AIDS. In one of the few references to HIV in his
journal, BrYaN reported to his father that he had twice been tested. Later,
while watching an episode of *Queer as Folk* about one of the characters
waiting for his HIV test results, BrYaN recalls the tension he and Matt had
felt while waiting for the results from their own HIV test.

For Matt's twenty-first birthday, BrYaN rented a suite in Kansas City's
most elegant hotel and arranged a superb dinner with the help of Matt's
father's girlfriend, who managed to secure a dinner reservation for them.
Later that night they went to the sports bar where their friends and fraternity brothers threw Matt a party. BrYaN continued to struggle with his
cast and crutches. Bringing Matt home for a weekend, he was amazed that
his mother was more civil to him. He learned that his brother was engaged;
later BrYaN realized that not only was he not invited to be a part of the
wedding party but he was not even invited to the wedding. Indeed, Adam's
fiancée was as critical of BrYaN's gayness as were Adam and his mother. At
one point Adam's fiancée actually called him abnormal. BrYaN's mother
continued to blame him for family difficulties because he had chosen such
a dirty way to live his life. She also maintained that BrYaN's difficulty with
his brother Adam was all BrYaN's fault for choosing to live as he has. Since
BrYaN's parents were planning to sell their house and move closer to the
center city, his mother insisted that BrYaN remove all his things from the
house. Adam and his fiancée intended to move in with his parents, although his father confided to BrYaN that this would not happen.

Even as there was increased difficulty in BrYaN's relationship with his mother and with both Adam and Adam's fiancée, things were ever more comfortable with both his own and Matt's father. Matt's father invited BrYaN to go skiing with him and his girl friend in Vail over the Christmas break, and carefully arranged a suite for BrYaN and Matt, which included a large bedroom with a big bed. During the day, BrYaN hobbled about on his crutches, wandering through the shops and reading while Matt and his father skied. Matt was in a particularly romantic mood, and the two 'of them intensely felt their intimacy as they embraced. BrYaN told Matt that Matt was cute enough to marry; Matt blushed and reassured BrYaN: "I love you." As BrYaN has observed, those are the three most important words anyone could ever say.

Returning to school from Vail, BrYaN, Matt, Jeff, and Tyler moved into their new apartment close to campus. All the parents helped with the furniture, and Matt scurried about cleaning and arranging the furniture as the movers brought it in. BrYaN looked at their new bed and observed that this was different from the dorms; he was moving in with his boyfriend with whom he would now be sharing all of his life. The moving-in finished, Jeff observed that it was much more BrYaN and Matt's apartment than it would ever be his and Tyler's. There were the usual problems: BrYaN and Tyler were not especially neat. This had been acceptable when they shared a room together, but in the apartment things would have to be orderly out of respect for Jeff and Matt. Matt continued to fuss when BrYaN and Tyler failed to pick up after themselves, and BrYaN was amused that Matt was neater than he was and that Matt would fuss at him to pick up his things. Soon their apartment became a hangout for the group. Lee, their gay foreign friend, and Nate, another coworker at the computer center and also gay, soon joined the circle of friends and often slept over at the apartment. Nate had been out in high school and was completely comfortable being gay.

Watching an episode of *Queer as Folk,* BrYaN and Matt commented that the Justin character, out in high school and later the subject of a life-threatening homophobic attack, certainly had a different set of experiences than had been their lot in high school. BrYaN observed that he was too busy questioning his own sexuality during his high school years and was terrified that he might be found out. He even had dates with girls so that he could fake being straight. He recalled hearing about another boy who had been outed and who became so despondent that he had cut his wrists. BrYaN remembered only one instance of bullying in high school when another boy called him a faggot, but more as a taunt than an accusation.

Meeting his former high school classmates some years later, his friend Eric told him that most people at school did know that he was gay, particularly since Adam had told them, but that it made little difference and that he should just be himself. BrYaN was also critical of the gay scene, particularly clubs where social position is determined by the number of men one has gone to bed with.

Watching *Queer as Folk* showing Justin and his lover having sex, Tyler and Jeff asked BrYaN and Matt—in all innocence and with good nature— if that was how they did it. While their roommates were just joking, BrYaN became acutely embarrassed. He reports having been uncomfortable watching this television series about the gay and lesbian community with his straight roommates. He also reports feeling somewhat uncomfortable in public with the gay thing, and that even watching the show makes him feel a little embarrassed about his own sexuality. On one occasion Matt and he were hanging out at the local bookstore; Matt had purchased a copy of the young adult gay magazine *XY,* and BrYaN felt uneasy that other customers would see them with the magazine. Another time, he purchased a copy of *XY* as Matt had requested but felt embarrassed walking up to the cash register with the magazine and so covered it up with the *Wired* magazine that he was also buying. As he says: "I guess by now I shouldn't feel this way about picking up a simple magazine, but I still get a lump in my throat every time. It's as if I'm panicked that someone is going to make some kind of cruel remark. I don't know why I would care if someone did but I do" (October 20, 2001). Matt lectured him that it was one thing to go around broadcasting that he was gay and another to hide from it.

As BrYaN and Matt moved toward their second anniversary, BrYaN observes:

One thing that was (and is) still bothering me was the amazement shown by Kristi's friends that Matt and I are moving toward our two-year anniversary. In fact, the amazement shown [toward] other gay people puzzles me. Is this some sort of a record or something? Do str8 people just assume that gay couples don't stay together while other gay people expect you to break up as soon as the next hot looking gay dude finds his way into your life? (April 8, 2001)

And:

And yes, being gay is only a part of my life. The gay factor is only a part of who a person is and it shouldn't be the dominating factor in a person's life. Does my being gay have anything to do with my progressing through college and graduate school? NO . . . I'm a person, a student, young, career minded, relationship oriented, a nervous wreck getting good grades, a Thunderbird enthusiast, a wannabe runner, a championship water skier dreamer, a person who enjoys the internet and on-line journaling . . . and I just happen to be a gay individual who is in a relationship with another guy who feels the same way. I'm all this, and al[l] these parts make up who I am. (April 7, 2001)

In this important passage, BrYaN also notes that he doesn't need to jump into bed with every good-looking guy who comes around:

I'm quite happy hopping in an[d] out of bed with Matt. So he happens to be a guy rather than a girl. BIG DEAL. I care for him, I love him, and there is nothing in the world I wouldn't do for him. There is much more to our relationship than sex. MUCH MORE . . . Sure, sex is a part of this (and great sex it is in case ya just have to know) but it is just part of the whole. . . . It is great to just be around Matt, to be in the same room, on the same running trail, in the same classroom. (April 7, 2001)

BrYaN describes how one night, waking up when a breeze stirred the Venetian blinds, Matt rolled over half asleep, put his arm around him and whispered "I love you so much," and then turned over and went back to sleep. BrYan also notes:

Matt has the warmest most caring disposition I've ever seen . . . he always knows just when to do the right thing. It is so great when for no apparent reason he will give me a kiss on the cheek or a hug. It's as if he sense[s] that I feel the need to be touched by him or feel the warmth of his body. Hmm, maybe I need some of his DNA. (June 1, 2001)

These vignettes sum up their tender feelings for each other. Each feels this presence of the other as providing an enhanced sense of completion of the self. Again, the feelings that the two boys have for each other was epitomized when BrYaN wore Matt's dirty clothes while running on those many weekend occasions when Matt had to be at home helping his mother. BrYaN says that wearing Matt's clothes makes him feel Matt's presence with him.

BrYaN reports that one day while driving about the suburb where the university is located, Matt talked about the two of them owning a condo with a two-car garage. In a later account, BrYaN mused after watching an episode of *Queer as Folk* that

Why is it so wrong for Matt and I to have successful careers, an expensive house, and to be like any other married couple out there? This is what both of us want and I do believe that it is entirely obtainable. The only time I feel defeated in reaching for these goals is when some narrow-minded writers of a corny second-rate show . . . were trying to say that a gay couple striving for a life *among the entire population* was impossible and that those who try are only fooling themselves. (January 20, 2002; italics added)

In this observation about living typically normal while loving another gay man, BrYaN both explains the title for his website and journal (the-populace.com) and the expectations of his generation that gay men want to live in the same manner as their straight counterparts, with the same hopes for self, family, and career. He does not believe that the future for gay people necessarily means living in a gay enclave as the producers of *Queer as Folk* seem to convey. He disputes their portrayal of gay men living "above an abandoned coffee shop or a noisy bar and fly[ing] a multicolored flag . . . A nice 'stately' house is exactly what I want and it is exactly what Matt wants" (March 10, 2002). This observation again reflects the goals of a self-identified gay man, born in the 1980s, rejecting the stereotype of a life confined to the gay ghetto, and realizing aspirations similar to those of straight-identified middle-class counterparts for a successful career and comfortable life (Dilley 2002).

When BrYaN finally turned twenty-one, a few months after Matt's own twenty-first birthday, BrYaN's father treated him to a fancy lunch. His father admitted that Adam was being immature about the wedding and re-fusing to invite BrYaN. His father did express some concern that BrYaN was making his own life much more difficult by choosing to be gay, noting that a junior partner in the firm might now be a full partner if he hadn't been gay. At the same time, his father was full of praise for Matt. The re-mainder of the day and evening (and the night in private) was spent party-ing in their room.

Throughout the spring of that year, BrYaN continued to excel in his classes and was kept busy at the computer center. He managed to design a senior project that would integrate his work on Oracle databases with a project designed by the Chair of the English Department. Word of his computer skill has spread beyond the university community; he has re-ceived several lucrative job offers in the computer industry that offer a gen-erous salary and benefits, but he feels that this might lead him away from his own goals. BrYaN celebrated his second anniversary with Matt at a downtown hotel; they enjoyed the embarrassment on the face of the waiter bringing them room service for two and, in return, BrYaN reports that he felt a bit uncomfortable with the waiter's reaction to them. Their conversa-tion that weekend was about them and their relationship, and BrYaN con-cludes: "I guess we just kinda decided that we love each other very much." Matt produced two rings, replacing the earlier ring with one with three small diamonds and a platinum streak across the band. As they placed rings on each other's ring finger, Matt said he wanted it clear that BrYaN was taken. BrYaN observed that he guessed he and Matt would be around for quite a while. He goes on to observe:

I explained to Matt that I really cared for him [more] than anything in the world and that I felt sort of goofy asking him to marry me. Matt just smiled and said that now [I] just have to figure out how to do it! I was so taken by Matt's views on marriage and he agreed with me that when two people love each other and care for each other then they should have the right to be married. He also said one more time that he didn't want to be with anybody else other than me . . . I couldn't help but get a few tears. (June 9, 2001)

BrYaN observes elsewhere that he and Matt both feel uncomfortable with the word "marriage," preferring instead commitment; it is the symbolic rather than the legal aspect of marriage that is important to him. He says he has problems with the term "boyfriend"; for some guys it means someone just to have sex with, but for others it means more than that but still implies that other guy is being kept at a distance and not really a part of a shared relationship. He reflects that Matt is more than a boyfriend, really his partner. He observes:

He is the one whom I choose to be with . . . partner/life partner/husband/sig. Other/mate? Hmm, a definition or term can be a hard one to grasp here. I hate husband that is way too gender specific. I'm just as much a husband as he is. Partner/life partner, to me sounds way too sterile. I also do not like the word mate. It has way too much of a simple sexual connotation to it. So, I guess for now the word couple comes to mind. It is also weak in its meaning. (September 9, 2001)

Matt then suggested that they look into becoming incorporated as a limited partnership (limited liability company, or LLC) since anyone can be a partnership. Matt and BrYaN invented the term Relationship Limited Partnership (RLLC™) for people who seek a legally recognized relationship that could buy property, obtain credit cards, and obtain health insurance.

The joy and passion of their anniversary weekend together was in sharp contrast to a rather unpleasant confrontation that BrYaN had with his father, who continued to be vaguely critical of BrYaN's life and confused about his relationship with Matt. He once again reiterated that BrYaN was making his life immensely more difficult for himself. They even disagreed about the cabin and the lake property. His father suggested that if a developer made an offer on the property, it would be hard to resist since real estate prices around the lake had risen dramatically since they purchased the property. However, later that summer his father decided to take his mother's name off the lake property and offered instead to make BrYaN a half owner, with a plan to buy out BrYaN's father's share over a fifteen-year period.

Both his mother and father tried to pressure BrYaN to come to Adam's wedding. But, BrYaN noted, Adam had actually never invited him. Instead, BrYaN arranged for his group of friends to join him at the cabin for the weekend of Adam's wedding. In contrast, Matt's father invited Matt, BrYaN, Tyler, and Kristi to join him and his girlfriend on a business and pleasure trip. BrYaN felt a bit embarrassed when Matt's father knocked on the apartment door and he sleepily arose, having just gotten out of the bed that he and Matt shared. Matt's father had thoughtfully arranged for Matt and BrYaN to have their own mini suite at the hotel.

As the summer progressed, BrYaN's father made increased efforts to seek him out. On several occasions he told BrYaN how proud he was of his achievements and how frustrated he was with things at home and with Adam's failure to show any initiative. He was quite clear that Adam and his wife were not moving with them to the new house they had purchased to be closer to the city. He also expressed some distaste that BrYaN's mother had bought Adam and his wife a new sports car as a wedding gift. It became increasingly clear that his father was moving emotionally closer to BrYaN while his mother was growing increasingly closer to Adam and his wife. Once, when Adam had been particularly nasty about his relationship with Matt, BrYaN hauled off and slugged him, leaving Adam with a black eye. While his mother was horrified, his father laughed and put his arm around him. BrYaN was aware that something was happening in his family, and it made him uneasy.

With the cabin now half his, BrYaN and Matt began making some changes, rearranging the furniture, making repairs, and bringing BrYaN's things from his room in the old house that his parents were selling. BrYaN looked forward to the time when the cabin would belong to him and Matt. He was pleased that Matt enjoyed the cabin and the lake property as much as he did. Over the summer, the group of friends spent many enjoyable weekends together at the cabin, with everyone comfortable living in tight quarters and aware of what was going on each night in the several bedrooms. BrYaN reports that both his and Matt's hormones were raging. Unfortunately, tempted by a last opportunity that summer for water-skiing, BrYaN attempted several jumps that, while nearly prefect, caused him to injure his fragile ankle once again.

As he entered his senior year that autumn, his relationship with Matt was one of the mainstays in BrYaN's life even as things were falling apart at home. BrYaN was immersed in his growing responsibilities at the computer center and reading through the genre of American twentieth-century novels. He was given early admission to graduate school by an appreciative English department at his undergraduate university. Gay themes occasionally were topics for course papers. BrYaN once wrote on Chaucer and the political aspects of love, implicitly an issue in being gay. As always, BrYaN supported his argument about the text, carefully supported by evidence from the secondary literature. Issues regarding being gay were not a prominent part of BrYaN's undergraduate studies in literature, however. His papers reflected a keen and sensitive critical appreciation well supported by perspectives founded in contemporary criticism. Although he worried a good deal about his academic record, he continued with a perfect A average. Fortunately, both Matt and Jeff scored well enough for them to get into the UMKC law school. Now the whole group could continue to be together following college graduation.

Politics seldom enter BrYaN's journal. He does report that he is fond of the works of Ayn Rand (BrYaN never does explain his interest in objectivism). The events of September 11 were troubling for BrYaN as they were for all of us. He reports feelings of grief, sorrow, anger, and pain, and wonders why it should take a tragedy of such magnitude to bring the country together.

BrYaN's parents invited Matt to spend Thanksgiving holiday at their new home. Since there was no room with Adam and his fiancée staying over the holiday, the two of them were put up at a nearby motel where they were able to have a king-size bed for themselves. At a reunion the night before the holiday, BrYaN's old high school friends again greeted them warmly, and Matt soon struck up conversations about sports with several of BrYaN's old friends. Matt also got along well with BrYaN's relatives where, again, his near-encyclopedic knowledge of sports was a big hit. They also visited with Matt's mother, who met BrYaN for the first time. There was some embarrassment when Matt's grandmother remarked that they were such a sweet and loveable couple. BrYaN observes that "IT" had been mentioned out loud, and everyone present looked embarrassed.

Matt was at first hesitant about fooling around in his own mother's house and insisted that there be nothing that would make the bed creak so that it could be heard in any adjoining bedroom. They also went dancing at a gay bar, amused that it really looked like Babylon from the *Queer as Folk* television series. On another night, BrYaN and Matt took Tyler to the gay dance bar. While a good sport, even dancing with Matt with his shirt open to his navel, Tyler was clearly taken aback by the overt display of gay sexuality, including the experience of a trip to the bathroom where he was the object of many stares and even a few propositions!

The year 2001 ended with a wonderful Christmas party attended by all the members of their circle, now called "the family," which now included Lee, the gay foreign student. It was not only a close family but an inclusive one as well. Among the presents that BrYaN and Matt exchanged, in addition to a large bottle of Wet (lubricant), was a matching Cross pen set with each of their names on it. The family Christmas was somewhat less satisfying; BrYaN particularly missed his friends who had scattered to their homes and vacations over the holidays. Matt was away with his father on their annual Christmas break ski trip, and BrYaN missed him but brightened considerably when Matt called him to say how much he missed him. Then, after he returned from his ski trip, Matt had to spend time with his mother. BrYaN describes the desire that each felt for the other. Lying in bed together following Matt's return from his ski trip, BrYaN reports:

It just felt so darn good to feel him next to me last night. I literally could not keep my hands off his smooth soft chest. It was so great just to run my hands through his hair and give him a hug . . . I really don't think our bathroom will ever be the same. There was a small flood beginning to form outside the shower on the floor . . . just watching Matt towel off was cause for another wild time in our room. This time Matt started it and I was only too happy to comply. (January 5, 2002)

In this and other reports in his diary of two young men, hormones raging and in sync, passionate and playful, BrYaN expresses the comfort of these two young men with their sexual desire. Visiting BrYaN's father with Matt over a weekend, and falling asleep in front of the television set in the family room, his father commented how comfortable BrYaN and Matt appeared to be with each other as they slept curled up together.

Transfixed by each other, enjoying their sexual play together, BrYaN reports that his closeness with Matt has increased over time. While BrYaN and Matt appreciate the interest occasionally shown in them by other gay men on campus and flirting in return, they demur, sometimes explaining that although pleased with the attention shown in them, they are "taken." BrYaN observes that, sure, he flirts sometimes, as does Matt, who thinks it is funny. He adds: "Do Matt and I check out the guys? Sure we do, so what? There isn't a couple out there who doesn't look around. Looking is one thing, appreciation is one thing but temptation is another" (May 11, 2002). He adds that Matt is so desirable he would have no need of being tempted by another man. He observes that every time he and Matt have sex it's like the first time and that Matt excites him to no end. BrYaN reports that they have enjoyed playing "Cowboi and Indian," and teasing each other by pretending to pick up the other one as a hustler. BrYaN observes about Matt's impact on him that "whenever we are that close to each other, I don't know what it is. His smell, his warmth, his closeness seems to put me in a trance and totally under his power. When we hold each other, I feel as if I just want to blend and mix with his being. I feel as if I am actually a part of his person. It's wonderful and exhilarating" (March 29, 2002). Understood from the perspective of psychoanalytic psychology of the self, BrYaN and Matt might be viewed as "essential others" or twinship for each (Kohut 1977; Galatzer-Levy and Cohler 1993). Their closeness fosters for each of them an enhanced sense of self-completion and integrity. At the same time, they also have separate interests. For example, BrYaN respects Matt's interest in film and the satisfaction that Matt gets from participation in his film club.

As the spring of his last college year approached, already struggling with feelings of sadness with the approaching graduation, BrYaN was additionally troubled to see the "For Sale" sign on their old house. However, he was impressed with his father's enthusiasm for the sophisticated new city home—a departure from the old family-oriented house. As the year progressed, heading toward graduation, the friends discussed their futures. Tyler asked if BrYaN and Matt would continue to share the apartment with him. In March, just before the move into the new house, his father told him that he would be moving in alone and that his parents had decided to divorce. His mother would be moving back to Iowa along with Adam and his wife to be near to her own family. BrYaN's response was to assume that he had been the cause of his parents' breakup. If he had not come out gay and had not created dissension in the family then his parents might not have quarreled and decided on divorce:

Everything seemed fine until Matt and I headed out to my family's house that Thanksgiving. That is when my mom seemed to really change. That is when the emotion just seemed to fade away from her personality. Quite honestly, that is when she quit being my friend and I still to this day believe that it was also when she quit being my mother. . . . I had come to one final decision. It's mom who is initiating the divorce; it's HER problem. If she wants to tell me about it, she will just have to call me. (March 23, 2002)

It is common that gay and lesbian offspring assume that they are the cause of problems in the family, and BrYaN's response to hearing the news from his father reflected this feeling of guilt. His father assured him, however, that problems between them were long standing and had little to do with BrYaN's sexuality. BrYaN notes in bold type that he won't air his family's problems in his journal; he says only that his conversation with his father did a great deal to bring them closer. At the same time, he was angry and disappointed with his mother, the perfect all-American housewife and mother who couldn't even call him to acknowledge what was happening. When BrYaN called his mother to talk with her, she simply hung up the phone. However, just as Matt's father had earlier taken BrYaN in and made him a part of his new family following divorce, BrYaN's father reached out to Matt and made it clear that Matt would always be welcome in his home. The impact of divorce in each family had been to bring the fathers and their gay sons together in a new family. Watching the movie *Billy Elliot,* about a boy who becomes a ballet dancer and whose father supports his decision to become a dancer, BrYaN was moved by the father's expression of care and concern, which he now understood.

With the last semester of Bryan's college career coming to an end and graduation approaching, BrYaN lamented that things seemed to be speeding along too rapidly; he did the best he could to slow it down, able for a change to "do nothing." BrYaN ended his college career with an enviable academic record of virtually all A's and accolades from his instructors and academic advisor. Tyler accepted the offer from BrYaN's father to work for him before attending business school; Jeff went to work as a paralegal for his own father. BrYaN observed that while he liked the idea that nothing had changed in his life, still he wondered if there was something wrong in his decision for the next phase of his life. His plan was to work full time for the computer center and finish his MA and perhaps a PhD in the English department. Although the group decided to move into a larger and better-appointed apartment a bit farther outside the campus, Tyler and Jeff sharing one room, he and Matt the other bedroom, in other respects things remained as before. His father had moved into his new place and was enjoying increased business in the wake of the Arthur Anderson accounting debacle, which had left a number of area companies without an auditing firm. His father worked frantically through the tax season and appreciated the fact that BrYaN often called and was concerned about his workload. The major tragedy was that BrYaN's beloved Thunderbird was totaled by an uninsured, drunken driver while parked in the lot at the lake resort. His father helped him get a replacement car (alas not a T-Bird). BrYaN was distraught over the demise of his car; that, together with other changes taking place in his own life and that of his friends, made him restive. Anxious to succeed at work and at school, BrYaN reports that he planned to relax following the exhausting time before graduation when he was overwhelmed with work. At the same time, he found time to listen sensitively to the problems of his friends also dealing with issues of graduation and career.

Following graduation and throughout the summer before starting graduate school, BrYaN worked full time in the computer center. Jeff and Kristi announced their engagement. BrYaN and Matt celebrated their third anniversary together at the lake and were later joined by their friends, who enjoyed coming down and partying with them. The highlight of this anniversary was Matt's gift of forms completed for the limited partnership of Phillips-Connelly, LLC. Jeff had asked his father to complete the necessary legal forms and filing; all that was required was BrYaN's signature, some technical accounting details that BrYaN's father delighted in completing, and a thirty-day waiting period. Noting that the major problem with the limited partnership was that there was no business or property as the subject of the partnership in the statement, BrYaN's father fixed that problem by including Matt on the lake property in the limited partnership of Phillips-Connelly, LLC. Matt's name was now on the title of the cabin as a one-fourth owner, and the state approved the limited partnership making Phillips-Connelly, LLC, official. By this time, BrYaN's father was completely supportive of BrYaN's relationship with Matt, although he sometimes looked a bit uncomfortable with the depth of BrYaN's expression of his love for Matt. BrYaN says the purpose of the partnership was "to further our current partnership in the life-long learning . . . this LLC is another block in a foundation we are assembling together: A LIFE TOGETHER" (June 10, 2002). BrYaN writes that it was particularly important that someone was so adamant about making him a part of his life. He was pleased that Matt enjoyed the cabin and the quiet time at the lake. BrYaN describes Matt as the force that keeps him going. He says that

Matt and I had no problems whatsoever in honestly expressing our feelings and desires to stay together . . . we also know that our life together is made up of so much more than sex 24-hours a day, even though it sounds like that as of late. There is much more to us than just seeing how much WET we can use up in a week. We are very perceptive of each other's feelings and I really do believe that on some level we can practically read each other's mind. (June 11, 2002)

Even the crowd at the lake accepted the easy relationship between BrYaN and Matt. They befriended another young gay man who had not really come out and gave him the courage to realize his own sexual desire. They even introduced him to Lee, the gay foreign student with whom they had become close friends.

With the approach of autumn and the new school year, Matt was a bit apprehensive about starting law school while BrYaN was concerned about doing well in graduate school. Matt and Jeff had two law school classes together, so they could help each other out. A last trip to the beloved lake and the cabin by the group of friends was highlighted by Matt's writing "I love you" in permanent felt-tip marker across BrYaN's chest while he was asleep. Growing closer to his father, BrYaN even attended Mass one Sunday, followed by watching football at his father's golf club. Alas, the summer's water skiing had taken its toll on BrYaN's vulnerable ankle, and he was ordered to stop running. BrYaN writes that he missed that special time with Matt running together in the cool of the morning air. The doctor recommended that he keep his ankle elevated. BrYaN notes if only the doctor knew that both he and Matt would be delighted that BrYaN was to keep both ankles in the air! However, BrYaN adds that

we don't spend every free minute of our time in bed doing the deed. We have though found ourselves drifting into our own world a little bit . . . we just find ourselves relying on each other almost exclusively. And considering that relying on each other is what makes up part of a healthy relationship, I think it to be a good thing . . . the warmth and togetherness seem to melt us into one unbreakable unit. (September 22, 2002)

BrYaN notes his tendency to brood over things, but is encouraged by Matt to talk things over.

During the autumn, BrYaN continued to work full time as a senior staff member in the computer center even while enrolled full time in the graduate English program. BrYaN was able to complete all his classwork ahead of schedule, carefully planning assignment due dates, immersed in the study of the southern American writer William Faulkner. Once again he earned perfect grades in all his graduate courses. Matt and Jeff were deep into their law books. After an initial period of adjustment, Matt and Jeff were both making high marks in their law courses. The group of friends did find time to get together and to help Tyler and Kristi as they planned for their wedding. Even though Tyler would be moving out, Jeff would continue to share an apartment with BrYaN and Matt.

In entries that celebrate Phillips-Connelly, LLC, BrYaN narrates a wonderful, warm, birthday dinner for Matt, now twenty-three, and BrYaN, hosted by the two fathers. BrYaN's father reported that he had heard from Tyler that BrYaN wasn't taking sufficient care of his ankle and, although BrYaN fiercely defended his target weight, was criticized by his father for continuing with a diet, which BrYaN's doctor believed would lead to an unhealthy weight loss. BrYaN's father gave Matt a birthday present, and it was clear that both fathers were delighted with their sons and their relationship and that the two fathers had themselves become good friends. BrYaN's father invited Matt's father and his fiancée to Thanksgiving dinner with BrYaN, Matt, and relatives on his side of the family. Throughout the fall, BrYaN and Matt spent time at the cabin getting the property ready for the winter and enjoying each other's company. BrYaN commented that "it was so great to see that sparkle in Matt's eyes, to see him want to take part . . . treating the place as OUR place." Most recently, as the two fathers had become good friends, Matt's father introduced BrYaN's father to a woman friend. BrYaN has chastised his father for beginning to date so soon following his divorce. His father, while telling BrYaN to mind his own business, commented that he hoped he could find a person for himself "as nice and considerate, polite and responsible as Matt." BrYaN says that this comment made him feel good inside.

Pleading overwhelming demands at work in the university's computer center and in his graduate study, BrYaN reported in January 2004 that he was ending his blog. He also reported that he and Matt journeyed to San Francisco where they were married. As he concluded his many years of faithfully recording his life and his life with Matt, he reported that the two of them still spend much time with their old friends. Tyler has since moved out, and Jeff and Kristi have married and moved into a loft, which was remodeled with the assistance of BrYaN, Matt, and their other friends. In his second year of law school, Matt and Jeff are flourishing; BrYaN continues his graduate studies in English. BrYaN and Matt's fathers continue as close friends, and Tyler works for BrYaN's father's accounting firm. BrYaN and Matt continue to work on their lake property and enjoy their summers at the lake.

After more than five years together, BrYaN and Matt have grown closer and more in love with each other. While other life-writers in this study have also realized close and caring relationships, what is distinctive of BrYaN and Matt's relationship, and characteristic of many gay relationships in these days, is the way in which their relationship is a part of their life with their close circle of friends, both gay and straight, and with their fathers. The comfort evident in the relationship of Bryan and Matt is also evident to their friends and family, whether they are together in their apartment, with friends at the sports bar, or at the cabin on the lake. Their fathers respect this intimacy and carefully provide them with a room together when they are invited to travel with their fathers, and even BrYaN's discreet yet explicit portrayal of his sexual intimacy with Matt all reflect the increased acceptance of gay life and relationships in contemporary urban society. BrYaN has observed that their sexual intimacy is a reflection of an emotional closeness in which their relationship fosters the sense of personal integrity and vitality for each of them.

BrYaN's portrayal of his intimacy with Matt is given in terms of currently understood concepts of intimacy among both gay and straight relationships. BrYaN is clearly aware, however, of the stereotyped view of gay relationships as inherently less stable than straight relationships. He goes to great length to show that the intimacy he shares with Matt is no different in kind from that of straight couples. In this, as in his many achievements at school and at work, BrYaN's life writing reflects a view of gay lives as typically normal, and he seeks to be a part of his generation rather than using his gay identity as the basis for a separate life "apart from the populace."

Voices from Oasismag.com

Oasismag.com is a website organized by and for queer youth that offers a number of typically continuing brief memoirs regarding the experience of coming out gay or lesbian and establishing a gay identity. Contributors to the website offer testimony that the discovery of this site has been important for them, not only in coming to terms with their gay desire and discovering that there were other men who felt as they did but also that being gay can become just another part of life. Two young adult gay life-writers provide memoirs that reflect the integration of being gay into a typically normal life in much the same manner as BrYaN's elegant and richly informative journal and website. Michael is a twenty-year-old college student in Portland, Oregon, interested in music, and Dane is nineteen years old, attending college in Arizona.

Michael

Born in 1982 and growing up in a small town in eastern Oregon, Michael, a talented musician, was awarded a scholarship for college in Portland, a four-hour drive across the state. Michael's interests include marathon running, the martial arts, and fishing, as well as tinkering with his car. Michael's chief passion in life is jazz (his nickname on the Web site is "Jazzer"), and he goes to local jazz clubs at every opportunity. His parents were divorced when he was still quite young, but he has known his stepfather and considers him his "real" father since he was seven. His natural father was abusive, and Michael recalls seeing him hit his mother (his mother reports that once Michael took a broom and began hitting his father). He recalls that ever since he was little he was interested in music, becoming an accomplished French horn player.

He also remembers that ever since he was little he was aware that something about him was different—that he preferred the company of other boys to that of girls, and was even aware of a sexual attraction felt toward these boys. At the same time, he didn't give this too much thought. He says he didn't know about sex and didn't care—but also observes wistfully that life was simple for him back then. He says that he misses the innocence of youth, a time of an untainted mind, and a time when he wasn't aware of Christian right antigay propaganda. In the same vein, he says he likes to be with younger guys because they still have some of the innocence that he believes he has lost. Younger guys are much more accepting of differences among people and still hold to ideals that seem to be lost with age. He recalls memories of a time when things were different for him; he still wants to be held as he was when he was a child. His earliest memory is of wanting and getting a bottle.

Even though there have been some dark moments in Michael's life, early memories of good and satisfying care reflect Michael's basic optimism in the present. He would "love to live my life at a time when the world was still so new to me. A world that still had things to discover. A world that hadn't turned against me." At the same time, he says that his struggles have made him into a kinder and more sensitive person. He told his mother he was gay while in high school, and his stepfather heard about it through the rumor-mill in his small town. Michael presently lives with a straight roommate whom he has known since grammar school. The roommate and his friends are comfortable with the fact that Michael is gay and out.

Michael credits the Internet with having saved his life. Feeling isolated in high school because of his gay desires, he discovered oasismag.com and realized that other teens were in a similar situation, which was comforting and affirming. He discovered that some other teens were even more in the closet than he was. One of his fellow journal writers from oasismag even visited him from Canada. Oasismag staffers and journal writers feel particularly protective of their Web site and each other, and believe they have a particular mission—helping other gay teens to find themselves. Michael reports he had three experiences of having a crush on another guy while in high school, including one who was briefly his boyfriend, but says that he doesn't feel comfortable talking about these earlier experiences. Seeing the movie *Billy Elliot* about a boy with gender atypical interests who was determined to become a ballet dancer was also an inspiration for him.

During the winter of his first year at college, Michael discovered the local gay men's chorus, and even though most of his fellow singers are older than he is, he reports that this is a nice group of guys to hang around with. A group from his chorus recently attended a mainstream gay movie together. He observes that being gay is a source of a natural bond since all gay men struggle with similar issues of how it is to live gay and to deal with harassment. He reports that his weekly chorus rehearsals are a high point of his week because he is with a core group of friends who are like him. His college is careful to protect diversity within the student group and does not permit anything that might interfere with a good learning and working environment. He also thinks that gay men have the particular ability to see through shallowness in relationships as a result of having been closeted earlier in life. Further, because there aren't preset patterns for dating within the gay community, gay men try hard to make relationships work, and most of them want more than simply a hot night of sex.

Michael's narrative begins with his first year in college where he is making friends and dealing with the reality that not everyone accepts homosexuality. He joined a gay club at college, even though still reticent about issues of dating and sexuality. His roommate keeps him informed about rumors related to Michael's sexuality. He tells of an incident at a college party when a girl in his circle of friends told him that rumors had been circulating that he was gay. He says that he answered in the affirmative and without hesitation (hoping that a guy he had a crush on, standing nearby, might hear as well), although he notes that he is a modest person; while he doesn't shout the fact from the rooftops, neither does he go out of the way to avoid telling people that he is gay. Later, he suggested to a friend, a fellow member of his orchestra, also possibly gay, that he was interested in him; to date he has not yet had a positive response from his friend. He notes that he is something of a geek since he doesn't drink or smoke pot. His attitude toward being gay is this:

As a gay male, my perceived gender role is different than that of my straight counterparts . . . I have never felt the need to make any sort of declarative statement about my sexual orientation without a direct need.

He says that he doesn't like stereotypes or gay people who maintain such stereotypes. Most people accept his being gay as just another aspect of who Michael is. Although he thinks about having a boyfriend, he says that he is not lonely and is confident that someday he will find his ideal man; a boy he had a crush on while in high school has finally come out gay and he thinks about having this boy attend his college and being his roommate.

His jazz band at college travels around and, on one recent trip he requested having a girl, a good friend, as his roommate. He says that he felt comfortable with this arrangement, more so than if he had had another man as a roommate.

By the end of his first year at college, Michael had achieved considerable success both in his schoolwork and also as a performer in the band. His plans for the summer included preparing for a marathon. He enjoyed participating in his first Gay Pride parade in Portland where he worked in the gay chorus booth and got to meet lots of other gay men who complimented his looks and expressed an interest in getting together with him. He enjoyed the attention! He served as a counselor at the music camp where formerly he had been a camper and was openly gay from the outset. Campers and counselors alike were completely accepting. He notes that in a perfect world this would always be the way things should be. The same campers who knew that he was gay still wanted him to practice with them and were not troubled by his occasional references that one or another boy was cute.

While he has not yet had a boyfriend, his most recent report concerns meeting another member of the gay chorus at a party for the chorus and agreeing to go home with him. He describes their mutual passion in detail. Reflecting back on this night spent enjoying their sexuality, Michael concludes: "I probably didn't put myself in the safest position of all, but then again, I just know I would have beat myself up if I didn't take the chance. And part of the thrill WAS the not-knowing aspect of things—very hot indeed!" Michael appears to be growing in his role as a gay man, both exploring his own sexuality and his place in the larger community while continuing with his studies in music and his close relationships with gay and straight friends. Michael's nonchalant attitude regarding safer sex may reflect the experience of a generation coming out after the antiretroviral medication had changed the course of AIDS and in which few young men actually know someone with AIDS.

Dane

Attending college in Phoenix, Arizona, nineteen-year-old Dane writes of his struggles in coming to terms with the reality that he is gay. His Web site includes brief diary entries for a period of about four months along with a number of comments in which he reflects on the problems and possibilities of being gay. He calls his site "Discovering me?" because he says that recognizing his own homosexuality has made him aware of the diversity the world has to offer. He is looking for someone to love and who will love him unconditionally, but he is concerned with what he perceives as the preoccupation within the gay community with sex. He speculates that it may just be his traditional Catholic upbringing, but he is saving himself for the person he will spend the rest of his life with to realize a number of "firsts" in gay sexual relations. Just as among other members of his generation, he has both gay and straight friends. When he told his best friend that he was gay, his friend assured Dane that his sexuality didn't matter and that he still loved him because had always loved Dane the person. Sometimes he wonders whether he is really gay, but then finds himself starring at a shirtless guy jogging past him and realizes all over again how attracted he is to other guys. He longs for the joys of parenthood and is concerned that he has traded being gay and happy for the possibility of having a family.

Dane grew up in a small town in Montana and moved with his family to Arizona. An ardent road and mountain cyclist, who also enjoys the companionship of a good friend in a coffee shop, Dane is out to both of his parents. Just as with many young men of his generation (Savin-Williams 1998, 2001), he elected first to come out to his sister and his mother, and only later to his father (who no longer lives with his mother). He reports that he had a long period of depression and anxiety over the past several years and had seen physicians and a psychologist but could never divulge to them that the source of his problem was his feeling that he was gay. When he was on his own in college, he was able to come to grips with this reality for himself and then to tell his family. He believes that he didn't make a choice to be gay; the only choice he made was to be honest both with himself and with others about being gay. He observes about himself that he faked being a hetero for so long that fake feelings of being straight linger on.

Acknowledging his gay desire only within the past year, when he was eighteen, his first realization of his gay desire was while sitting with his boyfriend in the parking lot of a fast-food place (appropriately named "In and Out"). He acted on the urge to kiss his boyfriend; that kiss in turn led to three hours of making out. For Dane, as for BrYaN, another member of the queer community, the alternative television series *Queer as Folk* has had an impact on his understanding of his own gay desire, and he recalls a statement from the character Emmette that it is better to come out as a teenager than to do so later in life and get stuck in a new adolescence. He reports that he forced himself to tell his mother. He notes it may have been a busy day for his mother, but he insisted that she listen to him as he confessed he was dating someone, and that someone's name was Tim. Although confessing to some confusion, his mother hugged him upon hearing his news and assured him that she loved him.

Dane and his father had difficulty talking with each other, which made the task of disclosure to him much more difficult. Finally, on Father's Day, after spending time together, Dane left him with a lengthy note explaining that he was in fact gay. He had composed the letter the previous February but was only able to part with the letter in June. Just as with his sister, his father confessed that he had suspected for a long time that Dane was gay. Although his father was initially unhappy that he had learned about Dane's sexual identity on such a special occasion, he seems to have had little difficulty over time dealing with this new reality.

Much of Dane's life writing concerns his effort to come to terms with his gay sexual identity. He reflects on the fact that he is a "homophobic homo" and finds himself engaged in not only self-loathing but also stereotyping the gay community. Then he realizes that the gay community is filled with many different types of people. He worries about being stigmatized, and is troubled by the belief that he is no longer one of the majority; he even harbors feelings of guilt about being gay as something he was not "supposed" to be. He wonders about wearing a rainbow ribbon on his book bag. He eschews all labels yet believes that this clue might help him find a guy. He confesses both to fascination and also to distaste for people who have such labels. However, he worries that otherwise no one will know that he is gay. He works in a sporting goods store where he is sure all the other workers are straight and can't imagine being out at work in such a store. He observes that he feels like there is something missing in his life, which is otherwise filled with adoring family and friends. That void is a loving gay relationship, and it continues to elude him.

Wrapping Up

Within the generation of gay men born in the 1970s and 1980s, coming of age around the millennium, their own life stories and the social contexts within which they lead their lives are significantly different from those of preceding generations. Within the family, across the university campus, and increasingly, the workplace, being gay is understood as only one of several alternative sexual lifeways. The media has played some role in this change. Even within the gay community, gay-themed movies and television shows have had an impact on the manner in which gay men understand and write about themselves. These media presentations have also sharpened the debate about what are often seen as stereotyped portrayals of the gay lifestyle. Concern with fashion, promiscuous sexuality, and self-preoccupation alternate with the wish to realize a permanent union and, often, attain parenthood as well. For members of this typically young adult cohort, focusing on a satisfying career, finding a meaningful relationship, and enjoying a fulfilling life have become important goals. Nowhere is this more clearly and colorfully expressed than in the life writing of sometime-escort and porn producer Aaron Lawrence. He seeks economic advantage through escorting and production of gay "amateur" videos in order to help his life-partner Jeff, who works in the arts, and in order for the couple to support a family.

Helping other young men to find their way within the gay community has become an important theme expressed by Kirk Read and oasismag .com Web site contributors alike. This concern with helping others to avoid the pain and pitfalls of the gay lifeway reflects a generative, mentoring perspective, which has been emphasized to a great extent in the life writing of this new generation, rather than that of preceding generations. Cautionary tales such as the posthumous account of '50s-generation life-writer James Melson, who died of AIDS, have little relevance for these young men coming of age at the millennium. The discourse of gay desire as dangerous has largely disappeared, replaced by discourse about gay desire, surrounded by friends, both gay and straight, and pursuing a satisfying career (Savin-Williams 2005). Nowhere has this change in the experience of homosexuality been better documented than in the life writing of BrYaN Phillips, who pursues a successful graduate career with his partner, Matt Connelly. This account portrays a young man with devoted family and friends, certainly aware of the impact of being gay upon his hopes and fears for the future.

For members of this millennium generation, debates such as those between Andrew Sullivan (1995) and Michael Warner (1999) regarding the future of gay culture seem dated and almost irrelevant. Even the term "postgay" fails to capture the aspirations of this generation. Gay men born in the '70s and '80s intend to lead full, satisfying lives, while clearly aware of the complex issues posed by the gay lifeway. While there is some marked variation within the members of this generation—Kirk Read in San Francisco and working on behalf of gay youth, and Aaron Lawrence in New Jersey and promoting gay sexuality (Cohler 2004c)—portrayal of the gay lifeway as either deviant or irrelevant to the course of adult life fails to capture the experience of self and others within this generation of characteristically gay men.

7 | Conclusion

Social science deals with problems of biography, of history, and their intersections within social structures. . . . The problems of our time . . . cannot be stated adequately without consistent practice of the view that history is the shank of social study, and recognition of the need to develop further a psychology . . . that is sociologically grounded and historically relevant.

C. Wright Mills, *The Sociological Imagination*

Cultural shifts of the past decade have helped to demystify homosexuality for many, and I'm less of an obnoxious brat these days, both of which are conducive to healing conversation. Coming out was in many ways the easy part. Going home is considerably more daunting.

Kirk Read, *How I Learned to Snap*

Lives, Times, and Gay Memoirs

Concern with the interplay of life story and historical and social change has assumed a preeminent place in the study of lives. Reviewing the self-life writing of men born across six successive generations or cohorts from the 1930s to the 1980s, it is clear that social change has had a dramatic impact upon the manner in which these men experience and write about self, sexual desire, and relationships with family, friends, and lovers or partners. Prior to the generation of men born in the 1950s, men seeking sex with other men most often viewed themselves as "homosexual." Men born in the postwar period most often eschew this term, which they associate with earlier efforts to stigmatize and denigrate their same-sex desire. For the most recent generations of men born in the 1970s and 1980s, the term "gay," counterposed to the term "straight," may pose a problem in defining their sexual identity and imply a natural, binary distinction (E. Stein 1999). Many men in this generation prefer terms such as "queer" or "spectrum," and avoid any label that implies difference.

Social Context, Generation, and Life Story

Two intellectual perspectives have provided the foundation for this study of history, social change, and writing about desire. One perspective, life-course social science, is concerned with the effect of social and historical change in understanding the trajectory of lives within and across generations (Elder 1996). Elder has suggested that we inevitably make meanings of particular sociohistorical events (period effect), but that persons of different generation-cohorts, understood as some particular span of birth years, experience these events in different ways and make somewhat different meanings of these events (cohort effect), which are different from the meanings of these events made by members of earlier and later generation-cohorts. Consistent with social philosopher Karl Marx (1845) and the concept of generational consciousness (Mannheim 1928; Ortega y Gasset 1921–22), the significance of intracohort variation within generations shows consistency in how they interpret the personal and shared past.

Consistent with contemporary study of memory and the importance of youth movements in fostering social change, events taking place during young adulthood inevitably serve as the filter for successive reinterpretations of subsequent experiences. Men born in the two generations prior to the emergence of the gay rights movement have made meaning of subsequent experiences in terms of the social opprobrium of their youth, whereas men born in the 1950s, coming of age in the 1970s, understand changes across their adult years in terms of the social activism of their youth. This recollection of the present in terms of the past provides the foundation for the fascinating problem of nostalgia in social life (Davis 1979; Boym 2001). For example, in an analysis of women college graduates, Stewart and Healy (1989) linked social and historical change to the meaning of work and family roles for women within contrasting cohorts across the first half of the twentieth century. They show that it is important to consider generational changes in understanding women's views of the relationship of family and work roles, together with the impact of these different views on reciprocal socialization across generations within the family.

The other perspective, the narrative study of a lifetime, is concerned with how we tell stories about our experiences. From earliest childhood to oldest age, we continue to tell a story of our lived experience (Bruner 1987, 1990, 2002). Life stories provide self-coherence even as the teller encounters both expected and eruptive life changes (McAdams 2001). Our identity is formed through the story we tell about ourselves and is remade across the course of life in order to preserve a sense of continuity as we encounter these life changes. In the view of such students of the life story as Bruner (2002); Cohler and Hammack (2006); Holland, Lachicotte, Skinner, and Cain (1998); McAdams (1990, 1997, 2003); Mishler (1999); and Plummer (1995), the activity of telling or writing a life story is itself a practice that fosters the construction of an identity. This life-story perspective provides an opportunity for understanding how social change and personal circumstances *together* have an impact upon understanding of self and lived experience across generation-cohorts. Handel (2000) notes that the life story reflects one's currently interpreted biography, and we strive to maintain a coherent story of our lived experience. Stories of the personal and collective past are rewritten over individual and historical time, and we continue to revise our life stories in the context of successive shared understandings of historical events.

Elder and O'Rand (1995) and Handel (2000) have observed that, while recognizing that particular lives are shaped by social circumstances, life course study has not attended in significant detail to the study of the activity of writing or telling about one's own life. The life story reflects the distinctive social and historical changes experienced by members of particular generations and cannot be understood apart from this social and historical context (Dannefer 1984; Elder, Johnson, and Crosnoe 2003). We make meanings of lived experience, including how we struggle to overcome adversity (Gergen and Gergen 1986; Lieblich, Truval-Mashiach, and Zilber 1998; McAdams and Bowman 2001). These life changes are integrated into a narrative, which itself changes throughout life as directed by social and historical circumstances. Further, as George (1996) and Settersten (1999) have observed, there is considerable intracohort variation that affects our life story. Such factors as geography, ethnicity, social status, and sexual orientation, together with social change, determine how we understand the course of our own life (Green 2002; Hostetler 2001; Sears 1991).

A life story must be understood not only in terms of the time and place of telling or writing but also in terms of the meanings of this account made by the reader who may be in a different place and time from that in which the life story was written (Iser 1978; Kaminsky 1992). The meaning that the author assumes in writing autobiographies and memoirs, and the meaning of these accounts for the reader, are each governed by particular historical and individual circumstances. As Tierney (2000) has shown in his experience of reading a recent biography of the early American explorer Meriwether Lewis (Ambrose 1996), a reader's sexual identity leads to a distinctive understanding of a life story.

The study of life stories written by homosexual men provides an ideal means for studying this interplay of writing personal accounts in the context of social change. I have suggested that two events have particularly marked the lives of these men over the postwar period: the beginning of the gay rights movement in the United States in the aftermath of the 1969 riots at New York's Stonewall Inn (Carter 2004; Duberman 1994), and the emergence of AIDS during the summer of 1981 (Moore 2004; Odets 1995). These two events affected everyone aware of homoerotic desire (period effect) but in distinctive ways for men in those generations who were young to middle-age adults at the time at which they occurred (cohort effect). I have followed the perspective of sociologist Howard Schuman and his colleagues (Schuman, Belli, and Bischoping 1997; Schuman and Scott 1989) and psychologist Martin Conway (Conway and Pleydell-Pearce 2000) in suggesting that those events taking place in young adults have particular impact upon the manner in which adults subsequently recount their life stories; these events provide a template for understanding the course of later experiences.

Events experienced in common by one generation, young adults at the time of occurrence, are experienced differently by preceding generations viewing these events in terms of those that their generation experienced in their young adult years. The impact of the Stonewall riots and the emergence of the gay rights movement was experienced differently by 1930s life-writer Martin Duberman, who reported that he could not even bring himself to watch the riots, presumably a result of his sense of shame about his sexual orientation, and Arnie Kantrowitz, 1940s-generation life-writer, who was inspired by the activism of the crowd in the days following the Stonewall raid to become an activist helping to shape the gay rights revolution.

Boxer and Cohler (1989) and Cohler and Galatzer-Levy (2000) note the importance of studying the contrasting meanings of sexual identity across generation-cohorts. Parks (1999), Rosenfeld (2003), and Stein (1997) have studied narratives of lesbians dealing with their sexual identity across several generations. Using narrative accounts, Sadownick (1996) has contrasted understandings of gay sexuality among men across generations from the postwar years to the present. With the exception of Sadownick (1996), who relied largely on archival life-story accounts, these other reports contrast conceptions of sexual identity among persons from different birth cohorts, all interviewed in the present. While providing generationally based narratives, these retrospective life-story accounts have been shaped by social changes experienced across a lifetime. It is important to understand how cohort membership determines meanings both of particular life circumstances and larger social change in the present life-story account across these groups.

The intersect of social and historical change in the construction of the life story has been particularly significant in the study of both life writing and told narratives among three generations of gay men and lesbians (Cohler and Hostetler 2003; Cohler and Galatzer-Levy 2000). The emergence of a gay rights movement over the past three decades, based on the model of the civil rights movement, has transformed the lives of this "invisible" minority: men and women with a same-sex orientation (D'Emilio 1983/1998; Kaiser 1997). Inspired by the social changes of the 1960s, including the civil rights movement, a visible social movement was created in the aftermath of patron resistance to the Stonewall Inn police raid. This spontaneous protest and the overzealous police response led to a series of riots that lasted for several days and inspired community activism spurred largely by young adults in a generation now labeling itself "gay." An anniversary parade and celebration in 1970 drew a crowd of several thousand men and women into Central Park and became the forerunner of the annual gay pride parade, now generally celebrated in many major cities in the United States and elsewhere on the last weekend in June.

The social and historical changes of the past three decades in the wake of the Stonewall riots have had quite different implications for the construction of the life story among women and men within two cohorts— those older men and women who were already middle-aged at the time of the Stonewall protest, and those now-middle-aged men and women who were the young adult activists at that time (Parks 1999; Rosenfeld 2003; Sadownick 1996; Stein 1997). Many men and women, understanding themselves as members of a sexual minority group and accepting the term "homosexual," (or among women, as "lesbian") were accustomed by midlife to living with inevitable stigma related to their sexual orientation. They avoided the social opprobrium expressed by a heterosexist society (Herek et al. 1996) and selected careers such as accountant or librarian, where anonymity was possible. These occupations made it possible to work alone and to avoid discussion of life outside of work. The homosexual men and women in this generation generally avoided any visible evidence of their sexual orientation in demeanor or lifestyle.

The current generation of middle-aged women and men, who came of age at the time of the Stonewall riots, generally defined themselves as "gay" or "lesbian" and were much more likely to follow the model of the civil rights movement by demanding respect and confronting the larger society. This confrontational style was more likely to engender social conflict than the invisibility sought by earlier generations (Rosenfeld 2003). Unfortunately, the increased visibility with the advent of the gay rights movement and legalization of bars and clubs (Sadownick 1996) resulted in the spread of the HIV virus, particularly within the generation born in the 1950s; this indeed had a dramatic impact upon the manner in which same-sex desire was written (Gagnon 1990; Moore 2004; Murphy 1993; Sadownick 1996).

Sadownick's report on two contrasting generations of gay men is particularly significant in reporting personal accounts within two contrasting generations, each young adults at the time their life stories were told or written. One generation, young adults during the postwar era, returning from wartime service, organized their life stories around discreet public sex experiences and visits to homosexual bars where payoffs to mob and police alike were common, and where police shakedowns and congressional crusades against homosexuality filled the pages of newspapers (Read 1973). Homosexuality was classified as a psychiatric disorder and homosexual men were remanded by family and community to the offices of psychiatrists seeking to convert gay to straight.

With this older generation of men, there were no chat lines, bulletin boards, community newspapers, or glossy national magazines filled with full-page advertisements by mainstream retailers. Difficulties in finding other gay men posed obstacles for men within this generation. A subculture of furtive cruising became a feature of urban homosexual life (Brown 2001, Read 1973). This generation was able to decode ambiguous symbols from men who might also desire sexual contact. Furtive, fleeting sexual contact was all that was possible, since men could not be seen being socially intimate. These clandestine experiences of sexuality led to the disconnect between sexuality and intimacy, which has echoed across succeeding generations of gay men struggling to reconcile sexual desire and enduring intimacy (Sullivan 1998).

Young adults at the time of the Stonewall riots enjoyed a heady revolution, which could not have been anticipated by the prior generation. Social change fostered a revised life story in which homosexual desire was more generally accepted; this change led to a gay culture spawning newspapers, magazines, gay rights organizations, and easily available gay community newspapers (Tobias 1998a). Removal of homosexuality from psychiatric nomenclature, together with passage of antidiscrimination laws that made it possible both to be "out" at work and to attain civil rights as a gay man, led to conflict with a conservative society expecting sexual orientation to remain secretive (Clendinen and Nagourney 1999).

Life writing regarding same-sex orientation in this generation reflected the significant social changes of the time. Memoirs, often published by mainstream publishers, reported on the impact of nonstereotyped childhood interests upon awareness of being gay (Corbett 1997). These accounts reported on the meaning of newly available explicit books and films portraying gay sex, which informed those men who were sexually uninitiated of what gay men did during sex, and structured what men expected during gay encounters and, more generally, the nature of gay intimacy (Burger 1995; Cohler 2004c; Harris 1997; Plummer 1995). Sadownick (1996, 107) reports that these men at midlife often feel guilty that their frenetic rush into readily accessible gay sex led to the AIDS pandemic, first evident in the early 1980s.

Study of personal accounts by Parks, Rosenfeld, Sadownick, and Stein necessarily focus on stories written backwards. The social changes over the past twenty-five years have made it possible for those whose voices were formerly stilled by an oppressive society to finally speak out. What was once written in opposition to mainstream society or counterhegemonic (Jolly 2001b) has become the story of just another sexual lifeway. While these social changes have made it possible for life-writers such as Kirk Read (2001) to publish their life stories nearly contemporaneous with events described in the story, older life-writers have been able to find their voices only in middle or later life. The life stories of these men, while only recently published, were written in the light of social and historical changes subsequent to events taking place earlier in the course of life.

It is inevitable that we continually rewrite the life story in the context both of personal development and social change. In what has become a classic example of this inevitable process of rewriting our accounts of our lives over time, Vaillant (1977) reported that the accounts of adolescence provided by men just starting college were markedly different from those provided by the same men at midlife. I would add only that for each generation of adolescents telling their life stories in their college years and again at midlife, the way the life story is rewritten at midlife is always a consequence of intervening social and historical change. While the life story is inevitably rewritten, the nature of changes observed from the college years to midlife will differ among other generation-cohorts.

Looking Backward, Looking Forward

The narratives that I have reviewed in this study confirm Sadownick's (1996) observations regarding the meaning made of alternative sexualities among men across generations in America since World War II. Among the men born in the 1930s and coming of age in postwar America, the lure of the city as a venue in which these men could realize their desire for sexual intimacy is most striking. Perhaps the most intense account of this world was that of Alan Helms's (1995) discovery of the underground colorful life of men enjoying sexuality with other men. As a young college student, Helms was transported into another world where other men eagerly sought his attention and where he discovered a social world that existed outside the purview of mainstream society. A decade later, 1940s-generation life-writer Arnie Kantrowitz (1977) reported on his discovery of the affirmation of his alternative sexuality while riding the bus from suburban New Jersey to New York's East Village. Just as Dorothy in the movie, Kantrowitz was transported over the rainbow to a Technicolor Oz.

Common to the two generations coming of age *before* Stonewall was an abiding sense of shame regarding same-sex desire. Life-writers from the 1930s and 1940s most often sought psychotherapy, either in an effort to rid themselves of their desire, or in an effort to make peace with what was regarded as personally and socially reprehensible. Perhaps the most painful life story is that of Martin Duberman, a member of the 1930s generation, whose upper-middle-class background, intelligence, and Harvard education provided access to low-fee psychoanalysis with senior but conservative psychiatrists who viewed his same-sex desire as evidence to psychopathology. This was at a time when psychiatrists still regarded such desire as evidence of illness (finally removed from psychiatric diagnostic nomenclature in 1973). Life writing from the generations growing up over the decades following the emergence of the gay rights era shows little of this earlier sense of shame regarding same-sex desire.

AIDS represents the second cohort-forming event for these life-writers. It was the generation of men born late in the 1940s and in the 1950s for whom this event was particularly painful. While Arnie Kantrowitz (1977) and Andrew Tobias (1998a) both note the terrible cost of the pandemic on their circles of friends, Mark Doty's (1996) first volume of memoirs portrays the personal cost in exquisite detail as he narrates an account of his lover's illness and death. Only Tim Miller (1997) focuses on AIDS as a political issue in both his narrative and his performance art, while Paul Monette's (1988) memoir, *Borrowed Time: An AIDS Memoir,* reflects a similar bitter political commentary on governmental indifference well into the AIDS pandemic. By the time the generations born in the 1960s and beyond write their memoirs, AIDS is hardly mentioned; the advent of the antiretroviral medication in the mid-1990s has, at least for the moment, turned an illness with a certain death sentence into a chronic disease with few visible symptoms.

Both the prejudice and stigma afflicting the men born prior to the gay rights movement and the AIDS pandemic lead to narratives emphasizing either redemption or contamination, as portrayed by McAdams and Bowman (2001). Psychotherapist Bill Borden (1992) has poignantly portrayed how men with AIDS were able to come to terms with their illness and to tell stories of redemption. Similar testimony is offered by Paul Monette (1988, 1994), himself destined to succumb to AIDS, and Fenton Johnson (1996) and Mark Doty, both of whom remained seronegative and wrote about caring for their dying lovers. In each instance, as psychologically painful as this caregiving was, these life-writers found new meanings for their lives and achieved enhanced self-affirmation through the act of caregiving. Johnson and Doty, sustained by the creative task of writing about their loss, fostered the work of mourning (Freud 1917; Pollock 1989). Psychologist Nancy Stein and her colleagues (Stein, Folkman, Trabasso, and Richards 1997) have shown that among caregivers for partners dying of AIDS, those who were able to look beyond the tragedy and set goals for themselves following bereavement were best able to maintain morale in the aftermath of their loss.

Writing also nourishes an increased sense of personal integrity (Bruner 2002; McAdams 2003). The action of life writing itself protects against a narrative of decline and a fragmented sense of self. Narratives of making a gay identity (Cohler and Hammack 2006) portray a turning point or epiphany. Most often the epiphany is phrased in terms of the decision to disclose or "come out" to self and others, particularly other family members. Coming out and facing the possibility of rejection and prejudice on the part of family and friends is still a risky proposition within many communities and families. While it is believed that personal disclosure fosters enhanced sense of congruence (Savin-Williams 1998), the activity of coming out and writing about an alternative sexual identity is a counterhegemonic activity. In the instance of Andrew Tobias's (1973) iconic memoir of coming out, influential among subsequent life-writers, Tobias was so concerned about the impact of his disclosure upon his family that he elected to use a pseudonym; he revealed his authorship only upon publication of his follow-up memoir (Tobias 1998a) nearly a quarter of a century later.

Social change across the intervening decades made it possible for Tobias (1998a, 1998b) to write more openly in his second account than in his
initial account. As the memoir of Marc Adams (1996) shows, even within
Christian Right families, changes in contemporary society and attitudes
have made possible to make such a disclosure, which ultimately leads to
reduced conflict with family and friends. Preserving the relationship with
their gay family member is more important than criticizing their sexual
identity (Dew 1994; Savin-Williams 2001). In the case of BrYaN Phillips,
disclosure has brought BrYaN and his father closer together even though
his mother still cannot accept her son's sexual identity.

This book has told of the journeys of men who have written about
their lives and their same-sex desire. Reviewing the life stories of these men,
we see that their journals, memoirs, and autobiographies all tell of the impact of both personal life circumstances and social and historical change
upon writing about self, relationships with others, and sexual desire. The
gay rights movement and AIDS, together with other social changes such as
the emergence of Conservative Christianity and the national debate over
same-sex unions, have influenced how these life-writers have understood
their lives. These accounts bear out Marx's (1845) observations regarding
the necessity of understanding of personal circumstances within the context of a systemic, historically conditioned relationship to the social sur-
round. Further, following Mannheim (1928), and systematically elaborated
by sociologist Glen Elder and his colleagues (Elder, Johnson, and Crusnoe
2003), material conditions govern conceptions of self and experience in
quite different ways over time as consequences of ever-changing social and
historical circumstances.

The timing of social changes among men born within some span of adjacent years, particularly influenced by events taking place in young adulthood, inevitably determines how this generation makes meaning of social
change across a life-time. For men born in the 1930s, writing retrospec-
tively in the context of later social change, which itself impacts both the
structure and content of the narrative, the experience of same-sex desire
was one of an enduring sense of shame leading to disavowal (Goldberg
1999), and a split-off aspect of their lived experience, which led to dimin-
ished morale. The narratives of this generation are in striking contrast with
authors born in the 1980s, coming of age at the millennium. Among this
youngest generation of life-writers, homosexuality is but one aspect of
their life.

This perspective on the significance of sexuality for understanding self
and social life is in marked contrast with such personal accounts as that of

Alan Helms (1995), a talented academic by day, who negotiated a secretive world of gay sex by night. In contrast, BrYaN Phillips's gay identity is accepted by his friends and is largely irrelevant within his academic and work life. BrYaN and his partner, Matt, plan on a life typical for his generation of well-educated and successful urban young men and women. For Helms, living in a world of furtive sexual expression, always risking criminal prosecution, the world was dangerous. For BrYaN, much of this sense of danger has disappeared from a world inclusive of both gay and straight friends, out at work and in school in ways that would have been difficult for Helms to have realized at a similar point in his own life.

For BrYaN, as for other life-writers in his web-ring, there is little danger beyond an occasional antigay remark, which his straight friends make clear is unacceptable. Narratives such as those of Kirk Read and BrYaN Phillips reflect a time when their gay lifestyle has become one of several possible sexual lifeways (Hostetler and Herdt 1998). Future life writing by gay men may focus directly on such issues as "gay marriage" (Whyte, Merling, Merling, and Merling 2000) or parenthood (Green 1999) rather than the search for self-acceptance and respect from the community. It is inevitable that life writing by gay men in future generations will show little of the subversive character of life stories written in earlier generations. These life stories may consider homosexuality as just one aspect of a life story in which marriage, work, and parenthood become more significant than the experience of same-sex desire in writing and reading a life story.

Bibliography

Adams, M. 1996. *The Preacher's Son*. Seattle, WA: Window Books.

Alexander, I. 1990. *Personology: Method and Content in Personality Assessment and Psychobiography*. Durham, NC: Duke Univ. Press.

Ambrose, S. E. 1996. *Undaunted Courage: Meriwether Lewis, Thomas Jefferson, and the Opening of the American West*. New York: Simon and Schuster.

Bargh, J. A., K. Y. A. McKenna, and G. M. Fitzsimons. 2002. "Can You See The Real Me? Activation and Expression of the 'True Self' on the Internet." *Journal of Social Issues* 58:33–48.

Baruth, P. E. 1996. "Consensual Autobiography: Narrating 'Personal Sexual History' from Boswell's London Journal to AIDS Pamphlet Literature." In *Getting a Life: Everyday Uses of Autobiography*, ed. S. Smith and J. Watson, 177–97. Minneapolis: Univ. of Minnesota Press.

Bayer, R. 1987. *Homosexuality and American Psychiatry: The Politics of Diagnosis*. Princeton, NJ: Princeton Univ. Press.

Bérubé, A. 1990. *Coming Out Under Fire: The History of Gay Men and Women in World War II*. New York: Free Press.

Bieber, I., H. Dain, P. Dince, M. Drellich, H. Grand, R. Gundlach, M. Kremer, A. Rifkin, C. Wilbur, and T. Bieber. 1962. *Homosexuality: A Psychoanalytic Study*. New York: Basic Books.

Birk, L., W. Huddleston, E. Miller, and B. Cohler. 1971. "Avoidance Conditioning for Homosexuality." *Archives of General Psychiatry* 25 (4): 314–23.

Birk, L., E. Miller, and B. Cohler. 1970. "Group Psychotherapy for Homosexual Men by Male-Female Cotherapists." *Acta Psychiatrica Scandinavicia* Suppl. no. 218, 1–36. Repr. as chap. 40 in *Progress in Group and Family Therapy*, ed. C. Sager and H. Kaplan. New York: Brunner/Mazel, 1972.

Blum, L. A. 2001. *You're Not from around Here, Are You?: A Lesbian in Small-Town America*. Madison: Univ. of Wisconsin Press.

Blumstein, P., and P. Schwartz. 1983. *American Couples: Money, Work, Sex*. New York: Morrow.

Borden, W. 1989. "Life Review as a Therapeutic Frame in the Treatment of Young Adults with AIDS." *Health and Social Work* 14: 253–59.

Boxer, A. M., and J. M. Carrier. 1998. "Evelyn Hooker: A Life Remembered." *Journal of Homosexuality* 36:1–17.

———, and B. Cohler. 1989. "The Life Course of Gay and Lesbian Youth: An Immodest Proposal for the Study of Lives." In *Gay and Lesbian Youth*, ed. G. Herdt, 315–55. New York: Harrington Park Press.

Boym, S. 2001. *The Future of Nostalgia.* New York: Basic Books.

Brodsky, J. I. 1993. "The Mineshaft: A Retrospective Ethnography." *Journal of Homosexuality* 24:233–51.

Brown, R. J. 2001. *The Evening Crowd at Kirmser's: A Gay Life in the 1940s.* Minneapolis: Univ. of Minnesota Press.

Brown, R. M. 1973. *Rubyfruit Jungle.* Plainfield, VT: Daughters, Inc.

Bruner, J. 1987. "Life as Narrative." *Social Research* 54:11–32.

———. 1990. *Acts of Meaning.* Cambridge, MA: Harvard Univ. Press

———. 2001. "Self-making and World-making." In *Narrative and Identity: Studies in Autobiography, Self, and Culture,* ed. J. Brockmeier and D. Carbaugh, 25–37. Philadelphia, PA: John Benjamins Pub.

———. 2002. *Making Stories: Law, Literature, Life.* New York: Farrar, Straus, and Giroux.

Burger, J. R. 1995. *One-Handed Histories: The Eroto-Politics of Gay Male Video Pornography.* New York: Haworth Press.

Carter, D. 2004. *Stonewall: The Riots That Sparked the Gay Revolution.* New York: St. Martin's Press.

Charmaz, K. 2002. "Qualitative Interviewing and Grounded Theory Analysis." In *Handbook of Interview Research: Context and Method,* ed J. F. Gubrium and J. A. Holstein, 675–94. Thousand Oaks, CA: Sage Publications.

Chauncey, G. 1994. *Gay New York: Gender, Urban Culture, and the Makings of the Gay Male World, 1890–1940.* New York: Basic Books.

Chodorow, N. 1994. *Femininities, Masculinities, Sexualities: Freud and Beyond.* Lexington: Univ. Press of Kentucky.

Clendinen, D., and A. Nagourney. 1999. *Out for Good: The Struggle to Build a Gay Rights Movement in America.* New York: Simon and Schuster.

Cohler, B. 2004a. "The Experience of Ambivalence within the Family: Young Adults 'Coming Out' Gay or Lesbian and Their Parents." In *Intergenerational Ambivalence: New Perspectives on Parent-Child Relations in Later Life,* ed. K. Pillemer and K. Lüscher, 255–84. Boston: Elsevier.

———. 2004b. "Memoir and Performance: Social Change and Self Life-Writing among Men who are Gay Pornography Producers and Actors." *Journal of Homosexuality* 47:7–43.

———. 2004c. "Saturday Night at the Tubs: Age and Cohort and Social Life at the Urban Gay Bath." In *Gay and Lesbian Aging: Research and Future Directions,* ed. G. Herdt and B. de Vries, 211–34. New York: Springer Pub. Co.

———, and A. M. Boxer. 1984. "Settling into the World: Person, Time, and

Context." In *Normality and the Life Cycle: A Critical Integration,* ed. D. Offer and M. Sabshin, 145–203. New York: Basic Books.

———, and R. M. Galatzer-Levy. 2000. *The Course of Gay and Lesbian Lives: Social and Psychoanalytic Perspectives.* Chicago: Univ. of Chicago Press.

———, and P. Hammack. 2006. "Making a Gay Identity: Life Story and the Construction of a Coherent Self." In *Identity and Story: Creating Self in Narrative,* ed. D. P. McAdams, R. Josselson, and A. Lieblich, 151–72. Washington, DC: American Psychological Association.

———, and A. J. Hostetler. 2002. "Aging, Intimate Relationships, and Life Story among Gay Men." In *Challenges of the Third Age: Meaning and Purpose in Later Life,* ed. R. S. Weiss and S. A. Bass, 137–60. New York: Oxford Univ. Press.

———, and A. J. Hostetler. 2003. "Linking Life-Course and Life-Story: Social Change and the Narrative Study of Lives Over Time." In *Handbook of the Life Course,* ed. J. T. Mortimer and M. J. Shanahan, 555–78. New York: Kluwer Academic/Plenum Publishers.

———, and A. J. Hostetler. 2006. "Gay Lives in the Third Age: Possibilities and Paradoxes." In *The Crown of Life: Dynamics of the Early Postretirement Period,* ed. J. James and P. Wink. New York: Spring Pub. Co.

———, A. J. Hostetler, and A. M. Boxer. 1998. "Generativity, Social Context, and Lived Experience: Narratives of Gay Men in Middle Adulthood." In *Generativity and Adult Development: How and Why We Care for the Next Generation,* ed. D. P. McAdams and E. de St. Aubin, 265–310. Washington, DC: American Psychological Association.

Conway, J. K. 1998. *When Memory Speaks: Reflections on Autobiography.* New York: Alfred A. Knopf.

Conway, M. 1997. "The Inventory of Experience: Memory and Identity." In *Collective Memory of Political Events: Social Psychological Perspectives,* ed. J. W. Pennebaker, D. Paez, and B. Rimé, 21–46. Mahewh, NJ: Lawrence Erlbaum Associates.

Conway, M. A., and C. W. Pleydell-Pearce. 2000. "The Construction of Autobiographical Memories in The Self-Memory System." *Psychological Review* 107: 261–88.

Coontz, S. 1992. *The Way We Never Were: American Families and the Nostalgia Trap.* New York: Basic Books.

Cooper, B. 1996. *Truth Serum: Memoirs.* Boston: Houghton Mifflin.

Corbett, K. 1997/1999. "Homosexual Boyhood: Notes on Girlyboys." In *Sissies and Tomboys: Gender Nonconformity and Homosexual Childhood,* ed. M. Rottnek, 107–39. New York: New York Univ. Press.

Cory, D. W. [Edward Sagarin]. 1951. *The Homosexual in America: A Subjective Approach.* New York: Greenberg.

Crowley, M. 1968. *The Boys in the Band: A Play in Two Acts.* New York: S. French.

Dane. "Discovering Me?" http://discoveringme.oasismag.com/stories/story Reader$21 (last accessed 2003; no longer available).

Dannefer, D. 1984. "Adult Development and Social Theory: A Paradigmatic Reappraisal." *American Sociological Review* 49:100–116.

———. 1996. "The Social Organization of Diversity, and the Normative Organization of Age." *Gerontologist* 36:174–77.

Davis, F. 1979. *Yearning for Yesterday: A Sociology of Nostalgia.* New York: Free Press.

Dawson, J. 2000. *Gay and Lesbian Online.* Los Angeles: Alyson.

Delany, S. R. 1999. *Times Square Red, Times Square Blue.* New York: New York Univ. Press.

Delph, E. W. 1978. *The Silent Community: Public Homosexual Encounters.* Thousand Oaks, CA: Sage Publications.

D'Emilio, J. 1983/1998. *Sexual Politics, Sexual Communities: The Making of a Homosexual Minority in the United States, 1940–1970.* Chicago: Univ. of Chicago Press.

———. 1989. "The Homosexual Menace: The Politics of Sexuality in Cold War America." In *Passion and Power: Sexuality in History,* ed. K. Peiss and C. Simmons, 226–40. Philadelphia, PA: Temple Univ. Press.

Dew, R. F. 1994. *The Family Heart: A Memoir of When Our Son Came Out.* Reading, MA: Addison-Wesley.

Dilley, P. 2002. *Queer Man on Campus: A History of Non-Heterosexual College Men, 1945 to 2000.* New York: RoutledgeFalmer.

Doty, M. 1996. *Heaven's Coast.* New York: HarperCollins.

———. 1999. *Firebird: A Memoir.* New York: HarperCollins.

———. 2001. *Still Life with Oysters and Lemon.* Boston: Beacon Press.

Drescher, J. 1998. *Psychoanalytic Therapy and the Gay Man.* Hillsdale, NJ: Analytic Press.

Duberman, M. 1972/1993. *Black Mountain: An Exploration in Community.* New York: W. W. Norton.

———. 1986/1991a. *About Time: Exploring the Gay Past.* Rev. ed. New York: Meridian.

———. 1991b. "Coda (Part 3)." In Duberman, *About Time,* 343–77.

———. 1991c. *Cures: A Gay Man's Odyssey.* New York: Dutton.

———. 1994. *Stonewall.* New York: Dutton.

———. 1996. *Midlife Queer: Autobiography of a Decade, 1971–1981.* New York: Scribner.

———. 1999a. *Left Out: The Politics of Exclusion: Essays, 1964–1999.* New York: Basic Books.

———. 1999b. "The 'Father' of the Homophile Movement." In Duberman, *Left Out,* 59–94.

———. 1999c. "Sex and the Military: The Matlovich Case." In Duberman, *Left Out,* 297–318.

Eakin, P. J. 1999. *How Our Lives Become Stories: Making Selves.* Ithaca, NY: Cornell Univ. Press.

Elder, G. H., Jr. 1974/1999. *Children of the Great Depression: Social Change in Life Experience.* Boulder, CO: Westview Press.

———. 1996. "Human Lives in Changing Societies: Life Course and Developmental Insights." In *Developmental Science,* ed. R. B. Cairns, G. H. Elder Jr., and E. J. Costello, 31–62. New York: Cambridge Univ. Press.

———, M. K. Johnson, and R. Crosnoe. 2003. "The Emergence and Development of Life Course Theory." In *Handbook of the Life Course,* ed. J. T. Mortimer and M. J. Shanahan, 3–19. New York: Kluwer Academic/Plenum Publishers.

———, and A. M. O'Rand. 1995. "Adult Lives in a Changing Society." In *Sociological Perspectives on Social Psychology,* ed. K. S. Cook, G. A. Fine, and J. S. House, 452–75. Boston: Allyn and Bacon.

Ely, S. E. 1996. *In Jewish Texas: A Family Memoir.* Fort Worth: Texas Christian Univ. Press.

Erikson, E. H. 1958. *Young Man Luther: A Study in Psychoanalysis and History.* New York: Norton.

———. 1982. *The Life-Cycle Completed: A Review.* New York: Norton.

Evans, A. 1999. "GAA and the Birth of Gay Liberation." www.gaytoday.com (accessed July 26).

Evans, M. 1999. *Missing Persons: The Impossibility of Auto/Biography.* New York: Routledge.

Fellows, W., ed. 1996. *Farm Boys: Lives of Gay Men from the Rural Midwest.* Madison: Univ. of Wisconsin Press.

Flannigan-Saint-Aubin, A. 1992. "The Mark of Sexual Preference in the Interpretation of Texts: Preface to a Homosexual Reading." *Gay and Lesbian Studies* 24:65–88.

Forster, E. M. 1921. *Howards End.* New York: Alfred A. Knopf.

Foucault, M. 1973. *The Order of Things: An Archaeology of the Human Sciences,* trans. E. Gallimard. New York: Vintage Books.

———. 1978. *The History of Sexuality,* vol. 1, *An Introduction.* New York: Random House.

Fraiberg, S., E. Adelson, and V. Shapiro. 1975. "Ghosts in the Nursery." *Journal of the American Academy of Child Psychiatry* 14:387–421.

Freeman, M. 1993. *Rewriting the Self: History, Memory, Narrative.* New York: Routledge.

———. 2002. "Charting the Narrative Unconscious: Cultural Memory and the Challenge of Autobiography." *Narrative Inquiry* 12:193–211.

Freud, S. 1914/1958. "Remembering, Repeating and Working Through: Further Recommendations on the Technique of Psychoanalysis." In *The Standard Edition of the Complete Psychological Works of Sigmund Freud,* vol. 12, ed. and trans. J. Strachey, 146–56. London: Hogarth Press.

———. 1917/1957. "Mourning and Melancholia." In Freud, *Complete Psychological Works,* vol. 14, 237–58.

———. 1935/1951. "A Letter from Freud." *American Journal of Psychiatry* 107:786.

Fricke, A. 1981. *Reflections of a Rock Lobster*. Boston: Alyson.

Friedman, R. C. 1997. "Response to Ken Corbett's 'Homosexual Boyhood.'" *Gender and Psychoanalysis* 2:487–94.

Frontain, R-W. 2000. "A Professional Queer Remembers: Bibliography, Narrative, and the Saving Power of Memory." In *A Sea Of Stories: The Shaping Power of Narrative in Gay and Lesbian Cultures: A Festschrift for John P. Dececco,* ed. S. L. Jones, 217–38. New York: Harrington Park Press.

Gagnon, J. H. 1990. "The Explicit and Implicit Use of the Scripting Perspective in Sex Research." *Annual Review of Sex Research* 1:1–43.

Galatzer-Levy, R., and B. Cohler. 1993. *The Essential Other: A Developmental Psychology of the Self.* New York: Basic Books.

———, and B. Cohler. 2002. "Making a Gay Identity: Coming Out, Social Context, and Psychodynamics." *Annual of Psychoanalysis* 30:255–86.

Gans, H. J. 1967. *The Levittowners: Ways of Life and Politics in a New Suburban Community.* New York: Pantheon.

Gay, P. 1977/1995. *The Enlightenment.* 2 vols. New York: W. W. Norton.

George, L. K. 1996. "Missing Links: The Case for a Social Psychology of the Life Course." *Gerontologist* 36:248–55.

Gergen, K., and M. Gergen. 1986. "Narrative Form and the Construction of Psychological Science." In *Narrative Psychology: The Storied Nature of Human Conduct,* ed. T. R. Sarbin, 22–44. New York: Praeger.

Gitlin, T. 1987. *The Sixties: Years of Hope, Days of Rage.* New York: Bantam Books.

Goldberg, A. 1999. *Being of Two Minds: The Vertical Split in Psychoanalysis and Psychotherapy.* Hillsdale, NJ: Analytic Press.

Green, A. I. 2002. "Gay but Not Queer: Toward a Post-Queer Study of Sexuality." *Theory and Society* 31:521–45.

Green, J. 1999. *The Velveteen Father: An Unexpected Journey to Parenthood.* New York: Villard.

Greenson, R. 1954. "The Struggle against Identification." *Journal of the American Psychoanalytic Association* 2:200–217.

Gusdorf, G. 1956. "Conditions and Limits of Autobiography." Repr. in *Autobiography: Essays Theoretical and Critical,* ed. J. Olney, 28–48. Princeton, NJ: Princeton Univ. Press, 1980.

Hagman, G. 2002. "Mature Selfobject Experience." In *Conversations in Self Psychology,* ed. A Goldberg, 85–107, vol. 13 of *Progress in Self Psychology.* Hillsdale, NJ: The Analytic Press.

Hall Carpenter Archives, Gay Men's Oral History Group. 1989. *Walking after Midnight: Gay Men's Life Stories.* New York: Routledge.

Handel, G. 2000. *Making a Life in Yorkville: Experience and Meaning in the Life-Course Narrative of an Urban Working-Class Man.* Westport, CT: Greenwood Press.

Harris, D. 1997. *The Rise and Fall of Gay Culture.* New York: Hyperion.

Harry, J., and W. DeVall. 1978. "Age and Sexual Culture among Homosexually Oriented Males." *Archives of Sexual Behavior* 7:199–209.

Harwood, G. 1997. *The Oldest Gay Couple in America: A Seventy-Year Journey through Same-Sex America*. Secaucus, NJ: Carol Publishing.

Helms, A. 1995. *Young Man from the Provinces: A Gay Life before Stonewall*. Boston: Faber and Faber.

———. 2003. "Reflections on Gay Male Porn from the Furtive '50s to Today's Explicit but Scripted Fare." *Gay and Lesbian Review* 10:27–30.

Henriksson, B. 1995. *Risk Factor Love: Homosexuality, Sexual Interaction and HIV Prevention*. Göteborg, Sweden: Göteborg Univ. Press.

Herdt, G. 1997. *Same Sex, Different Cultures: Gays and Lesbians across Cultures*. Boulder, CO: Westview Press.

———, and A. Boxer. 1996. *Children of Horizons: How Gay and Lesbian Teens are Leading a New Way Out of the Closet*. 2nd ed. Boston: Beacon Press.

———, and B. Koff. 1999. *Something to Tell You: The Road Families Travel When a Child Is Gay*. New York: Columbia Univ. Press.

Herek, G. M., J. B. Jobe, and R. M. Carney. 1996. *Out in Force: Sexual Orientation and the Military*. Chicago: Univ. of Chicago Press.

Holland, D. 1997. "Selves as Cultured: As Told by an Anthropologist Who Lacks a Soul." In *Self and Identity: Fundamental Issues,* ed. R. D. Ashmore and L. Jussim, 160–90. New York: Oxford University Press.

———, W. Lachicotte Jr., D. Skinner, and C. Cain. 1998. *Identity and Agency in Cultural Worlds*. Cambridge, MA: Harvard Univ. Press.

Holleran, A. 2004. "The Day After: On Presiding Over 'The Gay Table' 25 Years after Leaving Harvard." *Gay and Lesbian Review* 11:12–16.

Hooker, E. 1956. "A Preliminary Analysis of Group Behavior of Homosexuals." *Journal of Psychology* 42:217–25.

———. 1957. "The Adjustment of the Male Overt Homosexual." *Journal of Projective Techniques* 21:18–31.

———. 1968/69. "Homosexuality." Repr. in *National Institute of Mental Health Task Force on Homosexuality: Final Report and Background Papers,* ed. J. M. Livingood, 11–21. Rockville, MD: National Institute of Mental Health, 1972.

Horrigan, P. E. 1999. *Widescreen Dreams: Growing Up Gay at the Movies*. Madison: Univ. of Wisconsin Press.

Hostetler, A. J. 2001. "Single Gay Men: Cultural Models of Adult Development, Psychological Well-Being, and the Meaning of Being 'Single by Choice.'" PhD diss., Univ. of Chicago.

———, and G. H. Herdt. 1998. "Culture, Sexual Lifeways, and Developmental Subjectivities: Rethinking Sexual Taxonomies." *Social Research* 65:249–90.

Humphreys, L. 1970. *Tearoom Trade: Impersonal Sex in Public Places*. Chicago: Aldine.

Isay, R. A. 1986. "The Development of Sexual Identity in Homosexual Men." *Psychoanalytic Study of the Child* 41:467–89.

———. 1987. "Fathers and Their Homosexually Inclined Sons in Childhood." *Psychoanalytic Study of the Child* 42:275–94.

———. 1989. *Being Homosexual: Gay Men and Their Development*. New York: Farrar, Straus, Giroux.

Iser, W. 1978. *The Act of Reading: A Theory of Aesthetic Response*. Baltimore, MD: Johns Hopkins Univ. Press.

Johnson, F. 1996. *Geography of the Heart: A Memoir*. New York: Scribner.

Jolly, M. 2001a. "Lesbian and Gay Life Writing." In *Encyclopedia of Life Writing: Autobiographical and Biographical Forms*, vol. 2, ed. M. Jolly, 547–50. London: Fitzroy Dearborn.

———. 2001b. "Coming Out of the Coming-Out Story: Writing Queer Lives." *Sexualities* 4:474–96.

Jones, C., and J. Dawson. 2000. *Stitching a Revolution: The Making of an Activist*. San Francisco: Harper.

Josselson, R. 1996a. *Revising Herself: The Story of Women's Identity from College to Midlife*. New York: Oxford Univ. Press.

———. 1996b. "On Writing Other People's Lives." In *Ethics and Process in the Narrative Study of Lives*, vol. 4 of *The Narrative Study of Lives*, ed. R. Josselson, 60–71. Thousand Oaks, CA: Sage Publications.

Kaiser, C. 1997. *The Gay Metropolis: 1940–1996*. Boston: Houghton Mifflin.

Kaminsky, M. 1992. Introduction to *Remembered Lives: The Work of Ritual, Storytelling, and Growing Older*, by B. Myerhoff, 307–40. Ann Arbor: Univ. of Michigan Press.

Kantrowitz, A. 1977/1996. *Under the Rainbow: Growing Up Gay*. New York: St. Martin's Press.

Kaufman, M., and the Members of the Tectonic Theater Project. 2001. *The Laramie Project*. New York: Vintage Books.

Kohut, H. 1979. "The Two Analyses of Mr. Z." *International Journal of Psychoanalysis* 60:3–27.

———. 1984. *How Does Analysis Cure?* Ed. A. Goldberg. Chicago: Univ. of Chicago Press.

———. 1985. *Self-Psychology and the Humanities: Reflections on a New Psychoanalytic Approach*. Ed. C.B. Strozier. New York: W.W. Norton.

———, and E. S. Wolf. 1978. "The Disorders of the Self and Their Treatment: An Outline." *International Journal of Psychoanalysis* 59:413–25.

Kraut, R., S. Kiesler, B. Boneva, J. Cummings, V. Helgeson, and A. Crawford. 2002. "Internet Paradox Revisited." *Journal of Social Issues* 58:49–74.

Kutchins, H., and S. A. Kirk. 1997. *Making Us Crazy: DSM: The Psychiatric Bible and the Creation of Mental Disorders*. New York: Free Press.

Lawrence, A. 1999. *Suburban Hustler: Stories of a Hi-Tech Callboy*. Warren, NJ: Late Night Press.

Lee, J. A. 1991. "Can We Talk? Can We Really Talk? Communication as a Key Factor in the Maturing Homosexual Couple." *Journal of Homosexuality* 20:143–68.

Lieberman, M., and J. Falk. 1971. "The Remembered Past as a Source of Data for Research on the Life Cycle." *Human Development* 14:132–41.

Lieblich, A., R. Tuval-Mashiach, and T. Zilber. 1998. *Narrative Research: Reading, Analysis and Interpretation.* Thousand Oaks, CA: Sage Publications.

Linde, C. 1993. *Life Stories: The Creation of Coherence.* New York: Oxford Univ. Press.

Loffreda, B. 2000. *Losing Matt Shepard: Life and Politics in the Aftermath of Anti-Gay Murder.* New York: Columbia Univ. Press.

Loughery, John. 1998. *The Other Side of Silence: Men's Lives and Gay Identities: A Twentieth Century History.* New York: H. Holt.

Mann. T. 1912/1994. *Death in Venice.* Trans. C Koelb. New York: W. W. Norton.

Mannheim, K. 1928/1993. "The Problem of Generations." In *From Karl Mannheim,* 2nd ed., ed. K. H. Wolff, 351–98. New Brunswick, NJ: Transactions Books.

Marotta, T. 1982. *Sons of Harvard: Gay Men from the Class of 1967.* New York: William Morrow.

Marx, K. [1845] 1978. "The German Ideology." Part 1. In *The Marx-Engels Reader,* 2nd ed. Ed. and trans. R. Tucker, 146–200. New York: Norton.

Mass, L. D. 1990. *Dialogues of the Sexual Revolution.* 2 vols. New York: Harrington Park Press.

———. 1994. *Confessions of a Jewish Wagnerite: Being Gay and Jewish in America.* London: Cassell.

———, ed. 1997. *We Must Love One Another or Die: The Life and Legacies of Larry Kramer.* New York: St. Martin's Press.

McAdams, D. P. 1990. "Unity and Purpose in Human Lives: The Emergence of Identity as a Life Story." In *Studying Persons and Studying Lives,* ed. A. I. Rabin, R. A. Zucker, and R. A. Emmons, 148–200. New York: Springer Pub. Co.

———. 1997. "The Case for Unity in the (Post)Modern Self: A Modest Proposal." In *Self and Identity: Fundamental Issues,* ed. R. D. Ashmore and L. Jussim, 46–78. New York: Oxford Univ. Press.

———. 2001. "The Psychology of Life Stories." *Review of General Psychology* 5: 100–122.

———. 2003. "Identity and the Life Story." In *Autobiographical Memory and the Construction of a Narrative Self: Developmental and Cultural Considerations,* ed. R. Fivush and C. A. Haden, 187–207. Mahwah, NJ: L. Erlbaum.

———, and P. J. Bowman. 2001. "Narrating Life's Turning Points: Redemption and Contamination." In *Turns in the Road: Narrative Studies of Lives in Transition,* ed. D. P. McAdams, R. Josselson, and A. Lieblich, 3–34. Washington, DC: American Psychological Association.

———, H. M. Hart, and S. Maruna. 1998. "The Anatomy of Generativity." In *Generativity and Adult Development: How and Why We Care for the Next Generation,* ed. D. P. McAdams and E. de St. Aubin, 7–45. Washington, DC: American Psychological Association.

McCloskey, D. 1999. *Crossing: A Memoir*. Chicago: Univ. of Chicago Press.

McKenna, K. Y. A., and J. A. Bargh. 1998. "Coming Out in the Age of the Internet: Identity 'Demarginalization' through Virtual Group Participation." *Journal of Personality and Social Psychology* 75:681–94.

Melson, J. K. 1992. *The Golden Boy*. Binghamton, NY: Harrington Park Press/ Haworth.

Mendelsohn, D. 1999. *The Elusive Embrace: Desire and the Riddle of Identity*. New York: Alfred A. Knopf.

Meyer, I. H. 1995. "Minority Stress and Mental Health in Gay Men." *Journal of Health and Social Behavior* 36:38–56.

Michael. "Jazzer." http://jazzer.oasismag.com/stories/storyReader$82 (last accessed 2003; no longer available).

Miller, J. 1993. "Dante on Fire Island: Reinventing Heaven in the AIDS Elegy." In *Writing AIDS: Gay Literature, Language, and Analysis,* ed. T. F. Murphy and S. Poirier, 265–305. New York: Columbia Univ. Press.

Miller, N. K. 2002. *But Enough about Me: Why We Read Other People's Lives*. New York: Columbia Univ. Press.

Miller, T. 1997. *Shirts and Skin*. Los Angeles: Alyson.

———. 1999. "Memory and Facing the Future." *Harvard Gay and Lesbian Review* 6:34–36. Repr. in Miller, *1001 Beds.*

———. 2002. *Body Blows: Six Performances*. Madison: Univ. of Wisconsin Press.

———. 2006. *1001 Beds: Performances, Essays, and Travels.* Ed. Glen Johnson. Madison: Univ. of Wisconsin Press.

Mills, C. W. 1959/2000. *The Sociological Imagination.* Fortieth Anniversary Edition. New York: Oxford Univ. Press.

Minton, H. L. 2002. *Departing from Deviance: A History of Homosexual Rights and Emancipatory Science in America*. Chicago: Univ. of Chicago Press.

Mishler, E. G. 1990. "Validation in Inquiry-Guided Research: The Role of Exemplars in Narrative Studies." *Harvard Educational Review* 60:415–42.

———. 1999. *Storylines: Craftartists' Narratives of Identity*. Cambridge, MA: Harvard Univ. Press.

Monette, P. 1988. *Borrowed Time: An AIDS Memoir*. New York: Harcourt Brace.

———. 1992. *Becoming a Man: Half a Life Story*. New York: Harcourt Brace.

———. 1994. *Last Watch of the Night: Essays Too Personal and Otherwise*. New York: Harcourt Brace.

Moon, M. 1998. *A Small Boy and Others: Imitation and Initiation in American Culture from Henry James to Andy Warhol*. Durham, NC: Duke Univ. Press.

Moore, P. 2004. *Beyond Shame: Reclaiming the Abandoned History of Radical Gay Sexuality*. Boston: Beacon Press.

Moss, D. 1997. "On Situating Homophobia." *Journal of the American Psychoanalytic Association* 45:201–15.

Murphy, T. F. 1993. "Testimony." In *Writing AIDS: Gay Literature, Language, and*

Analysis, ed. T. F. Murphy and S. Poirier, 306–20. New York: Columbia Univ. Press.

Murray, H. A., et al. 1938. *Explorations in Personality.* New York: Oxford Univ. Press.

Nardi, P., D. Sanders, and J. Marmor, eds. 1994. *Growing Up before Stonewall: Life Stories of Some Gay Men.* New York: Routledge.

Neugarten, B. L. 1979. "Time, Age, and the Life Cycle." *American Journal of Psychiatry* 136:887–94.

Odets, W. 1995. *In the Shadow of the Epidemic: Being HIV-Negative in the Age of AIDS.* Durham, NC: Duke Univ. Press.

Olney, J. 1972. *Metaphors of Self: The Meaning of Autobiography.* Princeton, NJ: Princet on Univ. Press.

———. 1998. *Memory & Narrative: The Weave of Life-Writing.* Chicago: Univ. of Chicago Press.

Ortega y Gasset, J. 1921–22/1961. *The Modern Theme.* New York: Harper.

Parks, C. 1999. "Lesbian Identity Development: An Examination of Differences across Generations." *American Journal of Orthopsychiatry* 69:347–61.

Peck, S. 1995. *All American Boy: A Memoir.* Los Angeles: Alyson.

Phillips, Bryan. 1999–2004. "The Populace." http://the-populace.com (last accessed 2003; site now discontinued).

Phillips, S. H. 2001. "The Overstimulation of Everyday Life: I. New Aspects Of Male Homosexuality." *Journal of the American Psychoanalytic Association* 49: 1235–67.

———. 2003. "Homosexuality: Coming Out of the Confusion." *International Journal of Psychoanalysis* 84:1431–50.

Plath, D. W. 1980. "Contours of Consociation: Lessons from a Japanese Narrative." In *Life-Span Development and Behavior,* vol. 3, ed. P. B. Baltes and O. G. Brim Jr., 287–305. New York: Academic Press.

Plummer, K. 1995. *Telling Sexual Stories: Power, Change, and Social Worlds.* New York: Routledge.

———. 1996. "Intimate Citizenship and the Culture of Sexual Story Telling." In *Sexual Cultures: Communities, Values, and Intimacy,* ed. J. Weeks and J. Holland, 34–52. New York: St Martin's Press.

———. 2001. *Documents of Life 2: An Invitation to a Critical Humanism.* Thousand Oaks, CA: Sage Publications.

Pollock, G. H. 1989. *The Mourning-Liberation Process.* Madison, CT: International Universities Press.

Porter, K., and K. Weeks, eds. 1991. *Between the Acts: Lives of Homosexual Men, 1885–1967.* New York: Routledge.

Poster, M. 2001. *What's the Matter with the Internet?* Minneapolis: Univ. of Minnesota Press.

Propp, V. 1928/1968. *The Morphology of the Folktale.* 2nd. ed. Trans. L. Scott, ed. L. A. Wagner. Austin: Univ. of Texas Press.

Read, K. 2001. *How I Learned to Snap: A Small-Town Coming-Out and Coming-of-Age Story*. Athens, GA: Hill Street Press.

Read, K. E. 1973/1980. *Other Voices: The Style of a Male Homosexual Tavern*. Novato, CA: Chandler and Sharp.

Rechy, J. 1963/1984. *City of the Night*. New York: Grove Press.

Remafedi, G., ed. 1994. *Death by Denial: Studies of Suicide in Gay and Lesbian Teenagers*. Boston: Alyson.

Ricoeur, P. 1977. "The Question of Proof in Freud's Psychoanalytic Writings." *Journal of the American Psychoanalytic Association* 25:835–72.

Robinson, P. A. 1999. *Gay Lives: Homosexual Autobiography from John Addington Symonds to Paul Monette*. Chicago: Univ. of Chicago Press.

Rofes, E. 1998. *Dry Bones Breathe: Gay Men Creating Post-AIDS Identities and Cultures*. New York: Haworth Press.

Rosenfeld, D. 2003. *The Changing of the Guard: Lesbian and Gay Elders, Identity, and Social Change*. Philadelphia, PA: Temple Univ. Press.

Sadownick, D. 1996. *Sex between Men: An Intimate History of the Sex Lives of Gay Men Postwar to the Present*. San Francisco: Harper.

Savage, D. 1999. *The Kid: What Happened After My Boyfriend and I Decided to Go Get Pregnant*. New York: Dutton.

Savin-Williams, R. C. 1998. *"—And Then I Became Gay": Young Men's Stories*. New York: Routledge.

———. 2001. *Mom, Dad, I'm Gay: How Families Negotiate Coming Out*. Washington, DC: American Psychological Association.

———. 2005. *The New Gay Teenager*. Cambridge, MA: Harvard Univ. Press.

Schafer, R. 1981. *Narrative Actions in Psychoanalysis*. Worcester, MA: Clark Univ. Press.

Schiff, B., and B. Cohler. 2001. "Telling Survival Backward: Holocaust Survivors Narrate the Past." In *Narrative Gerontology: Theory, Research, and Practice*, ed. G. Kenyon, P. Clark, and B. de Vries. New York: Springer Pub. Co.

Schuman, H., R. F. Belli, and K. Bischoping. 1997. "The Generational Basis of Historical Knowledge." In *Collective Memory of Political Events: Social Psychological Perspectives*, ed. J. W. Pennebaker, D. Paez, and B. Rimé, 47–78. Mahwah, NJ: Lawrence Erlbaum Associates.

———, and J. Scott. 1989. "Generations and Collective Memories." *American Sociological Review* 54:359–81.

Sears, J. T. 1991. *Growing Up Gay in the South: Race, Gender, and Journeys of the Spirit*. New York: Harrington Park Press.

———. 1997. *Lonely Hunters: An Oral History of Lesbian and Gay Southern Life, 1948–1968*. Boulder, CO: Westview Press.

———. 2001. *Rebels, Rubyfruit, and Rhinestone: Queering Space in the Stonewall South*. New Brunswick, NJ: Rutgers Univ. Press.

Seidman, S. 2002. *Beyond the Closet: The Transformation of Gay and Lesbian Life*. New York: Routledge.

Settersten, R. A. 1999. *Lives in Time and Place: The Problems and Promises of Developmental Science.* Amityville, NY: Baywood Pub.

Shand-Tucci, D. 2003. *The Crimson Letter: Harvard, Homosexuality, and the Shaping of American Culture.* New York: St. Martin's Press.

Shelby, R. D. 1994. "Homosexuality and the Struggle for Coherence." In *Progress in Self Psychology* 10:55–78. Hillsdale, NJ: Analytic Press.

———. 2002. "About Cruising and Being Cruised." *Annual of Psychoanalysis* 30: *Rethinking Psychoanalysis and the Homosexualities,* ed. J. Winer, J. W. Anderson, B. Cohler, and D. Shelby, 191–208. Hillsdale, NJ: Analytic Press.

Shilts, R. 1987. *And the Band Played On: Politics, People, and the AIDS Epidemic.* New York: St. Martin's Press.

Shyer, M. F., and C. Shyer. 1996. *Not Like Other Boys: Growing Up Gay: A Mother and Son Look Back.* Boston: Houghton Mifflin.

Signorile, M. 1998. *Life Outside: The Signorile Report on Gay Men, Sex, Drugs, Muscles, and the Passages of Life.* New York: HarperCollins.

Singer, J. A., and P. Salovey. 1993. *The Remembered Self: Emotion and Memory in Personality.* New York: Free Press.

Socarides, C. W. 1988. *The Preoedipal Origin and Psychoanalytic Therapy of Sexual Perversions.* Madison, CT: International Universities Press.

Stein, A. 1997. *Sex and Sensibility: Stories of a Lesbian Generation.* Berkeley: Univ. of California Press.

Stein, E. 1999. *The Mismeasure of Desire: The Science, Theory, and Ethics of Sexual Orientation.* New York: Oxford Univ. Press.

Stein, N., S. Folkman, T. Trabasso, and T. A. Richards. 1997. "Appraisal and Goal Processes as Predictors of Psychological Well-Being in Bereaved Caregivers." *Journal of Personality and Social Psychology* 72:872–84.

Stewart, A. J., C. Franz, and L. Layton. 1988. "The Changing Self: Using Personal Documents to Study Lives." *Journal of Personality* 56:41–74.

———, and J. M. Healy Jr. 1989. "Linking Individual Development and Social Changes." *American Psychologist* 44:30–42.

Stierlin, H. 1981. *Separating Parents and Adolescents: A Perspective on Running Away, Schizophrenia, and Waywardness.* Rev. ed. New York: Aronson.

Styles, J. 1979. "Outsider/Insider: Researching Gay Baths." *Urban Life* 8: 135–52.

Sullivan, A. 1995. *Virtually Normal: An Argument about Homosexuality.* New York: Alfred A. Knopf.

———. 1998. *Love Undetectable: Notes on Friendship, Sex, and Survival.* New York: Alfred A. Knopf.

Terry, J. 1999. *An American Obsession: Science, Medicine, and Homosexuality in Modern Society.* Chicago: Univ. of Chicago Press.

Tierney, W. G. 2000. "Undaunted Courage: Life History and the Postmodern Challenge." In *Handbook of Qualitative Research,* 2nd ed., ed. N. K. Denzin and Y. S. Lincoln, 537–54. Thousand Oaks, CA: Sage Publications.

Tipton, S. M. 1982. *Getting Saved from the Sixties: Moral Meaning in Conversion and Social Change*. Berkeley: Univ. of California Press.

Tobias, A. (a.k.a. John Reid) 1973/1993. *The Best Little Boy in the World*. Rev. ed. New York: Ballantine.

———. 1998a. *The Best Little Boy in the World Grows Up*. New York: Random House.

———. 1998b. "Gay Like Me." *Harvard Magazine* 100 (Jan–Feb 1998): 50–59.

Tóibín, C. 2002. *Love in a Dark Time*. New York: Scribner.

Tolpin, M. 1997. "Compensatory Structures: Paths to the Restoration of the Self." In *Conversations in Self Psychology*, ed. A. Goldberg, 3–19, vol. 13 of *Progress in Self Psychology*. Hillsdale, NJ: Analytic Press.

———. 2002. "Doing Psychoanalysis of Normal Development: Forward Edge Transferences." In *Postmodern Self Psychology*, ed. A. Goldberg, 167–92, vol. 18 of *Progress in Self Psychology*. Hillsdale, NJ: Analytic Press.

Vaillant, G. E. 1977. *Adaptation to Life*. Boston: Little, Brown.

Warner, M. 1999. *The Trouble with Normal: Sex, Politics, and the Ethics Of Queer Life*. New York: Free Press.

Weinberg, M. S. 1970. "The Male Homosexual: Age-Related Variations in Social and Psychological Characteristics." *Social Problems* 17:527–38.

Weintraub, K. J. 1978. *The Value of the Individual: Self and Circumstance in Autobiography*. Chicago: Univ. of Chicago Press.

Weston, K. 1991. *Families We Choose: Lesbians, Gays, Kinship*. New York: Columbia Univ. Press.

Whisman, V. 1996. *Queer by Choice: Lesbians, Gay Men, and the Politics of Identity*. New York: Routledge.

White, M. 1994. *Stranger at the Gate: To Be Gay and Christian in America*. New York: Simon and Schuster.

Whythe, D., A. Merling, R. Merling, and S. Merling. 2000. *The Wedding: A Family's Coming Out Story*. New York: Avon Books.

Williams, R. 1977. *Marxism and Literature*. New York: Oxford Univ. Press.

Winnicott, D. W. 1953. "Transitional Objects and Transitional Phenomena." In *Collected Papers: Through Paediatrics to Psycho-Analysis*, 229–42. New York: Basic Books.

———. 1960. "Ego Distortion in Terms of the True and False Self." Repr. in *The Maturational Processes and the Facilitating Environment: Studies in the Theory of Emotional Development*, 140–52. New York: International Universities Press, 1965.

Woods, W. J., and D. Binson, eds. 2003. *Gay Bathhouses and Public Health Policy*. New York: Harrington Park Press.

Young, I. 1995. *The Stonewall Experiment: A Gay Psychohistory*. New York: Cassell.

Young, P. D. 1973. "So You're Planning to Spend a Night at the Tubs?: Here's Some Advice Your Mother Never Gave You." *Rolling Stone*, February 15, 1973.

Index

activism, *xii;* 1960s as social climate for, 16, 64–65, 133–34, 155, 219; ACT-UP and, 82, 122, 129–30; antidiscrimination ordinance in New York, 78–79, 135–36, 221; birth cohorts and, 63, 134, 155, 216; "coming out" as social activism, 65; life writing as political act, 12–13; Mattachine Society and political activism, 28; medical, 82; political, 12–13, 16, 68. *See also* gay rights

ACT-UP, 82, 122, 129–30

Adams, Marc, 135; childhood of, 147; early sexual experiences of, 148–49, 150; family of, 146–47, 148–49, 155, 224; long-term relationships of, 154–55; Read compared to, 164–65; religious fundamentalism and, 13, 156, 224; suicide attempts, 146; violence in family life of, 146, 147–48

aging: Helms "golden boy" persona and, 59–60. *See also* midlife

AIDS, 22; ACT-UP (AIDS Coalition to Unleash Power), 82, 122, 129–30; antiretroviral therapies for, 20, 98, 101, 131, 133, 161, 223; as apocalypse, 106, 107, 119; caregiving and loss as subject of life writing, *xiii–xiv,* 13, 104, 106, 116–21, 223; as context, 158; as creative context, 106, 118; desire and writing of desire in context of, 130; documentation of epidemic, 82 *(see also under specific authors);* Doty as chronicler of, 106, 108, 116–21; epidemiology of pandemic, 16, 18; as focus of life writing, 12–13; Gay Men's Health Crisis (GMHC) and, 82; as generation-defining event, 15, 18–19, 36, 100, 134, 169, 214, 218, 222–23; government policy as failure, 123; guilt and, 118, 221; Helms as chronicler of pandemic, 45, 61; Kantrowitz as chronicler of pandemic, 70; life writing as mourning, 13, 106, 223; Monette as chronicler of pandemic, 106; monogamous relationships as response to, 129; Odets as chronicler of pandemic, 103–4; as punishment,

103, 104, 147, 151–52; Religious Right and, 152; safe sex practices and, 20, 82, 129, 160–61; sexual inhibition and, 128; sexual practices and, 18; social contexts of pandemic, *xii;* systematic misinformation campaigns by Religious Right, 149; testing for HIV, 129, 134; Tobias as chronicler of pandemic, 84, 94, 96, 97–98

AIDS Coalition to Unleash Power (ACT-UP), 82, 122, 129–30

Allport, Gordon, *ix*

alter egos, 10, 153

ambivalence, 155

American cultural diversity: counterculture, 168; social acceptance as regionally diverse, 160, 165; southern culture, 110, 160, 165. *See also specific cities*

anonymity: intimacy as elusive, 143; sexual encounters as anonymous, 11–12, 73, 127; shame and, 137; urban life and, 27, 113

antidiscrimination ordinances, 78–79, 159

antiretroviral therapies, 20, 98, 101, 131, 133, 161

anti-Semitism, 74

apocalypse: as AIDS metaphor, 119; in Doty's works, 106, 107, 119

assimilation of gay culture, 159

audience: Internet access to life stories, 11; for life writing, *vi,* 5–6, 7, 21, 115, 217–18; sexual identity as lens of, 218; straight readers as, 85. *See also under specific authors*

autobiography, 5–6, 20–21; Kantrowitz on, 70. *See also* life writing

aversive conditioning, *x,* 56

backward socialization between generations, 63

Baker, Gilbert, 160

Bargh, J. A., 174

bath houses: bodily attractiveness and, 58; intimacy and, 79–80; as social venue, 11–12, 79–80, 81

Index

community *(continued)*
  66, 79, 101; gay community as asset to
  at-large, 160; Internet technology and
  creation of, 161–63, 173–75, 176; Mendelsohn on gay community, 141; Phillips and rejection of gay community,
  193–94
confession in life writing, 12, 31, 68
conservatism, social, as context, 81, 124,
  135, 156
contemporaneous forms of life writing,
  6–7, 17, 68, 84, 163–64, 221
conversion therapy, 150, 152, 156
Conway, Martin, 14–15, 41, 218
Coontz, Stephanie, 105
Cooper, Bernard, 133
Corbett, K., 48, 71–72
Cory, Donald Webster (Edward Sagarin),
  28, 67
counterculture, 12, 115, 120; 1990s and
  mainstreaming of, 169; gay community as, 101; identity of generational
  cohorts and, 22–23; in San Francisco,
  66, 90, 114
criminalization of same-sex desire, *xii,* 18;
  police raids, 55–56, 66, 92, 220
Crowley, Mart, 67
cruising, intimacy and, 40–41, 220
Cures: A Gay Man's Odyssey (Duberman),
  29, 30

Dane: coming out to family and friends,
  212; gay identity of, 211–12; on passing as heterosexual, 212; self-loathing
  and stereotyping of gay community,
  213
Daughters of Bilitis, 16
death: desire linked to, 121, 137, 138–39;
  mourning, 13, 103, 108, 116–21; writing linked to, 117
D'Emilio, J., 28, 66, 68
Depression, as generation-defining event,
  15
desire: as expression of vitality, 119–20; psychology of, 8–9; writing of desire, 130.
  See also same-sex desire
Dew, R. F., 156

diaries, 5; Duberman as diarist, 30, 34–35,
  42; in Miller's performance art, 126
discrimination: antidiscrimination ordinances, 78–79, 135–36, 159, 221; anti-
  Semitism, 74; in employment, 36,
  38, 66; in immigration policy, 122–
  23, 132; by NEA, 122, 130; Religious
  Right and, 130; suicide as reaction
  to, 151
diversity in American culture, 13, 22
Doty, Mark, 3, 9, 13, 103; academic career
  of, 116, 118; AIDS pandemic chronicled by, *xiii,* 103, 106, 108, 116–21, 134,
  222, 223; apocalypse, 106, 107, 119;
  on audience for life writing, 115;
  body consciousness of, 111–12, 113,
  114; childhood of, 107–13; color as
  metaphor in works of, 107, 108–9,
  111, 115, 119, 120, 121; counterculture
  of 1960s as context for, 113–15, 133;
  as dancer, 107, 113; death, grief, and
  mourning as subject in works, 103,
  108, 116–21; depressive episodes, 113;
  early sexual experience of, 112; epiphanies of, 107–8, 119; family of, 108–13,
  113, 114–15, 116; films and, 111, 112;
  heterosexual experiences of, 107; on
  life writing as memorial or grieving
  experience, 116–18; long-term relationships of, 106–8, 116–21, 133; marriage to Ruth, 115–16; memory in
  works of, 107–8, 117, 121; as poet, 115,
  118; on sexual awakening as a child,
  111; sexual identity of, 114; shame
  and, 109, 111–12, 115; suicide attempts of, 114; violence in family
  dynamics of, 112, 115
drugs, 57, 80, 115, 159; 1960s drug scene,
  75, 76
Dry Bones Breathe (Rofes), 158
Duberman, Martin, *x;* academic career of,
  36, 37; as activist, 29, 32–33, 35, 38,
  39, 41; childhood of, 30, 35; coming
  out (revelation of sexual identity), 31–
  32; "cure" for same-sex desire sought
  by, 25, 29–30, 33–36, 38–39, 40, 42–
  43, 222; as diarist, 30, 34–35, 42; early

sexual experience of, 30; efforts to "pass" as heterosexual, 35; family of, 30, 37, 41; Helms compared to, 62–63; as historian, 29, 31–32, 38, 39, 41; intimacy and long-term relationship experiences, 36, 40–41; Kantrowitz compared to, 76, 218; New York and, 27; as playwright, 30, 31–32, 37–38; psychotherapy experiences of, 35–36, 38–39, 43; quotes from works of, 25; Robinson on, 42–44; as self-loathing, 33–37, 39, 42–43, 218; "split life" of, 37; works of, 25, 29–30

education: academy as relatively accepting social milieu, 32; as escape, 50–51
effeminacy, 110; as sign in master narrative of gay boyhood, 111; as stereotypical, 86
eighties (1980s). *See* 1980s *at beginning of index*
Elder, Glen H., *ix–x,* 14, 15, 216, 217, 224
The Elusive Embrace: Desire and the Riddle of Identity (Mendelsohn), 135, 136–37
employment discrimination, 36, 38, 66
"essential others," 9–10, 203
Evans, Mary, 18–19

Falwell, Jerry, 147, 150, 153
family: acceptance by, 13, 20, 224; "family by choice," 173. *See also* parents; *specific authors*
father/son relationships, 110, 136, 154; 1970s and 1980s birth cohorts and expectations of, 159, 224; between adult children and parents, 95; body consciousness and, 142; same-sex desire and, 170; shame and, 184. *See also* parenthood; *specific authors*
Fellows, Will, 13–14, 15
fifties (1950s). *See* 1950s *at beginning of index*
film: Doty and, 111, 112; Helms and, 49–50, 69–70; Horrigan on, 69–70; as impact on development, 49, 69–70; Kantrowitz's use of *The Wizard of Oz* as theme or metaphor, 69–70, 72, 77;

pornography and gay self-acceptance, 162; as sexual education, 162–63
Firebird (Doty), 3, 106, 107
the Firehouse, 78
Fire Island, 80; gay community in, 96
Fitzsimons, G. M., 174
Flannigan-Saint-Aubin, A., 21
Forester, E. M., 42, 57
forties (1940s). *See* 1940s *at beginning of index*
Frank, Barney, 88
Freeman, Mark, 5, 12
Freiberg, Selma, 171
Freud, Sigmund, 4–5, 8, 120, 159
Fricke, Aaron, 163, 170
"fruit" as term for same-sex desire, 124–25

Galatzer-Levy, R., 9, 218
Garland, Judy, 69, 70, 74
gay: Duberman's self-identification as, 33; use of term, *ix,* 6, 65–66, 98, 215–16, 220
Gay Academic Union, 39
Gay Activists Alliance (GAA), 32–33, 77, 78, 79, 100
gay bars: open operation of, 136, 220; police raids and harassment, 38, 55, 92, 100; as social milieu, 11–12, 35; Sporters in Boston, 91, 92; Tobias's experience in, 91, 92
gay identity: in 1990s, 163; academic interest in, 155; ambivalence within, 136–37; as dual existence, 135; family and community acceptance and, 155–56; gay pride, 74, 76–77, 160; labels resisted, 176; life writing and construction of, 223; mentoring and, 164, 169–70; pornography and gay self-acceptance, 162; "postgay" movement, 159, 214; rainbow as icon of, 160, 198, 213; self-acceptance and, 135. *See also under specific authors*
Gay, Lesbian and Straight Education Network (GLSEN), 20, 163
Gay Liberation Front (GLF), 77, 100
Gay Men's Health Crisis (GMHC), 82
Gay, Peter, 4

secrecy *(continued)*
for, 55–56, 66, 148–53; pseudonyms and, 83–84, 94, 223; religious persecution as context for, 148–53
seduction, heterosexuals and fear of, 32, 36
self-loathing: 1930s birth cohort and, 25, 33–34, 61–62, 63; AIDS epidemic and, 103; the body and, 36–37; Duberman as, 33–37, 39, 42–43; exacerbated by psychotherapy, 38; Kantrowitz as, 73; political ideology as context for, 104–5; psychiatric professional as, 74; stereotyping linked to, 213
self or selfhood: false vs. true self, 72–73; life writing and, 21; life writing as self-making, 3–4, 59–60, 121, 216–17, 223; memory as self-making, 121; parenthood as self-effacing, 144; personal coherence and, 21
self-psychology, *xi,* 78; self-vitality or coherence and, 8–10
Settersten, R. A., 217
seventies (1970s). *See 1970s at beginning of index*
Sex between Men (Sadownick), 158
sexuality: heterosexuality as norm, 30. *See also* same-sex desire
sexual stories, 10, 21; "coming out" narratives, 11; journeys of self-acceptance, 45, 62, 69, 99–100; master narrative of gay boyhood per Corbett, 48–49
shame: access to information and, 28; Adams and, 146, 151–52; AIDS and, 83, 104, 160; as barrier to intimacy, 145; bathhouse culture, 93; body consciousness linked to, 142; in Doty's works, 109, 111–12, 115; Duberman and, *x,* 35, 45, 63, 218; father/son relationships and, 184; generational contexts and, 60, 175, 222, 224; Kantrowitz and, 74, 83; life writing and reconciliation, 11–12; paradox of social acceptance and personal, 136–37; Phillips and, 175, 184; pre-Stonewall generations and, 222; psychotherapy and, 8–9; religious contexts for, 146,

151–52, 165; self writing and resolution of, 12, 115; Tobias and, 87, 93. *See also* secrecy
Shand-Tucci, D., 95
Shelby, R. Dennis, *xi*
Shepard, Matthew, 20, 163
Shilts, Randy, 16
Shirts and Skins (Miller), 124, 125, 127–28
Signorile, Michael, 159
silence: 1930s cohort and, 39; AIDS and, 80; as disapproval, 30
sixties (1960s). *See 1960s at beginning of index*
Skinner, D., 217
Socarides, Charles, 37, 43, 159–60
Socarides, Richard, 99
social acceptance: generational experiences of, 223–25; as norm for 1970s and 1980s birth cohort, 213–14; as regionally variable, 160, 165; of same-sex desire, 99, 136–37, 160, 213–14, 223–25
social changes: during 1960s, 16, 64–65, 76, 133–34, 155, 219; during 1970s, 81, 125; as contexts, *x,* 21; historical contexts of generational cohorts, 6–7, 215, 223–25; life writing and, *xii,* 5, 18–19; personal disruption and, 4; political activism and, 16; during postwar period, 25–26; reduction in prejudice during postwar period, 68; social conservatism, 81, 124, 135, 156; tolerance of same-sex desire, 99, 100
The Sociological Imagination (Mills), 215
Sons of Harvard: Gay Men from the Class of 1967 (Marotta), 64–65, 88–89, 99
spectrum, as term of sexual identity, 216
Spielberg, Steven, 4
Stein, A., 218, 221
Stein, Nancy, 223
stereotypes of male homosexuality, 86, 178, 198, 208, 210, 213; effeminacy, 86, 110, 111
Stewart, A. J., 216
stigmatization: AIDS and, 13, 17; generational differences and, 13–14, 20, 22, 27, 32, 100, 213, 223; "homosexual"

Wisconsin Studies in Autobiography

William L. Andrews
General Editor

Robert F. Sayre
The Examined Self: Benjamin Franklin, Henry Adams, Henry James

Daniel B. Shea
Spiritual Autobiography in Early America

Lois Mark Stalvey
The Education of a WASP

Margaret Sams
Forbidden Family: A Wartime Memoir of the Philippines, 1941–1945
Edited, with an introduction, by Lynn Z. Bloom

Charlotte Perkins Gilman
The Living of Charlotte Perkins Gilman: An Autobiography
Introduction by Ann J. Lane

Mark Twain
*Mark Twain's Own Autobiography: The Chapters
    from the* North American Review
Edited, with an introduction, by Michael Kiskik

Journeys in New Worlds: Early American Women's Narratives
Edited by William L. Andrews

American Autobiography: Retrospect and Prospect
Edited by Paul John Eakin

Caroline Seabury
The Diary of Caroline Seabury, 1854–1863
Edited, with an introduction, by Suzanne L. Bunkers

Marian Anderson
My Lord, What a Morning
Introduction by Nellie Y. McKay

American Women's Autobiography: Fea(s)ts of Memory
Edited, with an introduction, by Margo Culley

Frank Marshall Davis
Livin' the Blues: Memoirs of a Black Journalist and Poet
Edited, with an introduction, by John Edgar Tidwell

Joanne Jacobson
Authority and Alliance in the Letters of Henry Adams

Cornelia Peake McDonald
A Woman's Civil War: A Diary with Reminiscences of the War, from March 1862
Edited, with an introduction, by Minrose C. Gwin

Kamau Brathwaite
The Zea Mexican Diary: 7 Sept. 1926–7 Sept. 1986
Foreword by Sandra Pouchet Paquet

Genaro M. Padilla
My History, Not Yours: The Formation of Mexican American Autobiography

Frances Smith Foster
Witnessing Slavery: The Development of Ante-bellum Slave Narratives

Native American Autobiography: An Anthology
Edited, with an introduction, by Arnold Krupat

American Lives: An Anthology of Autobiographical Writing
Edited, with an introduction, by Robert F. Sayre

Carol Holly
Intensely Family: The Inheritance of Family Shame and the Autobiographies of Henry James

People of the Book: Thirty Scholars Reflect on Their Jewish Identity
Edited by Jeffrey Rubin-Dorsky and Shelley Fisher Fishkin

G. Thomas Couser
Recovering Bodies: Illness, Disability, and Life Writing

José Angel Gutiérrez
The Making of a Chicano Militant: Lessons from Cristal

John Downton Hazlett
My Generation: Collective Autobiography and Identity Politics

William Herrick
Jumping the Line: The Adventures and Misadventures of an American Radical

Women, Autobiography, Theory: A Reader
Edited by Sidonie Smith and Julia Watson

Carson McCullers
Illumination and Night Glare: The Unfinished Autobiography of Carson McCullers
Edited by Carlos L. Dews

Marie Hall Ets
Rosa: The Life of an Italian Immigrant

Yi-Fu Tuan
Who Am I?: An Autobiography of Emotion, Mind, and Spirit

Henry Bibb
The Life and Adventures of Henry Bibb: An American Slave
With a new introduction by Charles J. Heglar

Suzanne L. Bunkers
Diaries of Girls and Women: A Midwestern American Sampler

Jim Lane
The Autobiographical Documentary in America

Sandra Pouchet Paquet
Caribbean Autobiography: Cultural Identity and Self-Representation

Mark O'Brien, with Gillian Kendall
How I Became a Human Being: A Disabled Man's Quest for Independence

Elizabeth L. Banks
*Campaigns of Curiosity: Journalistic Adventures of an American Girl
    in Late Victorian London*
With a new introduction by Mary Suzanne Schriber and Abbey L. Zink

Miriam Fuchs
The Text Is Myself: Women's Life Writing and Catastrophe

Jean M. Humez
Harriet Tubman: The Life and the Life Stories

Voices Made Flesh: Performing Women's Autobiography
Edited by Lynn C. Miller, Jacqueline Taylor, and M. Heather Carver

Loreta Janeta Velazquez
The Woman in Battle: The Civil War Narrative of Loreta Janeta Velazquez,
   Cuban Woman and Confederate Soldier
With a new introduction by Jesse Alemán

Cathryn Halverson
Maverick Autobiographies: Women Writers and the American West, 1900–1936

Jeffrey Brace
The Blind African Slave: Or Memoirs of Boyrereau Brinch,
   Nicknamed Jeffrey Brace
as told to Benjamin F. Prentiss, Esq.
Edited and with an introduction by Kari J. Winter

Colette Inez
The Secret of M. Dulong: A Memoir

Before They Could Vote: American Women's Autobiographical Writing, 1819–1919
Edited by Sidonie Smith and Julia Watson

Bertram Cohler
Writing Desire: Sixty Years of Gay Autobiography